**LEW WALLACE
HIGH SCHOOL LIBRARY**

Minds and Motion

Also by D. Scott Rogo

NAD: A STUDY OF SOME UNUSUAL OTHER-WORLD EXPERIENCES
A PSYCHIC STUDY OF "THE MUSIC OF THE SPHERES"
METHODS AND MODELS FOR EDUCATION IN PARAPSYCHOLOGY
THE WELCOMING SILENCE
AN EXPERIENCE OF PHANTOMS
PARAPSYCHOLOGY: A CENTURY OF INQUIRY
IN SEARCH OF THE UNKNOWN
EXPLORING PSYCHIC PHENOMENA
THE HAUNTED UNIVERSE
MIND BEYOND THE BODY
THE HAUNTED HOUSE HANDBOOK

D. SCOTT ROGO

MINDS AND MOTION
THE RIDDLE OF PSYCHOKINESIS

Taplinger Publishing Company / New York

First Edition
Published in the United States in 1978 by
Taplinger Publishing Co., Inc.
New York, New York

Copyright © 1978 by D. Scott Rogo
All rights reserved. Printed in the U.S.A.

No part of this book may be reproduced or transmitted in any form or by
any means, electronic or mechanical, including photocopy, recording,
or any information storage and retrieval system now known or
to be invented, without permission in writing from the publisher,
except by a reviewer who wishes to quote brief passages
for inclusion in a magazine, newspaper, or broadcast

Library of Congress Cataloging in Publication Data

Rogo, D. Scott.
    Minds and motion.

    Bibliography: p.
    Includes index.
    1. Psychokinesis.   I. Title.
BF1371.R63   1978   133.8'8   77-92816
ISBN 0-8008-2455-5

To the team of people who have done so much to help my career:
TERRY, BOBS, MOLLIE, AND ROY

Contents

	PREFACE	11
1.	FROM SKEPTICISM TO BELIEF	15
2.	PK IN EVERYDAY LIFE	26
3.	THE MYSTERY OF THE POLTERGEIST	42
4.	SCIENTISTS, MEDIUMS, AND PK	66
5.	NINA KULAGINA: THE SOVIET PK BREAKTHROUGH	102
6.	THE PK EPIDEMIC	118
7.	EXAMINING THE GELLER EFFECT	139
8.	GROUP PK	167
9.	PK AND HEALING	198
10.	THE RANGE OF PK	216
11.	PK THEORIES: MIND ENERGY? PHYSICAL ENERGY? OR COSMIC ENERGY?	235
	REFERENCES	259
	INDEX	267

Acknowledgments

THE AUTHOR would like to thank the following authors and publishers for allowing use of copyrighted material in this volume:

Portions of Pamela Painter de Maigret's article, "PK Training in Russia," are reprinted by special permission of *Fate* magazine (May 1976). Several extracts concerning experiments with Uri Geller and the Geller effect which appear in Chapter 7 are drawn from Charles Panati's (editor) *The Geller Papers* (Houghton Mifflin Company, 1976) and are reprinted by permission of the publisher. For allowing use of material which originally appeared in C. G. Jung's *Memories, Dreams, Reflections,* translated by Richard and Clara Winston (revised edition, 1973), acknowledgment is due to Pantheon Books, Inc., and also to Scarecrow Press, Inc., and Dr. Gertrude Schmeidler (editor) for extracts from *Parapsychology: Its Relation to Physics, Biology, Psychology, and Psychiatry* (1976). Selections drawn from Louisa Rhine's *Mind over Matter* (Macmillan, 1972) and *ESP in Life and Lab* (Macmillan, 1967), as well as excerpts from Iris Owen and Margaret Sparrow's *Conjuring Up Philip* (Harper & Row, 1976), appear by permission of the publishers. Extracts from Benson Herbert's "Spring in Leningrad" are printed by permission of the Parapsychology Foundation and the *International Journal of Paraphysics* (Paraphysics Laboratory, Downton, Wiltshire, England).

Portions of Chapter 3 originally appeared in the October 1977 issue of *Human Behavior* and in the September 1976 issue of *Probe* magazine.

Preface

DURING THE LAST one hundred years, parapsychologists have made two major discoveries about man, his mind, and his world. First, they have learned that somehow we can communicate with one another through a mysterious faculty which bypasses the five physical senses. The second discovery psychical investigators have made about the human psyche is even stranger. There now exists considerable evidence that, by sheer conscious or even unconscious mental intent, we can actually influence physical matter. This book is concerned with this second great discovery.

I need hardly point out that we do not know how psychokinesis, as this phenomenon is usually called, is able to manipulate matter. We do not know what laws govern its operation, nor even why humankind possesses this strange ability in the first place. However, I do not think that PK should be considered a total enigma to science. To the contrary, I think we know a great deal about this unusual phenomenon. In fact, we might well be on the very verge of unraveling the PK mystery.

It was this realization that encouraged me to write this volume. So in this book I will be chiefly focusing on those aspects of the PK enigma which I feel helps us to understand the very nature of psychic energy.

Until recently, most PK tests have been designed to see if people could make rolling dice, or other moving objects, land on certain faces or on designated areas of a landing platform more often than chance would account for. A formidable log of such research has been published, and this work constitutes an important chapter in the history of PK research. However, although I will often cite this research in this volume, I will not dwell upon it. My decision was mediated by two factors. First, while this research serves as good scientific evidence for PK, it tells us relatively little about the nature and modus operandi of the phenomenon. I am afraid that much laboratory PK can be criticized on the same grounds, so I will bring in this kind of laboratory PK research only when the findings from a specific experiment make a notable contribution to our understanding of PK. Second, all of this research has been presented in eminently readable form by Dr. Louisa Rhine in her *Mind Over Matter* (New York: Macmillan, 1970). This excellent book will serve as a complete guide to this phase of PK research.

I need hardly bring up the fact that there has been an upsurge of interest in PK during the last two decades, not only within parapsychology but within the scientific community at large. This new interest has been sparked by three factors: (1) the appearance of gifted psychics, mainly in the Soviet Union, who claim the ability to move objects by willpower; (2) the recent appearance of Uri Geller on the psychic scene and the incredible controversy he has prompted; and (3) a new interest among parapsychologists to study and report poltergeist cases. Naturally, I will focus on these three areas of PK research in some depth. These reports, in turn, cast new light on much PK research carried out around the turn of the century with psychics who could apparently levitate tables, materialize phantom forms, float objects about, and perform other séance-room wonders. So, in a way, this book will concentrate mainly on two avenues of PK research—the very new and the very old.

My plan while writing this book has not been to prove the existence of PK. (However, I do cite what I feel to be the best laboratory evidence for its existence in chapter 1.) Instead, I hope to make a little sense out of the PK mystery. Throughout our research over the last hundred years, we have hit upon certain clues now and then which might help us begin to understand the very nature of PK. These clues are just waiting to be extracted and correlated. While I cannot claim that I have in any way discovered how or why PK operates, I hope that in the course of this book I have at least been able to shed a little new light on a very unusual and exciting phenomenon.

D. SCOTT ROGO

1

From Skepticism to Belief

IN THE SOVIET UNION, a housewife stares intently at a matchbox on a table in front of her. All of a sudden, the cardboard box slides across the table by itself in little spurts of motion.

In Chicago, Illinois, a middle-aged bellhop stares into a Polaroid camera. When the shutter is snapped and the self-processing print is ejected, the photograph shows a picture of a building miles away. All it should have shown is a blurred image of the people in the room.

In Toronto, Canada, a group of people sit around a table, resting their hands gently atop it. At first it rocks to and fro, then knocking sounds resound from its center, and, on rare occasions, the table hoists and suspends itself briefly in the air.

At Maimonides Medical Center in Brooklyn, New York, a psychic concentrates on a complicated machine. Suddenly, although the psychic is sitting several feet from it, the machine goes haywire.

In Olive Hill, Kentucky, a family looks on with terror as objects fly around their home as though thrown by an invisible force, and furniture is overturned violently. Parapsychologists rush to investigate.

In each of these cases a very bizarre force is at work. The laws which we have always believed control our universe are being suspended or violated. A new and hardly understood power is gaining the attention of science. This is the challenge of mind over matter.

This book deals with a very unusual subject. It concerns a phenomenon in which we, in our Western culture, both believe yet disbelieve. That may sound like a hopeless paradox, but it really isn't.

Do you believe that, by merely willing it, you can make a little bottle slide across a table several feet away? You most likely do not. Would you believe that by mental concentration you could make dice fall on the same sides several times in a row? Again, probably not. Nor probably do most of the people whom you see in the course of your day-to-day life.

Yet, on the other hand, have you ever prayed with the hope that somehow your thoughts might have some influence on your material situation? Or that of a friend's? Have you ever hit a golf ball or thrown a bowling ball and given it a little body English to help it along a bit if it seemed headed to miss the mark?

Just as you would unhesitatingly say no to the first group of questions, you might feel no embarrassment in answering affirmatively to the latter ones. This is the paradox. On a conscious level, the idea that we can influence material objects merely by an act of mind or will is so counter to our materialistic, matter-of-fact way of looking at the world that we reject it out of hand. Yet, on an intuitive level we do seem to realize that somehow our thoughts can break out of the private world of our minds and actually act upon the physical world.

In ancient times, philosophers would argue days upon end over such issues as the relationship between the mind and body, the mind and the brain, the mind and the outside world, *ad infinitum.* However, the rise of the Renaissance in Italy after the Dark Ages brought with it the realization that it was better to test a theory experimentally than just to argue over it theoretically. And it was at this time that scholars and philosophers first began seriously to consider whether or not the mind could influence the outside world through some hidden force.

The concept that the mind can directly manipulate physical matter is not an idea that sprang full grown. For centuries scientists and scholars alike have been dimly aware that mind over matter is a distinct possibility. But it has been only recently that scientists have been trying to demonstrate mind over matter in the laboratory experimentally. This search has now gone on for over a century. Mind over matter is not a philosophical issue, to be

From Skepticism to Belief   17

debated with hypotheses, rebuttals, theorems, or polemics, but a scientifically testable theory. And the results of these experiments and observations constitute the core of this volume.

Even before the Industrial Revolution and the resurgence of interest in the methods of science which it brought, there were stories of people with very peculiar abilities and tales of houses struck with very peculiar infestations. According to Catholic records and testimony, many saintly people, such as St. Teresa of Avila and St. Joseph of Cupertino, were seen to levitate and float in the air by scores of witnesses. Even the writers of the Egyptian papyruses recorded reports of houses which were plagued by demons who threw objects around and broke furniture. And by the Middle Ages, scientists were well aware that some psychic force, hidden within man's mind, could be coaxed out into the open by direct willpower. For example, in his posthumously published work entitled *Sylva Sylvarum,* Francis Bacon (1561–1626) wrote that there was a physical force within man's imagination that could be tested, ". . . upon things that have the lightest and easiest motions . . . as upon the sudden fading or coming up of herbs; or upon their bending one way or other . . . or upon the casting of dice."

Bacon's words were certainly prophetic. I am sure that Bacon did not realize that three hundred years later just these types of experiments would be run by scientists with astounding success. Dr. Bernard Grad, a biologist working at McGill University in Canada, has now shown irrefutable evidence that a psychic's will can help plant growth. Likewise, J. B. Rhine, working at his laboratory at Duke University in the 1930s and 1940s, demonstrated that subjects could psychically influence the fall of dice so that they would land with a certain face upright more often than chance could account for.

But why, in the face of evidence such as this—and the evidence which will follow—do we still tend to disbelieve in this power of the mind which parapsychologists have dubbed telekinesis (to move at a distance) or psychokinesis (to move by the mind, PK for short)? The roots of our disbelief are both psychological and emotional.

Any psychoanalyst will tell you that believing that our thoughts can influence the outside world is merely a carry-over from a very childlike, egocentric view of the world. Infants inherently believe that they can manipulate the world with their thoughts. They lose this belief as they begin to test the reality around them and learn the rather unsettling lesson that the world just doesn't work that way. However, lurking within the child's mind is still that belief in the omnipotence of his thoughts. In fact, if a male child during the Oepidal conflict (during which he unconsciously sees his father as a rival for his mother's love, and would like to see the old boy conveniently out of the way) should lose his father to death or accident, it may take years of psychotherapy to help him overcome his guilt. This guilt is engendered by that primitive, though repressed, belief that somehow his thoughts caused the misfortune. So, psychologically we disbelieve in psychokinesis because (1) we don't like to believe that we are thinking like children and (2) over the years our reality testing has proved to us that, by and large, our thoughts cannot normally affect the world around us. We conveniently ignore or disbelieve any evidence to the contrary, no matter how strong that evidence may be.

On an emotional level we tend to reject the notion of psychokinesis out of fear. It is a rather terrifying idea that our private thoughts—unspoken and unacted upon—can actually produce a physical effect on an object or a person. I might be able to make this point a little clearer by narrating a personal incident. Some years ago I discovered that a very good friend of mine had acted quite dishonorably toward me, which angered me no end. He had just bought a Mercedes-Benz which was, of course, his pride and joy. I was miles away in a different city at the time and, very childishly, I couldn't keep from thinking how I would like to wreck the car in order to get even. When I arrived back home only a few days later, I learned that, at the very time of my mental vendetta, the car had been completely destroyed in a freak accident. I was unnerved, for I could not help but feel that somehow my thoughts had helped precipitate the accident. Those who disbelieve in psychokinesis will have no problem in dismissing this sequence of events as coincidental. The psychiatrist will contend that I was regressing to primitive thinking. This accident probably was coincidental, but if psychokinesis is an accepted fact, can we be sure? However, I have recounted this story only to illustrate a very important emotional point: how many of us are willing or prepared to accept responsibility for *this* kind of outcome of our thoughts?

Dr. Jule Eisenbud, a Denver-based psychoanalyst who has written extensively on the relation of psychiatry to psychic phenomena, believes that some of his patients' thoughts and obsessions have actually influenced the outside world in just this way. He had dubbed these people "typhoid Marys," whose mental rages often erupt symbolically, and psychically attack the physical world. As he writes of one such person victimized by PK:

> My attention was drawn to the possibility of Typhoid Marys in the sphere of the paranormal through observing an obsessional neurotic woman among whose acquaintances and relatives, and in whose immediate life space there occurred what seemed to be an unusually high number of illnesses, injuries, and fatal accidents, including the murder of her maid on her doorstep; the crash of a plane in her back yard, with the loss of several lives; and, in fact, the vehicular death, during a previous period of treatment, of her unlucky psychiatrist. . . . The patient herself, outside of her compulsions and obsessions, remained extraordinarily well and free of mishap. What alerted me to the paranormal possibilities in the case was the breaking off of one of the pieces in the toilet tank assembly and the flooding of the toilet in my office on the day following the patient's dream of compulsively checking several toilets (she lived in dread of bowel accidents.)

Here again, we cannot authoritatively say that this incident was coincidence, PK, or one of C. G. Jung's acausal synchronicites (remembering all the while that the word coincidence is only a label and not an explanation for anything). But the real lesson to be learned from Dr. Eisenbud's account is, again, if we accept the existence of psychokinesis we must admit that we might be causing all sorts of god-awful things to occur to ourselves and to others. Is it any wonder then that we immediately reject the idea of PK despite the scientific evidence?

Psychokinesis is only one of a variety of interrelated phenomena we term "paranormal" or "psychic." Parapsychologists study PK right along with telepathy, clairvoyance, precognition, haunted houses, and so forth. Even though PK is a physical phenomenon while extrasensory perception (ESP) is a purely mental one, there is an intrinsic relationship between the two. Barriers do not seem to limit the efficacy of either ESP or PK which can freely penetrate obstacles of any sort. Neither does distance have any great effect. And both phenomena represent some sort of interaction between mind and material objects. This is probably the most striking parallel between the two.

Take clairvoyance, for example, where it appears as if the mind is interacting with a material object and directly assimilating information from it. One popular type of clairvoyance test is called the DT, or down-through. The experimenter shuffles a deck of cards and then places it facedown on the table. No living mind knows the order of the cards, yet some gifted psychics are nonetheless able to report the order of the numbers, symbols, or colors on the cards accurately. How? We don't know, but somehow the subject's mind is directly interacting with the deck.

An even more baffling experiment for clairvoyance is the "psychic shuffle" technique. The experimenter shuffles a deck of cards and lays them flat down. Then the subject shuffles another deck of cards and stops when he believes that he has shuffled his deck to match the order of the cards in the target deck as closely as possible. Some of the statistics from these tests are staggering. The Trinidad psychic, Sean Harribance, was pitted against the psychic shuffle by experimenters at the Institute for Parapsychology at the Foundation for Research on the Nature of Man in Durham, North Carolina. (This is the old Duke University parapsychology laboratory.) A deck of Zener cards (twenty-five cards to the deck, randomly printed with any one of five geometrical figures) was shuffled blindly by the experimenter. Then the same experimenter shuffled another deck until Harribance suddenly called for him to stop when the psychic felt there was a close coincidence between the order of the two. Fifty "runs" were made of twenty-five guesses each. In the first series Harribance was able to get 50 percent more correspondences between the cards than the expected 20 percent due to chance. As the tests proceeded, he got higher and higher scores. He was also successful when he shuffled the deck himself, stopping to match the target order. Even when the experimenter and target deck were in another room, Harribance was able to succeed at the psychic shuffle.

This experiment might strike the reader as just another trite experiment whose only purpose was to "prove ESP." But this simple test is pregnant with horrendous implications. First of all, it demonstrates that Harribance's mind had some direct link to the decks of cards, and was able to keep track constantly—albeit unconsciously—of their shifting order as the shuffling proceeded. There was a direct information flow between the decks and the psychic's mind.

From the notion of clairvoyance it is only a very short step to the concept of psychokinesis where there is also some link between an object and the mind. When PK occurs, however, it looks as though the mind is actually manipulating (not merely interacting with) physical matter. As J. B. Rhine, the founder of modern parapsychology, writes in his *The Reach of the Mind:*

> The PK hypothesis is a logical follow-up of the ESP work itself. In the clairvoyance perception of objects there has to be some operation between the mind and the material objects. Each must have an effect on the other; at least that is the way all known reactions work. The mind, therefore, does something to the object, even though that something be too slight to be observed. The clairvoyance test, of course, was not designed to discover any such effect; what was needed was a means of measurement sensitive enough to register any such mental effect on the physical object. We would expect psychophysical interaction to show effects on the physical side as well as on the psychical. Why not extra*motor* as well as extrasensory perception?

As is well known, the first attempts to demonstrate PK scientifically at Duke University, where Rhine had set up his lab, were through rolling dice. Several types of tests were run. Subjects threw dice in mechanical apparatuses, trying to make selected die faces come up more often than any others; or for doubles to result more often than chance could account for; or to make the dice land on certain positions on a landing platform. All of these tests were ultimately successful. The mind really could exert a psychical force onto the physical world. For years there had been reports of people with such miraculous powers, but now Rhine had demonstrated it to the scientific community.

One of the major upshots from the Duke PK work was that a clear connection between ESP and PK was found to exist. Somehow, for instance, the mind had to keep track of the rolling and bouncing dice as they fell so it could make them land in the required position. Obviously, the ESP faculty had to take over this chore. As Rhine commented, ". . . if PK had been discovered without any previous knowledge of ESP, the latter would immediately have had to be assumed, to make the former intelligible."

The evidence of a cofunction between PK and ESP was wrapped up when experimenters both in this country and in Great Britain designed experiments which required subjects to use PK and ESP simultaneously. For these tests, subjects had to roll dice to make them land (the PK task) on sides which would match a list of numbers in sealed envelopes (which they had to determine by ESP). Again, the results were positive.

It is very hard to isolate PK from other forms of psychic phenomena. They all form a vast network by which we interact with one another and the world in which we live. What little children and primitive peoples know instinctively, Western science has now begun to prove scientifically.

Dice-rolling PK effects are, however, only a measure of PK. The effect is meager, we don't really see it, we only *infer* it. The only way we know that PK has been operating is to run the test over and over again until we can measure how much the dice have departed from the way they should have landed randomly as they fell. However, in looking over the history of psychic studies, there are many reports of much more sensational PK effects. It would be hard to make a topology of all the effects noted, but here are only a few:

As I indicated before, people have been known to move objects across counters and tables through PK. This phenomenon is not limited to matchboxes or other small objects. Some psychics have, under good control and observation, caused tables to levitate, caused their mental pictures to appear on photographic film, created glowing lights in the room, swung pendulums in sealed containers, or caused temperatures in the room to fluctuate. Sometimes when someone has died, a friend or relative will note that a clock has stopped in his home, or he will hear pounding noises on the walls. There is now evidence that some people can use PK to help animals and plants recover from biological damage, and this has given the concept of psychic healing its first scientific credence. Today we are being besieged by people who claim that, by merely stroking hard metal, they can cause it to break, bend, or contort. Even cases of teleportation, where an object suddenly appears in a sealed room as though penetrating solid matter, are on record. Other psychics are able to produce humanlike voices on blank tape spools. The various forms of PK are almost limitless. But all of these effects point in the same direction . . . that within us is a physical force which can transcend the laws of physics.

Before going on to explore all these bizarre forms of psychokinesis, I would like to summarize a few experiments which aptly illustrate how the PK ability has been captured in the laboratory. The following three experiments were all carried out specifically to prove PK by taking into account any possible criticisms that the results could be due to error or fraud. Before trying to evaluate the phenomena in the chapters to come, keep these three startling experiments in mind:

The first of what I feel to be a foolproof demonstration of PK was an experiment run by Laura Dale at the American Society for Psychical Research and was an outgrowth of the Duke dice-rolling work. Mrs. Dale's work took every experimental precaution possible into account.

Fifty-four New York college students were the subjects, each of whom was tested to see if he could influence the fall of dice. Four ordinary commercial dice were used. They were placed on an elevated ledge which was connected to a plank corrugated by several baffles. The dice were randomly tossed about by hitting the baffles as they tumbled down the plank. At the bottom of the chute was a landing platform on which the dice would ultimately fall and come to rest. Each subject threw the dice 96 times trying for a specific die face. Then the subject would throw 96 times for *another* die face until all 6 die sides had been thrown for. (All told, there were 31,104 die readings for the experiment.)

These precautions had to be so stringent for several reasons. First, using the baffled chute ruled out any possibility that the subjects could throw the dice in certain ways to bias how they would land. Using all the die faces equally as targets circumvented the argument that the dice were biased or loaded.

After the test was concluded, it was found that the group had achieved 171 more direct hits than would be expected by chance. That may not sound like much, but statistically such a result would only occur by chance 5 times in 1000 experiments. Neither were the dice biased, for subjects scored equally well on the 2, 4, 5, and 6 faces. Not only that, but there were some interesting post hoc findings within the results. Those who believed in PK seemed to do better than those who rejected the possibility. Furthermore, subjects uniformly did better on their first set of throws than at any other time during the test. (Each group of subjects began their PK trials using a different face for the target.)

In light of results such as these, it is difficult to believe that PK was *not* operating.

A second and vastly more complicated foolproof PK test was the brainchild of Dr. Helmut Schmidt. Dr. Schmidt is a brilliant physicist, originally at the Boeing Laboratories in Seattle, who turned his attention to the problem of PK from the physicist's viewpoint. First working at the Institute for Parapsychology in Durham, Dr. Schmidt now carries out his research at the Mind Science Foundation in San Antonio, Texas.

Schmidt's experiment pitted man against his old nemesis . . . the machine. He built a machine with an internal oscillator (coin flipper) which speeds back and forth between two positions about one million times per second. One could say that the machine oscillated between a heads or tails position. The device was hooked up to a piece of radioactive strontium 90. As the strontium 90 decays, it randomly throws off electrons. No one can predict when an electron will shoot off, but whenever one does and the machine has been activated, it stops the oscillation. So in any given time period, say five minutes, the machine will randomly stop 50 percent of the time in the heads position and 50 percent of the time in the tails position. The PK subject has to try to use his psychic ability to alter the decay rate of the particle so that the machine will stop in one position significantly more often than in the other.

To give the subject a morale booster, the whole apparatus is connected to a panel of circular lights, nine in all. If the subject can make more heads than tails come up, the lights will flash in one direction. If more tails come up, the lights will travel in the other direction. So the PK testee is told to try to make the lights flash in one general direction and move around the circle progressively. Under normal circumstances, the lights will illuminate back and forth randomly. Again, remember, the subject can only succeed at the test by using PK on the radioactive element within the machine.

As you might expect, Schmidt found one psychic subject who could succeed at the task. Somehow her mind was actively interfering with a subatomic, quantum process.

A third, but little less complicated, experiment into the realms of PK was designed by Dr. Gertrude Schmeidler, a psychologist at the City College of the City University of New York. She was testing the claims of New York psychic Ingo Swann who claimed that he could alter the surface temperature of an object while sitting several feet away from it. So, Dr. Schmeidler set up a series of pieces of Bakelite and graphite, hooking each to a sensitive thermistor which continually recorded their temperatures. Swann sat twenty-five feet away. According to a prearranged sequence, he was asked to make a specific piece of the material either warmer or cooler by willing it to happen. Swann was amazingly proficient at carrying out the test. As he concentrated, the target objects would fluctuate either warmer or cooler according to the experimenter's demand. There was another outcome of the experiment as well which was not predicted. When one object altered in temperature, other objects in the vicinity also changed temperature, but in the opposite direction. It was a sort of psychic version of robbing Peter to pay Paul.

These three experiments represent three very different ways that the PK function can work. In one, falling dice are somehow diverted from their course. In another, mind is shown to influence subatomic particles and processes. Lastly, PK can alter temperature.

What are the implications of these tests? If PK can be shown to deflect a pair of rolling dice, it is just as possible that it can slide them across a desk from a stationary position. If the mind can directly interfere with a tiny particle, it can levitate a table or heave a chair across the room. If PK can alter the surface temperature of a piece of plastic, it can alter the temperature of a whole room such as is recorded in haunted houses and during the Spiritualism séances of the Victorian era.

The laboratory work with the PK effect offers credence to tales of mediums who levitate tables and create materializations out of thin air, of poltergeists who ravage a house by breaking everything in sight by an invisible force, and to people who claim to bend metal by just touching it. This indeed is the challenge of mind over matter.

2

PK in Everyday Life

"ONE NIGHT . . . in our bedroom," wrote the bewildered mother of the famous French astronomer, Camille Flammarion, "we were awakened by a great noise; we had heard a mirror on the mantlepiece fall down, as well as your father's watchstand. I got up, and found that the mirror had fallen upon the hearth; the watch had been thrown upon the floor on one side and the watchstand on the other. I thought that everything was broken, and, most annoyed, I must say, I went back to bed without further investigation. In the morning when we got up, we found that nothing had been broken."

So far there is nothing out of the ordinary in this account. Mirrors fall from walls all the time, you might be thinking to yourself. But, it is the sequel to this episode which commands our full attention.

"The same morning the postman brought us a letter," continued Mme. Flammarion, "telling us of the death of your Aunt Boyet, your father's sister, who had died that very night, in Montigny. What did this manifestation mean? The coincidence is, at least, strange."

This account is an example of one of the commonest forms of spontaneous PK. Scattered throughout not only the literature of parapsychology but throughout recorded history itself are accounts of strange psychic happenings which occur in a person's home at the exact moment someone he knows has died miles away. It seems almost a common occurrence. In fact, every time I speak to a group of people about psychic phenomena, at least two or three members of the audience will come up to me afterward to recount such "death coincidences" which occurred within their own families. Death coincidences come in all sorts of guises. Odd noises, violent poundings, flying or spontaneously breaking objects; clocks stopping and starting on their own accord—these are all types of PK effects which have been recorded by the more than startled witnesses. A friend and colleague of mine, Raymond Bayless, who is a seasoned psychical investigator himself, recounted to me how at the moment his aunt died he heard what sounded like a great gong struck in his room.

Before modern parapsychology began delving into these reports, it was automatically assumed that these eerie effects were caused by the souls of the dead seeking to announce their demise to their friends and relatives. One correspondent wrote to Camille Flammarion, who collected and investigated many such accounts at the turn of the century, about a friend of his who had been so ill that he had not been able to attend his seminary classes. His illness lingered on for months. Each student had a nail on the wall of the classroom upon which to hang his coat and hat, so the sick student's space was always vacant. One day a fellow student decided to take advantage of the vacancy and placed his own hat on the nail.

"Now one day," wrote the witness, "between eleven o'clock and noon, while the entire class was attentively following the professor's course, the hat on the absent pupil's nail suddenly began to turn, without the least plausible reason being discernible. This motion was so energetic, and lasted for so long (almost a minute) that it drew the pupils' attention, and even the professor's, and made such an impression that they talked of it the whole day."

Later that afternoon a cable arrived announcing that the ill student had died at that very time.

Direct physical PK effects are not the only type of death coincidences that have been reported. Inexplicable sounds are also quite commonly reported, such as Bayless's gong which I mentioned above. One of Flammarion's acquaintances reported to him how, one day during evening prayers, his entire family was shocked when "an extraordinary noise made itself heard . . . as though the heavy counter had been violently shaken, making the scales and everything upon it resound noisily." The family all ran into the office, no doubt expecting to find something broken or at least in disarray. To their disquietude, everything was in perfect order. News arrived that evening announcing the death of a relative.

Other effects could be cited in which human cries were heard, footsteps stalked about, or shutters were mysteriously jiggled.

More importantly, however, than merely recording these cases (and literally dozens have been published) is trying to figure out what they mean and why they occur.

Early psychical investigators felt that these incidents were caused psychokinetically by the dying or deceased person. To them, these cases indicated the physical release of some component of the dying person's mind which had survived death and which traveled to a relative's house in order to produce the physical manifestation. The reason, of course, was the desire of the liberated soul to announce its earthly demise. Actually, these investigators supported their theory with some fascinating and valid points.

As was just pointed out, one of the first investigators to collect accounts of spontaneous PK was Camille Flammarion, one of the most celebrated astronomers of his day and an astute student of psychical research. Flammarion published several of these accounts in his books, *L'Inconnu et les Problemes Psychiques,* and in the second volume of his three-volume set, *La Mort et son Mystère.* A detailed analysis of Flammarion's cases was made by Emile Laurent. Writing in the February 1907 issue of *The Annals of Psychical Science,* Laurent argued that death coincidences actually do show some sort of intention or mark of identity indicating that the dying person was willfully responsible for the PK. One of his strongest points was that the PK manifestations will often continue until the witness realizes the significance and message of the disturbance. If, say, a bell rings by itself when a relative has died unbeknown to the witness, it is likely to keep ringing until the witness correctly understands the sign being communicated. The following example is typical of this type of case which suggested to Laurent and others that death-coincidence PK demonstrated survival of death:

> François M. was awakened one night at 11 o'clock by hearing three distinct raps on the door of his room. He opened it and found no one—three further raps were then heard, followed by a further

search. When for a third time this sound was made on his bed, he had presentiments associated with his mother, whose death, however, he was not expecting. About five or six days after he learned that his mother had died at that hour, making special mention of him.

In this account it is clearly implied that the noises ceased when François received the impression that his mother had died. In other cases, the PK will cease the minute the witness explores for the source of the noise. The effect will then repeat itself if the witness shrugs off the incident as probably due to a normal cause. To Laurent, this illustrated a cognitive and willful intelligence behind the affair.

The study of spontaneous PK had progressed very little since Flammarion's day until after the beginnings of experimental ESP and PK research at Duke University in the 1930s. It was only in the 1940s or so that parapsychology began looking back at these cases and collecting new ones. The chief modern case collector has been Dr. Louisa Rhine, wife and co-worker of Dr. J. B. Rhine, who soon formulated an entirely different theory about the nature of death coincidences, one that radically differed from Laurent's or Flammarion's. However, this new understanding of spontaneous PK was partly an outgrowth of the Rhines' ESP experiments.

When the Rhines began their experimental work at Duke University, their plan was to demonstrate the existence of ESP, and later PK, to the scientific community at large. They therefore embarked on a rigid experimental attack on the phenomena, using the methodology of experimental psychology. But by the 1940s the active debate over the ESP problem was over for all practical purposes. The PK controversy ended later. The evidence was all in, evaluated, and the resistance to the acceptance of psi had become more emotional than logical. At the time, the Rhines felt that it was time to turn away from research and projects designed merely to prove ESP and PK and to start exploring questions such as how and why these abilities manifest. While J. B. Rhine still confined himself in the laboratory in pursuit of these enigmas, Louisa Rhine began collecting cases of ESP and PK occurrences in everyday life to search for further clues. Her collection soon soared into the hundreds. (Once while I was in Durham I asked Mrs. Rhine if she had any accounts of one type of psychic phenomenon I was interested in. The next day she handed me a folder chock-full of them!)

Mrs. Rhine soon discovered that many types of psychic occurrences grouped around death. When a person dies, she ascertained from her studies, a friend or relative is likely to learn of the event psychically through a variety of channels. He might have either a symbolic or realistic dream of the death, a sudden intuition or hunch about it, or even a full-blown hallucination. Finally, Mrs. Rhine collected several accounts of PK activity at the moment of death, very similar to the type of cases Flammarion had published. Now, this created a curious puzzle. What was the connection between these ESP cases and the PK ones? Why was ESP the vehicle of communication in one instance, but PK in another? There had to be a connection and Mrs. Rhine set about to discover it.

The key to the enigma came not from PK research, but from some of the Duke ESP work. In his original ESP experiments, Rhine had been experimenting to demonstrate telepathy. The subject had to guess what symbol was printed on a card the agent was concentrating upon. However, he soon discovered that no agent really had to be employed at all; subjects could guess the symbols correctly even if no human being knew the order of the ESP cards. Clairvoyance had been demonstrated. This may not sound very exciting to us today, but in the 1930s this was an unexpected revelation. Back in Victorian times when psychical research was born, it was generally believed that telepathy occurred when an agent actively tried to send his thoughts to a percipient who merely waited passively for the impression to reach him. It was the agent who was the active partner, or so it was believed. Some early investigators didn't even believe in clairvoyance. However, the Duke work pointed in a new direction. Now it seemed that the agent's role was obscure; it was the percipient who was the key player in the ESP drama and who actively initiated the ESP. Somehow the percipient's mind reaches out and scans (like a psychic form of radar), latches onto any pertinent ESP signal, and brings it back home and pushes it into consciousness.

Good illustrations of this percipient-initiated process can be found all through the history of ESP experiments. Especially pertinent was a group of long-distance telepathy tests carried out in 1937 between Harold Sherman, who was in New York, and Sir Hubert Wilkins who was in the arctic regions. They recorded these experiments in their joint book, *Thoughts Through Space*. Several times a week Wilkins tried to send telepathic messages to Sherman by concentrating on noteworthy activities in which he had been involved during the day. What usually occurred, though, was that Sherman invariably bypassed Wilkins's thoughts and reported *other* experiences Wilkins had undergone. Sherman, therefore, did not respond to Wilkins's thoughts, but seemed to scan psychically for other relevant information.

A similar type of process cropped up again only recently during ESP experiments conducted at Stanford Research Institute in Palo Alto, California. Two physicists, Russell Targ and Harold Puthoff, have been experimenting with a procedure they call "remote viewing." For these tests, the agent is asked to drive to a distant locale and the subject tries to visualize and describe the geography of the agent's location. Targ and Puthoff discovered that the subject would often describe geographical features of the locale which were not within the agent's visual range. Pure telepathy could not explain such results. The subject might describe a tree behind a house, for example, while the agent, from his own vantage point, would only be able to see the building. So here again it looks as though some psi component of the subject's mind, not the agent's, is the carrier of the ESP information.

Mrs. Rhine discovered that a similar process was evident in her spontaneous cases. She came to the conclusion that death coincidences are not due to the influence of the dying person, but are produced by the witnesses themselves. Her theory is that the witness unconsciously receives an ESP impression of the death and then projects PK to carry out a physical phenomenon to jolt the message into consciousness. We know that ESP is an unconscious process and represents a two-stage assimilation. First the ESP impression is received unconsciously, and then it moves into consciousness. It is for this reason that ESP so often manifests in dreams, hunches, hallucinations, and so forth, which are all unconscious processes. At other times, the ESP message may never emerge into conscious recognition. In death-coincidence cases, PK is the vehicle of expression instead of a dream or hallucination. As Mrs. Rhine herself explains, ". . . the crises of close friends and relatives seem particularly likely to be picked up by ESP, although in cases of ESP they are expressed in dreams, intuitions, and ESP hallucinations. We thus come to the suggestions that these physical or *motor* effects could be simply another way besides those of ESP of expressing or registering a psi message."

Mrs. Rhine's theory makes good sense parapsychologically. There are even direct suggestions within the cases themselves which point to this process. In one case on record, a man passionately fond of money heard noises like coins tossed about when a relative died. According to another case, a child with an inordinate fondness for birds heard bird cries at the moment of a death miles away. In each instance, the effect was obviously architectured for prime emotional effect. The fact that PK molds itself to fit the emotional precoccupations of the witness would indicate that he is himself the producer of the PK.

Even though PK effects at death manifest in very personal ways, there is one type of death coincidence which occurs so often that it represents a phenomenon in its own right. No discussion of spontaneous PK can go by without taking a detailed look at *the* most prevalent form of death coincidence . . . spontaneous clock stoppings.

There is a worldwide folk tradition that clocks will stop mysteriously when someone in the house dies. I am sure everyone reading these pages sang that delightful German children's song in grade school, "My Grandfather's Clock," which "stopped, short, never to run again when the old man died." This little song exemplifies the vast tradition associated with PK-induced clock phenomena. Let's look at a few cases.

The following incident is almost a classical example of this phenomenon. The percipient, who reported the case to Mrs. Rhine, was the proud owner of a gold pocket watch which had been given to him by his brother.

> I took leave from my job and sat up nights to help my sister-in-law during the last two days of my brother's terminal illness. He breathed his last at six-twenty-five in the morning. I called the family immediately and we phoned for the doctor and the undertakers. At about seven-thirty we were sitting around a rush breakfast—my two brothers, the widow, and the nurse.
>
> Arrangements had previously been made to be at the undertaking parlors at nine-thirty, so as the wall clock neared nine o'clock, I suggested it was about time the widow and my brothers made arrangements to get started for the funeral parlor. Some one asked me how much time we had, and I took out the pocket watch mentioned

above, when, lo and behold, it had stopped at the exact minute of his death. I called the attention of those gathered around the table to the phenomenon and in order to show that it was no common occurrence, asked my brother to wind the watch to make sure it had not run down. It was three quarters wound.

According to another case collected by Mrs. Rhine, an Indian man died at 9:35 P.M. on October 3, 1953, at the hospital which had been caring for him. His family testified in their report that, as soon as they got home, they discovered that the man's favorite cuckoo clock had stopped exactly at the minute of his death.

Sometimes PK-induced clock-stopping cases can become enormously complex. In some of these instances it actually looks as if a dead, but surviving entity, really was masterminding the clock stoppings, as in the following case:

James H. Hyslop, one of this country's pioneering psychical investigators, died in 1920. Soon after his death, Gertrude Tubby, his former secretary, was visiting his longtime friend, Dr. Elwood Worcester, when she suddenly felt Hyslop's discarnate presence in the room with them. (Worcester, I might add, was the founder of the Emmanuel Movement in New England, which attempted to join together religion and psychology to help administer to man's mental and spiritual needs.)

"Very well, Hyslop, if you're near and understand what I say, show some sign to let us know that you remember us," Worcester declared aloud, half in jest and half seriously.

Nothing did happen, but the Worcesters were in for a surprise when the next morning two clocks started acting bizarrely. One stopped dead for no apparent cause. The other timepiece, a grandfather clock, began to strike and chime repeatedly, necessitating the removal of part of the mechanism responsible for the chiming in order to stop the din.

What is of considerable interest is that, at the moment of Hyslop's death, his daughter's watch had suddenly stopped. Did the surviving personality of Hyslop cause the PK, or did Worcester use his own PK to give himself the sign he had requested? There is no easy answer to the question.

Just whose agency is responsible for these clock-stopping cases is, of course, a question of considerable interest. But there is another question just as tantalizing. *Why* are clocks so often affected?

There might be several answers to this query, and several plausible theories have come to my own mind in the years I have been considering these cases. First, there are both obvious and symbolic meanings communicated in clock stoppings. If the witness, or the dying person, uses PK to make a death known, it would seem likely that the PK would seek to bring the witness's attention to the exact time of the death in the most expedient way. Stopping a clock or watch would be the most overt way of getting the message across. However, there is another and more symbolic meaning as well.

Everybody knows the old euphemism for death, "his time has run out." This phrase emphasizes the fact that we symbolically associate death with the stopping of time. These PK clock stoppings are perhaps literal allusions to how we feel about death—that time has stopped for the dead person. At a deeper level, man has always had a strange fascination with time. We judge everything by it. Dying persons often talk about wishing they could stop time. Maybe at death, either we or our friends and relatives use PK in a futile and abortive attempt to do just that on a symbolic level. Nothing can be more final than the end of time, nor the finality of death. The stopping of time is symbolic of the very act of dying.

On a purely mechanical level, timepieces might also be easier to manipulate by PK than for it to create any other type of disturbance. Very few people seem to be able to move an object from a stationary position by PK. Yet Rhine and other parapsychologists have found that many people seem to be able to exert a PK influence on rolling dice, spinning coins, and oscillating machines. We can draw an obvious conclusion from this fact: somehow it is easier for us to use PK to disrupt a moving system than to influence a stable one. A moving object is actively converting potential energy to kinetic energy while a stable system is not. To initiate movement by PK is probably infinitely more difficult to manifest than merely deflecting an object already in motion. Now, by and large, watches and clocks are a network of moving parts, and the disruption of any one of them would cause them to stop. Coils unwind, hands tick away, levers go back and forth, and so on. I cannot think of any household object that is more constantly in motion than a timepiece. When PK manifests at death in order to give the witness a sign, it would appear likely that it would take the path of least resistance. And that would direct it right to a clock as it searched out the easiest thing to disrupt.

In all fairness to this theory, however, I should add that there are cases on record when, at the moment of death, clocks which *had not run* for years began to tick joyously away! So, at this stage of our research, the mystery must remain still unpenetrable.

Not all cases of spontaneous PK focus on death. PK can occur quite spontaneously and having nothing at all to do with it. Even some of these well-familiar clock cases illustrate this. In her book, *ESP in Life and Lab*, Mrs. Rhine quotes one rather revealing case which was reported by a woman who had an absolute psychic penchant for fouling up her household clock:

> We have a clock over a hundred years old which belonged to my father before me and to his mother before him. A few years ago my parents were living with us, and the clock rested on the mantel in the front hall. We lived in a home in Chicago, Illinois.
>
> The day of mother's death in 1952 the clock stopped at the exact time of her passing. I rewound the clock and the next day it stopped at that exact time. It has never since stopped at that time. The clock uses more than twenty-four hours to run down before stopping, so that would eliminate its second stopping at that exact time from being run down.
>
> We were living in the same house about three years later when our eldest daughter's first baby was born. When my husband and I returned from the hospital, I noted that the clock had stopped at the exact moment the baby was born. I rewound the clock, and the following day it again stopped at that exact time. It has never again stopped at that time.
>
> A few years later, in 1956, we moved from Chicago to our present home in the suburbs about twenty miles distant. The clock was placed in the front hall. In 1958 our youngest daughter was married at our church in Chicago. When we returned home, the clock had stopped at the exact time the minister had pronounced them man and wife, as I had glanced at my wristwatch at that time. I rewound the clock, and it has never again stopped from being run down, as time proved it doesn't stop running in twenty-four hours after winding. It takes much longer.

This case tells us a great deal about the PK process. Even though the first incident was a conventional death coincidence, the number of repeated clock stoppings indicate that the narrator was the likely source of the PK. It also shows that in daily life we can use PK unwittingly. (I would suggest that the symbolic meaning of the latter two incidents was a figurative attempt to "make time stop," the old saying for when we are enjoying ourselves.) Lastly, these incidents demonstrate that we can project PK over great distances. This is a mind-boggling realization. We know from research that ESP is not hampered by distance. It would appear that neither is PK.

There is quite a bit of experimental evidence that shows PK is not barred by distance. Carroll Nash, an experimental parapsychologist now at St. Joseph's College in Philadelphia, tested the relationship between distance and PK with subjects who were asked to try to influence the fall of dice. The group score for the entire number of subjects was well above chance. But they did just as well when thirty feet from the dice as they did when only three feet away from them. In fact, in a second test run by Nash, the subjects did even better at the greater distance.

An even more bizarre distance test was run by Dr. R. A. McConnell at the University of Pittsburgh. In his experiment, subjects tried to influence the fall of dice at the university while they remained in their own homes and were asleep! The subjects chose their target numbers beforehand and gave themselves suggestions to use PK before they retired. One subject, McConnell himself, succeeded admirably.

In England, two members of the Society for Psychical Research, G. W. Fisk and A. M. H. Mitchell, carried out dice-rolling tests and discovered that subjects over three hundred miles away could still influence the falling cubes. (It could be argued, of course, that Fisk used his *own* PK on the dice to get extra chance scoring. This will be a question raised and discussed later.) One of Fisk's subjects, Dr. J. Blundon, turned out to be a phenomenal long-distance PKer.

So, here we see that both spontaneous case reports and experimental research point in the same direction—that no matter how odd it may seem, PK can function over tremendous distances.

Like death coincidences, spontaneous PK unrelated to death can take a variety of forms as well. The following are just a few typical cases which have been reported to Mrs. Rhine:

One woman reported that as she was washing and stacking

dishes one of them literally jumped out of the cupboard, landing noisily on a stack of plates below. At that moment the woman had a sudden intuitive flash (ESP?) that something had happened to her hospitalized sister. At that time the sister had hemorrhaged during an operation and almost died, but recovered.

One perplexed woman wrote to tell of a lamp in her room which couldn't decide whether it was going to turn itself on, or turn itself off. The witness couldn't find any normal cause for the lamp's curious antics, but she later learned that her husband had been involved in an accident at the time of the incident. He was shaken up, but unhurt.

One cannot help but notice that these cases all seem to dwell on crises which, as stated before, often act as the basis for many ESP experiences.

Admittedly, these types of cases may not seem overly dramatic, though no doubt very startling to the percipients. But remember, these effects might only be the tip of a great psychic iceberg. Although minor, these reports are vastly important to our understanding of PK. To quote Mrs. Rhine again, "For that matter, the sparks from Franklin's electric machine were small too, compared to the power of electricity in a thunderstorm."

There is, on the other hand, a whole different order of unconscious or spontaneous PK which often goes unnoticed. Let's say you were going to run a PK dice-throwing test with several subjects. Their task would be to make the number 5 come up as much as possible. You stand by and record the results. After you have run all your subjects and tabulated the results, you see that your subjects have done very well on the test. Fine and good. But now comes the question, whose PK was active? Your subjects' or your own? Could you have used PK to make sure you got the results you were hoping for? Today, parapsychologists are becoming very well aware of this problem.

Let me cite a beautiful example of how we can use PK—totally inadvertently—to manipulate the world around us and to satisfy our own needs.

I was running an experiment in precognition at the Division of Parapsychology and Psychophysics of Maimonides Medical Center in Brooklyn, New York. I wanted to see if I could get my subjects to visualize about a target picture that I would select after they had gone through a period of imagery generation. I had over a thousand pictures to choose from. The subjects were instructed to try to see in their mind's eye the picture I would choose when they were done. Now it was important that the choice of the target picture be completely random. I had to use some impartial way of picking it. Charles Honorton, the director of the division, had eschewed my plan of choosing the target on the basis of a code which was in turn based on the license plate numbers of passing cars. He felt my procedure was too unwieldy and suggested instead that I use a random number generator similar to the Schmidt coin flipper I described in the previous chapter. By activating the machine ten times I would get a succession of red and green lights in random order. This would give me a coding such as 0011010001 or 111001110. This coding would designate one of 1024 targets in the target files.

Well, frankly I balked at this. After all, I told Chuck Honorton, we know that these machines can be influenced by PK such as in Schmidt's experiment. Maybe I would use PK myself to rig the machine to come up with a target that would match what I knew my subjects had reported. If one saw an apple, maybe I would use my PK and cause the generator to choose a target with an apple in it. I would not really be testing precognition at all.

Well, to make a long story short (actually, it became an argument), I acquiesced to using the generator despite my misgivings. The basic reason I did so was that I'm a pretty lousy PK subject. My worries were unfounded, for the results of the test were not very striking. But one night just before I was about to leave the lab, I decided to look over some of the targets in the target pool. As I thumbed through them, one picture caught my eye which was so foul and tasteless that I couldn't keep my eyes from it. It was a picture of a naked, obese, smiling man with a pumpkin next to him. It really was ghastly. (I happen to have an aversion to naked, obese people.) I shut the file and went home with that picture clinging to my mind like a leech.

The very next morning I arrived at the lab and sat down to run my first precognitive session for the day. When it came time to choose the target, I made my ten activations on the generator, got my coding, and went to the target files. Then came the shock. I took out the appropriate target and there he was . . . my old, obese, naked nemesis, smiling as ever, with that damnable pumpkin sitting by his side. The generator had come up with that target out of 1024 available ones.

Since we know that the target-selecting device can be affected by PK, I don't think this all was mere coincidence. The choice of that particular target was most likely due to my unconscious use of PK to rig the generator so I would have to confront the taboo target. Also, I might add, I was able to flaunt the incident to Chuck as proof for my distrust of the machine.

Several other parapsychologists have come across similar effects in their own work. My favorite one came from one experimenter who wanted to see if cockroaches had PK ability. (No, I'm not joking.) He placed the insects on a grid which was randomly given electrical shocks. During any given period of time the grid would either be shocked or passed in a random order. The experimenter wanted to determine if the cockroaches could use PK to inhibit the generator and make it give fewer shocks than it was programmed for. When the test was over it was found that the cockroaches had apparently PKed the machine to give *more* shocks than chance would explain. Now, cockroaches do not usually go around shocking themselves, so it seems likely that the experimenter himself had used his own PK unconsciously to torture the poor creatures which he detested.

One researcher, Dr. Rex Stanford of St. John's University in Jamaica, New York, is actually trying to carry out PK and ESP tests in such a way as to prove that we can unconsciously use our psi capacities to fulfill our own needs. Stanford was well aware that ESP and PK often occur when there is a need for it to happen. So, he went about trying to create just such a need-oriented situation artificially in the laboratory, and designed a most interesting PK experiment.

First, each of the several subjects involved carried out a conventional PK test by trying to make a machine depart from randomness. Afterward, when the student thought the test was over, he was taken to an adjoining room and required to carry out a horribly monotonous task. Unbeknownst to the student, he could get out of the task if, by ESP, he learned that the machine was still running in the next room and could use PK to influence it. Stanford theorized that the subjects would be so bored by the job assigned to them that they would use ESP unconsciously to scan for any way to get out of it. He hoped that after the subject had unconsciously figured out what was going on through ESP, he would then use PK to carry out the experimental goal. As an added inducement, anyone who unconsciously manipulated the machine by PK would not only be released from the boring task, but given a very pleasant one to do instead.

This all may sound like a little too much to expect from ESP and PK, but the experiment worked. Some subjects did discern the secret experiment by ESP and then used their PK to manipulate the machine. As I warned earlier, the results of parapsychology experiments are often mind-boggling.

If we take into account results and reports such as these, it seems plausible that PK occurs much more often in our daily lives than we have been led to believe. Perhaps many little incidents occur which we dismiss as inconsequential, but which are actually genuine, though minor, PK occurrences.

Thomas Tietze, a historian of parapsychology, was writing a paper on the contributions to parapsychology of W. Franklin Prince, one of the pioneers of American psychical research. One of Prince's books which Tietze was analyzing dealt with paranormal raps. As Tietze tells it:

> As I turned today (August 11, 1974) to consider Prince's own experiences with "raps", I myself heard several loud, cracking noises, as of the splitting of wood, in my second floor hallway, just outside my study. Although I have no evidence whatever to indicate that the sounds were anything but normal, this was the sort of coincidence Prince so loved to record. I have lived in the house for two and a half years and have never heard any such noises before.

Of course, not all incidents of everyday PK are so minor, or disputable. Sometimes the PK can be incredibly powerful. The great explorer of the mind C. G. Jung admitted that his home became the scene of stormy PK activity during a time in his student days when he was preoccupied with psychic studies. Writing in his autobiography, *Memories, Dreams, Reflections,* he admitted that these youthful encounters with PK were "destined to influence me profoundly." Here, in his own words, is what happened to him:

> One day I was sitting in my room, studying my textbooks. In the adjoining room, the door to which stood ajar, my mother was knitting. That was our dining room, where the round walnut dining table

stood. The table had come from the dowry of my paternal grandmother, and was at this time about seventy years old. My mother was sitting by the window, about a yard away from the table. My sister was at school and our maid in the kitchen. Suddenly there sounded a report like a pistol shot. I jumped up and rushed into the room from which the noise of the explosion had come. My mother was sitting flabbergasted in her armchair, the knitting fallen from her hands. She stammered out, "W-w-what's happened. It was right beside me!" and stared at the table. Following her eyes, I saw what happened. The table top had split from the rim to beyond the center and not along any joint; the split ran right through the solid wood. I was thunderstruck. How could such a thing happen? A table of solid walnut that had dried out for seventy years—how could it split on a summer day in the relatively high degree of humidity characteristic of our climate? If it had stood next to a heated stove on a cold, dry winter day, then it might have been conceivable. What in the world could have caused such an explosion? "There certainly are curious accidents," I thought. My mother nodded darkly. "Yes, yes", she said . . ., "that means something." Against my will I was impressed and annoyed with myself for not finding anything to say.

Some two weeks later I came home at six o'clock in the evening and found the household—my mother, my fourteen-year-old sister, and the maid—in a great state of agitation. About an hour earlier there had been another deafening report. This time it was not the already damaged table; the noise had come from the direction of the sideboard, a heavy piece of furniture dating from the early nineteenth century. They had already looked all over it, but had found no trace of a split. I immediately began examining the sideboard and the entire surrounding area, but just as fruitlessly. Then I began on the interior of the sideboard. In the cupboard containing the bread basket I found a loaf of bread, and, beside it, the bread knife. The greater part of the blade had snapped off in several pieces. The handle lay in one corner of the rectangular basket, and in each of the other corners lay a piece of the blade. The knife had been used shortly before, at four-o'clock tea, and afterward put away. Since then no one had gone to the sideboard.

As Jung's experiences reveal, not all outbreaks of PK are single events. Sometimes our PK abilities seem to erupt from our minds and bodies without our realizing it, unleashing a virtual attack of PK manifestations. Objects are hurled about, furniture overturned, lights smashed, walls pounded upon, and countless other types of disturbances blow up. This is the eerie spectacle of the poltergeist.

3

The Mystery of the Poltergeist

ON NOVEMBER 25, 1974, the wire services in just about every major U.S. city carried a story as bizarre as it was unbelievable. It concerned a little house in the small, scenic city of Bridgeport, Connecticut, which, for all practical purposes, was haunted. Witnesses claimed, among other things, that objects were tossing about the house, that silverware was shooting around like makeshift missiles, and that a TV had jumped from a table by itself. The news story closed with the report that both police and clergymen were on the scene looking for a likely cause. Already over a hundred onlookers had swarmed to the house like ants over a lump of sugar.

Onlookers or not, the "ghost" certainly didn't seem to be gun-shy, and was literally wreaking havoc in the house. According to subsequent news bulletins released the same day, even the police—who had been called to the scene of the manifestations by the occupants of the house—couldn't come up with any solutions to the mystery. Nonetheless, the long-awaited denouement of the story came the next day. As the November 26, 1974, issue of the *Los Angeles Times* reported:

"Police today said that the unnatural happenings witnessed by police and firemen in a private home were a hoax perpetrated by a 10-year-old girl. Detective Capt. Anthony Fabrizi said that the girl, Meredith Goodin, adopted by Mr. and Mrs. Gerald Goodin admitted tossing around furniture in the home when no one was looking."

However, the case was far from settled. Not everyone, apparently, was happy with the official police explanation. The Reverend William Charbomneaux, a Roman Catholic priest who had been called in by the family to observe the preternatural force at work, was not in the least impressed by the police statement. Reverend Charbomneaux told reporters that he had deliberately checked the house for wires and trick devices which could account for the phenomena, but failed to uncover anything that looked suspicious. Besides, he pointed out, he had actually seen household objects move by themselves when little Meredith was under his direct observation. In one instance the girl was standing right next to him holding a bracelet in both hands. Suddenly a heavy dresser started to move from behind her. The priest also said that when he was holding vigil on another occasion, a TV slid off a table and fell to the floor. Meredith wasn't even in the room at the time.

Mr. and Mrs. Goodin were left as perplexed as ever. On one hand, the police were claiming that the whole haunting was a fraud, while their priest was maintaining, just as staunchly, that it was genuine. The crowds outside the house apparently sided with the police and dispersed, leaving the Goodins in peace. The police closed their files on the case and left as well. Unfortunately, the object throwings continued and the Goodins were left wondering what in God's name was happening to them.

Was some sort of PK force flinging household items about or was little Meredith playing tricks? Going over the case today, we might be able to come to a less biased conclusion.

The whole terrifying ordeal started for the Goodins on November 23. Late that night the entire family heard what they described as "pounding noises" emanating from the walls of the house. The knockings were not stationary and moved freely from one room to another.

It wasn't too long after the rappings began that household items commenced to move by themselves. Eight o'clock the next morning, Goodin heard a crashing noise from an adjoining room. He rushed onto the scene and found that a table had fallen over. Other tables and chairs followed suit as the bewildered man looked on. The Goodins were so unnerved by the events that they called in two friends, Harold and Mary Hoffman. By the time the couple arrived, the Goodin household looked as though it had been singled out by a tornado. According to the Hoffmans, cutlery, dishes, and furniture were scattered in disarray. Something had been flinging every conceivable item in the house about in fury.

As fortune would have it, an off-duty policeman happened to be passing by as the Goodins were trying to size up their situation. They quickly beseeched him to come inside, hoping that he could be of help. Policeman John Holsworth answered the frightened call . . . and became the first disinterested party actually to watch the antics in progress:

"I saw the heavy refrigerator lift slowly off the floor, turn, and then set down again," recounted Holsworth. "There was no one else around. Then the big TV set seemed to float in the air and crash to the floor."

Time was moving fast. Holsworth had hardly finished making his observations when more police arrived. Police Officer Joseph Tomek was the next law-enforcement officer to confirm Holsworth's observations. He told reporters:

"I just couldn't believe what I saw. Shelves fixed to the walls began to vibrate until they broke loose, then flew through the air. I looked for evidence that someone was making it happen, but I couldn't find anything—no wires, nothing. Then I watched as a big TV fell over."

By noon that day police, the fire department, and well-wishers were at the scene, all searching for an explanation for the outbreak. It didn't take police long to find a mundane explanation which they could report to the media whose interest had been aroused by the reports. The next day, Bridgeport's superintendent of police announced that the Goodins' daughter had hoaxed the whole affair.

Even the police couldn't get by with that one. One police sergeant, who had been on the scene of the outbreak for several hours, took strong exception to his superior's statement. Another policeman, Cal Leonze, had actually seen pictures fly off the walls and told reporters that he didn't think the girl was responsible. However, the police withdrew from the case, even though the eerie antics were continuing to plague the house. The Goodins eventually wired their furniture to the floor and began making plans to move.

In rereading all the collected testimony on the Bridgeport case, one has to be impressed. There were over forty visitors to the house, and while some of them thought the entire outbreak was a fake, many others were equally sure that some supernatural force was rampaging in the Goodin home. Some of these witnesses included fire and police officials. So why then did the police dismiss the case so quickly?

One reason is obvious. Very few people are aware that hauntings and kindred phenomena have been scientifically studied for nearly a hundred years. The police, I am afraid, have little official policy when it comes to the paranormal. When they were called into the Goodin home, they went with one thing in mind: if objects were being thrown around, somebody must be throwing them. Notice that I said some*body*, not some*thing*. So they immediately looked for a likely candidate. The Goodins' daughter was the likely suspect, and she became the police scapegoat.

The police announcement may also have actually been made out of genuine concern for the family's welfare and safety. Swarms of people invaded the Goodins' property when the news of the mysterious events hit the radio and papers. One or two overenthusiastic thrill-seekers even tried to break into the house, while crank telephone callers bombarded the Goodins with talk of evil spirits. The police probably knew that they could disperse the crowd by declaring that the whole thing was a hoax. For all intents and purposes, their strategy worked very well.

The Goodins are certainly not unique. They are not the first family that has suddenly found itself in the middle of a psychic eruption. Reports of homes besieged by inexplicable noises, object throwings, and even more bizarre phenomena have been recorded for centuries and from every part of the world. Let's go back some eighteen years and examine a similar report.

In March 1958, reports were carried coast to coast about a house on Long Island which was being plagued by some rather bizarre manifestations. The family reported that they had seen objects moving about the house, bottles propelling from countertops and popping their tops, and furniture shifting around the floor.

The police were soon called in, but could offer no explanation for the outbreak. They did note, however, that a twelve-year-old son seemed linked to the phenomena. The odd displays seemed only to occur when the boy was home and awake, so the police grilled him intensely for a confession. The boy only cried and insisted that he wasn't responsible for the manifestations.

The police did everything in their power to discover a natural cause for the outbreak. First they checked to see if anyone was operating a radio set in the neighborhood which might be emitting high-frequency waves which could possibly account for the disturbances. When that theory fell through, the Long Island Lighting Company made a gallant entrance, hoping to find an electrical malfunction in the home. But everything checked out O.K. Fireboxes, water leaders, and ground connections were all eyed as likely culprits, and even the chimney was capped to eliminate the possibility of freak downdrafts. The Town of Hempstead Engineers' Office made a check and found no underground water or streams around the land on which the house was built which might be setting off unusual seismic activity. One by one any normal explanations for the family ghost were laid to rest.

Despite these, and many other investigations, there was no reprieve from the nightmare. Bottles kept crashing into walls, and furniture moved about as noisily as ever. News accounts of the disturbances came to the attention of Dr. Rhine at Duke who quickly dispatched two parapsychologists, Dr. J. G. Pratt and W. G. Roll, to the scene of the action. After examining witnesses and weighing the evidence, the investigators could come up with no normal cause for the incidents. In short, they diagnosed the case as a possible poltergeist.

Poltergeist is a funny German word which, when roughly translated, means "noisy ghost." Poltergeist outbreaks represent the next step in our study of PK. Outbreaks similar to the ones which terrified the Goodins and the Long Island family have been reported for centuries, and accounts dating back to the first century A.D. can be traced. Every year two or three new cases hit the press.

So just what is a poltergeist?

Poltergeist disturbances are a form of spontaneous PK which usually erupt in a family setting. The unfortunate family will suddenly find itself victimized by any number of a vast range of manifestations. Raps resound over the house, objects move or fly about by themselves, furniture shifts position, objects disappear and reappear, mysterious fires break out, rocks bombard the house, and so on. In some cases the poltergeist harasses the family with only one type of phenomenon, but in other cases several different manifestations will join forces in an all-out assault on the hapless home.

In the usual poltergeist case, the disturbances are directly linked to the family under attack. If the family flees, the phenomena will more than likely follow them wherever they go. There are many cases on record where poltergeist outbreaks have followed a poor family from home to home as they tried to outrun the PK. More specifically, the poltergeist usually focuses on one member of the household, usually an adolescent. These victims become either the focus of the attack, or the phenomena usually occur only when they are present and awake. If they are sent away from the family, for example, the outbreak will most likely abate only to renew itself when that person returns. On a more optimistic note, however, poltergeist infestations are usually brief and rarely last more than a few weeks to a couple of months.

In short, the poltergeist does follow a particular and even predictable pattern. It is a PK syndrome in its own right and the above-mentioned features crop up in case after case. Nevertheless, the poltergeist is anything but stereotyped and each case will be marked by its own peculiarities. The Goodins and the Long Island family were victimized by object-throwing poltergeists. This is perhaps the most common form the outbreaks take. Objects of all sizes—from kitchen utensils to large pieces of furniture—will be hoisted about, float, or will be flung across the room. However, there are many other types of poltergeists as well. So before trying to understand the nature of the poltergeist, let's first take a look at five different additional types: (1) rapping poltergeists, (2) stone-throwing poltergeists, (3) teleporting poltergeists, (4) water poltergeists, and (5) fire poltergeists.

A typical rapping poltergeist made an appearance in the little German town of Pursruck in November 1970 and continued well into the next year. The scene of the infestation was an old schoolhouse which had been converted into an apartment building where two girls, Helga, aged thirteen and Anna R., aged eleven, were staying with their grandmother. After a member of a downstairs family had died, tappings were heard over the building but faded out after a few weeks. Apparently, nothing more happened that year.

The poltergeist began its real siege in May 1971 when raps,

scraping noises, and sawing sounds were heard in the elderly woman's apartment each night after the girls had retired. The noises were not stationary. Sometimes they came from under the girls' beds and at other times erupted from cupboards and doors. The noises became so loud that onlookers claimed that they sounded like machine-gun fire.

The first outside investigator to confront this poltergeist was a local village priest, Reverend Jakob Wolfsteiner, who took both girls, along with their parents, to his hometown of Lintach where he could better observe the phenomena. The raps continued there as well. Wolfsteiner had the children lay down on a table or on the carpet in his parsonage so they could be carefully watched. Nonetheless many witnesses heard the knocking sounds which would invariably start when the children were lying quietly. Reverend Wolfsteiner reported:

> In the evening of June 9, 1971, I went to Pursruck with the agreement of the parents and the children of the family R. I took along my Contaflax camera with long distance objective, and electric flashlight, and a tape recorder. The girls were in their beds. In the first minutes, they were covered with their blankets, holding their hands folded on their foreheads. Later on, the girls' father took away the blankets so that their feet and their whole body [sic] would be seen. Tappings were to be heard . . . I observed the girls in the light of an electric torch. Tappings appeared when the girls lay completely quiet in their beds and went on when I spoke to them. After these adventures I was definitely convinced that the girls could not possibly have caused the phenomena with their hands or other parts of their bodies.

The priest called a psychologist into the case so that a clinical assessment of the girls could be made. The psychologist, in turn, quickly discovered that the raps had begun after Anna had been frightened by a series of nightmares. These dreams, of a man standing by her bed shaking snakes at her, indicated that the girl was having psychological difficulties coping with her pubertal development.

It was at this time that the Pursruck case came to the attention of Professor Hans Bender, a German psychologist who heads a division of parapsychology at the University of Freiburg. Bender was able to hear the raps for himself when he investigated, but the poltergeist soon degenerated as the girls, overcoming their fears, began faking the raps themselves.

We really shouldn't be surprised that the girls eventually resorted to fraud. In many poltergeist cases the children involved will often deliberately begin to imitate the acts which they have seen the poltergeist carry out. Why, you may ask? There are several reasons for this common behavior. First, the child gains attention and, second, it keeps the fun going. In one case I personally investigated, a young girl was faking a poltergeist after the genuine PK had petered out in order to stay home from school! Fraud is probably the most difficult problem the poltergeist investigator must confront, for not only will children (and adults too, for that matter) manufacture poltergeists, but they will resort to fraud even when genuine activity is plaguing their homes.

From rapping poltergeists it isn't too far a journey to object-throwing ones. The Goodin case is a good example. As dozens of witnesses watched, objects fell from shelves, furniture hurled through the air, and kitchen utensils were thrown at them. Sometimes the objects came so quickly and from so many different directions that it was difficult for the onlookers even to keep track of everything.

One special type of object thrower which is commonly reported is the stone-throwing poltergeist during which stones, and oftentimes nothing else, will constitute the projectiles. There are generally two types of stone throwers. In the first type, stones bombard the *outside* of the house. For several days there might be periodic showers of hundreds of stones which will fall on the roof or catapult against the sides of the structure. The stones have been seen to fall in zigzag motion, sometimes do not bounce when they strike the ground, will fall abnormally slowly, and are often warm to the touch.

One of the most celebrated stone-throwings recorded in this country was the Big Bear, California, case of 1962 during which stones mysteriously attacked a mountain cabin. Both family members and sheriff's deputies witnessed the showers. The rocks would just suddenly appear over the house and then "float" down and strike the roof. One witness told reporters that he watched a rock suddenly appear out of nowhere and "float" down to the ground at a 30-degree angle. When he picked up the rock, he found it warm to the touch. Sheriff's deputies were called in and they immediately blamed the disturbance on a prankster armed with a slingshot. But they could find no culprit even though they scoured the area. In fact, one rock shower even damaged a deputy's car.

The family just couldn't handle the ordeal. They packed up their belongings and moved. Two college students were the next to rent the cabin and, even as they helped the family remove the last vestiges of their possessions, watched a rock come right through a window, smashing it to bits.

After that, the poltergeist seemed vanquished. A few more stones fell . . . and the case was over.

Even more fascinating than this type of rock-throwing poltergeist is another form which I call the "indoor stone-thrower." In these cases, as the name would imply, the rocks suddenly appear and fly about *inside* the house. These cases pose a double enigma. First, we have to ask, what force is throwing the rocks? Second, and even more perplexing, how do the rocks get into the house in the first place? In some cases it is highly likely that the rocks are actually teleported into the house. In other words, they are brought into the house right through solid matter such as doors and walls.

A good example of a teleporting stone-thrower was reported by W. G. Grottendieck, a Dutch traveler who was persecuted by a poltergeist for only one night in the jungles of Sumatra. He had settled down in a hut, expecting no doubt to pass a blissfully uneventful night when the poltergeist struck:

> I put my bullsack and mosquito netting on the wooden floor and soon fell asleep. At about one o'clock at night I half awoke, hearing something fall near my head outside the mosquito curtain on the floor. After a couple of minutes I completely awoke and turned my head half around to see what was falling on the floor. They were *black stones* from ⅛ to ¾ of an inch long. I got out of the curtain and turned up the kerosene lamp that was standing on the floor at the foot of the bed. I saw than that the stones were falling through the roof in a parabolic line. They fell on the floor close to my head-pillow. I went out and awoke the boy (a Malay-Pelamdang) who was sleeping on the floor in the next room. I told him to go outside and examine the jungle up to a certain distance. He did so whilst I lighted up the jungle by means of a small "ever-ready" electric lantern. At the same time that

the investigation came to a halt. When the children begin to fake, it is a sure sign that the poltergeist has ebbed.

So far we have surveyed the more commonly reported types of poltergeistery. However, sometimes the poltergeist will resort to extremely bizarre forms of persecution. The following cases represent one of the rarest forms of poltergeist attacks . . . the water poltergeist, in which instead of throwing things about, the poltergeist precipitates water all over the house. Only a few cases are on record, such as the following one:

According to the Lawrence, Massachusetts, *Eagle-Tribune*, the poltergeist started plaguing one family in October 1963. It all started unexpectedly when the family noticed a peculiar "wet spot" on the wall of the TV room in their apartment. Only a few moments later they heard a "pop" like a firecracker going off, and a jet of water squirted from the wall! This almost humorous incident was only the beginning of what turned out to be quite an ordeal. For the next three days water ejected from the walls almost continually. Finally, the family fled the apartment.

With the exception of this case, water poltergeists seemed to have become as nearly extinct as the ivory-billed woodpecker in the last fifty years. But the water poltergeist made a sensational comeback in Germany in 1972.

The scene of this poltergeist was a home in the little village of Scherfede. Small puddles of water began to form on the floor of the house in September. Mechanics were called in to check over the pipes and heating tubes. They found nothing awry. The local magistrate, realizing something mysterious was going on, eventually called in investigators from the Freiburg Institute for the Study of Border Areas of Psychology.

By October, though, the phenomena had taken on a new twist. Humid moist spots started to appear on the walls, and damp spots began to precipitate on the carpets. This is very reminiscent of the Massachusetts case.

By December 10 the poltergeist had really begun its attack. As Hans Bender describes it:

> . . . In intervals of 20-30 minutes, big water puddles appeared in the drawing room of the house. The family K.—father, mother and a 13-year-old girl Kerstin—heard a splashing when they were in another room. Nothing happened when they were present, and no one has even seen a pool in formation. Technicians came and admit-

ted that they were completely puzzled and could not find any cause. Trickery was excluded by carefully observing the room in question. At 7:30 P.M. neighbors of the next but one house came and asked for help: floods of water had suddenly appeared on the second floor and were coming down the staircase. There was too much to mop up with floor cloths. Helpers formed an echelon and brushed it out of the house. They were still at work when an hour later help was claimed for the next house where unexplainable water pools and splashes appeared and, another hour later, the same happened in the adjoining house, the last one of the row. This continued, more or less intensely, for three days.

So, in this case water phenomena infested an entire block of row houses. At first glance this might indicate that the water had a normal source such as bad plumbing, since poltergeists are not normally contagious. But this theory can't explain some of the more bizarre aspects of the case. When the water main was cut off to the K.'s house, water gushes continued nonetheless. Analysis of the water showed it to be identical to that of the local spring. By this time, building technicians, geologists and hydrologists were all on the scene scratching their heads in bewilderment.

It was at this time that Professor Bender got into the case. He and his colleagues soon isolated little thirteen-year-old Kerstin as the paranormal source of the infestation. They uncovered the revealing fact that she had often used the lavatories in the other victimized homes, and in two cases the water appeared in houses right after Kerstin had visited them. The one house on the block Kerstin had never visited was the only one to escape the contagion.

Like most poltergeists, this one was short-lived as well. The water manifestations soon ebbed. The case, though, has still not been resolved and Bender is still studying it and the role Kerstin obviously played.

Some poltergeists seem to be self-restrictive. That is, they rely on only one effect. The Massachusetts case is a good one in point. It *only* used water. There are other cases where the only phenomenon used is fire igniting, another form of nuisance—but an even more vicious and destructive one. Fire poltergeists, as the name implies, delight in setting fires one after another in the victimized home. Forty to fifty fires a day is not unheard of and sometimes even nonflammable objects will burst into flames. Fire officials are usually called in, but no normal cause for the blazes are ever found.

The fire poltergeist to end all fire poltergeists was the Macomb, Illinois, case of 1948. As Vincent Gaddis states in his book, *Mysterious Fires and Lights,* "Every daily newspaper in the United States and the leading journals of Europe carried day to day reports, most of them on their front pages."

The horror all started the first week of August when the Willey family noticed spots appearing on the wallpaper of their five-room farmhouse. These brown spots would get hotter and hotter and then—in an instant—burst out in flames. The fires were witnessed by the entire household: Willey himself, his wife, his brother-in-law, his nephew who was eight, and his little niece.

All day the brown spots and fires erupted. The family had to keep on their toes to stem each new blaze before it got out of control. Neighbors soon came to the aid of the puzzled family, buckets in hand, eyes constantly patrolling the house for the next brown spot to appear. Pans of water actually had to be stationed throughout the house as a safeguard. Of course, fire inspectors were on the scene in no time. Their advice? Strip the wallpaper off the walls, suggested Macomb fire chief, Fred Wilson. Unfortunately, denuding the walls made little difference. The fires just burst forth from the walls anyway. Even the ceiling had its share of fires. And what did Chief Wilson have to say about all of this?

"The whole thing is so screwy and fantastic that I'm almost ashamed to talk about it," he admitted.

The mysterious fires expanded their scope during the second week in August. Now fires began to ignite outside the house. The porch flared up, an ironing board outside was set on fire, and, back inside, the curtains were badly burned. Fire officials estimated that over two hundred fires had plagued the Willey house during the course of the epidemic. By August 14—two weeks after the brown spots first appeared—it was no longer any use even to try to contain the blazes. The house was finally consumed in flames and gutted.

The Willeys, homeless and hapless, took up rather rugged living accommodations in a large tent that they pitched on their property. Willey's brother-in-law and his family moved into a nearby garage. Despite the fact that the Willeys had no home in which to live, the fires still did not abate. The very day after their house was destroyed, the barn burned down. Two days after that the flames destroyed the milkhouse, tried to burn up the chicken house, and finally succeeded in burning down a second barn on the property. The only things that were left of the Willey farm were six outhouses. The poltergeist, it would seem, is a great respecter of privacy.

Everyone got into the act trying to find a rational explanation for the constant fires. One investigator thought that overhead airplanes were causing the fires by emitting high-frequency waves. That didn't explain anything because only the Willey farm, and no others in the area, was being affected. Flammable insecticides were blamed and freak gas deposits were checked for. In the meantime, fire officials, keeping their feet firmly on the ground during the crisis, started looking for arson suspects. They soon found one. They immediately focused on the Willeys' thirteen-year-old niece, Wanet, and hauled her before the media claiming that she was responsible for the entire affair. But how? No one really knew. Although the girl had been constantly underfoot during the entire episode, no one had ever seen her toying with matches or flammable chemicals.

Altogether twelve major and well-documented cases have been reported in the United States and Canada since 1940. The number of fires per case ranges from three to thirty. In one case, the Macomb incident, there were too many fires to count. On the average (discounting the Macomb case), the number of fires per case was 13.3 The average length of the cases was between a few days to two weeks.

How do we know that these incendiary reports are poltergeists at all and not just some freak physical phenomenon? Fire cases certainly seem to be different from the usual rampaging poltergeists we read about so often. There are several reasons why we believe that these epidemics are, in fact, a genuine form of poltergeist effect. First, mysterious fires will occur during more conventional poltergeist outbreaks. In one case I know of, the poltergeist first pounded on the walls, then threw things, and finally set a series of fires in the house. Second, the fire outbreaks conform to a typical poltergeist pattern. They usually occur in a family setting where children are present, rarely last very long, and—most significantly of all—will follow the family if they move. During one famous Alabama case the fires destroyed five houses in which the family had taken up residence. Third, these fires often consume totally noncombustible objects. Within the accounts I have collected are reports of loaves of bread, wet laundry, and even a household pet or two that have caught fire. Normal fires just do not act that way.

So, where does all of this lead us? We've now taken brief looks at rapping spooks and stone-throwing villains, teleporting objects and water sprites, and even thrown in a hell-fire or two. So we end up with that million-dollar question: What actually causes the poltergeist?

Anyone who has carefully read the foregoing accounts should have realized that adolescents were conspicuously present in almost every case I've summarized. As I stated at the onset of this chapter, this pattern crops up in case after case. So it is obvious that somehow these adolescents are intrinsically related to the poltergeist. In the Bridgeport case, the poltergeist focus was the adopted daughter. Two children were present in the Pursruck case. Even in rock-throwing poltergeists, we find the identical pattern. The Big Bear outbreak attacked a family which consisted of several children, including an adopted daughter. Even though W. G. Grottendieck was alone in his room when the black stones fell from the ceiling, he was accompanied on his jungle expedition by an adolescent native boy. The Nickleheim poltergeist focused on a child, and in both water poltergeist cases I cited a child was present. A child was present in the Macomb fires.

It is apparent that adolescents are almost always present when the poltergeist strikes. Even at the turn of the century psychic investigators were aware of the fact. Recently W. G. Roll, project director of the Psychical Research Foundation, and one of this country's leading poltergeist experts, reevaluated 102 poltergeist cases and found that 82 percent of them focused on a particular family member or members in the household. Although in the previous century more boys than girls became poltergeist foci, this sex differentiation has evened out over the years. According to his calculations, the ratio of male to female poltergeist children is 40 percent to 59.5 percent, and the average age of the focal person is between thirteen and fourteen years of age. Oddly enough, Roll found that over the years the age of the victim has increased steadily.

These children are the key with which we have begun to

unlock the mystery of the poltergeist. Since children always seem to be around when the poltergeist strikes, it is logical to assume that the youngsters are, in fact, producing the disturbances by PK, even though they seem to be unaware of it. Far from being caused by spirits or demons as was once widely believed, the real root of the poltergeist is the poltergeist victim himself. This concept will be easier to understand if you think back to the many instances of spontaneous PK. These cases would seem to prove that we use PK unconsciously to carry out a physical act in the world around us, such as making a clock stop, when someone we know has died. Poltergeists represent a similar process, but in these cases, the PK runs rampant, upsetting everything in the household.

But why?

Psychoanalyzing the poltergeist agent has been a parapsychological pastime for years, and many independent investigators have tried to figure out what psychological motivation would cause innocent children to unleash such a horrible force. Today, more and more cases are being studied and parapsychologists and psychologists alike are getting to the root of the poltergeist syndrome by clinically interviewing and testing the agents involved. These studies are telling us quite a lot about the dynamics of the poltergeist and what causes it to erupt.

The fact that the poltergeist uses a form of unconscious expression has been suspected for years. For example, Harry Price, a well-known British poltergeist hunter, investigated the strange case of Eleanore Zugun back in the 1920s. Eleanore was a Rumanian girl who was so victimized by a poltergeist that her parents had her committed. Luckily she was rescued and brought to Price's attention. He found that the PK followed Eleanore wherever she went—from Vienna to London and right into his own laboratory—and he felt that the PK was probably caused by conflicts arising from the girl's sexual maturation. Sure enough, the poltergeistery ceased when the girl's menstruation began. In the 1930s the Hungarian-born psychoanalyst, Nandor Fodor, probed a London poltergeist that centered on a neurotic and sexually disturbed woman. He uncovered evidence that the PK antics were psychological projections reflecting the woman's repressed hostility over sexual and interpersonal conflicts. Fodor called the poltergeist "a bundle of projected repressions." This definition neatly sums up what we think the poltergeist represents and what it is trying to express.

The general theory that the poltergeist represents a form of psychological expression has had startling confirmation over the last few years. Two contemporary investigators, W. G. Roll in this country and Dr. Hans Bender in Germany, have not only witnessed several modern cases, but in each instance have taken detailed psychological looks at the agents around whom the PK focused. Interestingly enough, most of these agents have shown similar psychological profiles when clinically examined. In case after case it has been found that the agents are the center of strong conflicts and hostilities, usually projected toward authority figures such as parents or employers. However, these agents also reveal an abnormally strong use of such defenses as repression, sublimation, and denial in order to deal with these frustrations. All of these defenses are used for a similar goal. They push this strong underlying anger out of the conscious mind and into the mysterious realms of the unconscious. Since this pattern has emerged in a number of poltergeist children (and adults!), it is now clear that this psychological setting is intrinsically related to the poltergeist itself.

These profiles tell us a great deal about the poltergeist. When the PK erupts, it looks as if it is caused by an agent who is seething with unconscious rage. The poltergeist is born as an unconscious form of expression. When the victim can no longer control his intense anger, even on an unconscious level, the PK is unleashed as a safety valve and as a means of venting the pent-up frustration. It is also a safe method of expression as well. The agent remains unaware that he is causing the disturbance and can unwittingly express his hostility without guilt or the threat of punishment or reprisal. Often the adolescent himself becomes the focus of the poltergeist and is singled out for persecution. In these cases, it appears as if the anger is directed inwardly.

This general theory also explains the psychological meaning behind the antics of the poltergeist. When a child is angry he exhibits his emotions by pounding on walls, throwing things in a rage, slamming doors, and even stealing. Notice that these are the same acts which the poltergeist performs. It, too, pounds on walls, throws things, and steals. So we might say that the poltergeist or

PK force carries out the very actions and nuisances that the agent would like to carry out consciously but doesn't dare. This pattern of hostility and repression has appeared in several cases where Rorschach inkblot, Thematic Apperception Test, Sentence Completion Test, and other evaluations have been made of the poltergeist focus. (In the Thematic Apperception Test [TAT] the subject makes up stories about ambiguous picture scenes placed before him. In the Sentence Completion Test he fills in a key word to a sentence where many emotionally charged words could be used. In both tests, the subject will tend to choose verbal responses which reveal his psychological needs.) Sometimes, though, the agents are somehow dimly aware that they are causing the commotion. One poltergeist agent told W. G. Roll that he actually enjoyed the phenomena. "It makes me feel happy; I don't know why," he candidly admitted.

A well-publicized poltergeist broke out in a Miami warehouse in 1967 where a youthful employee was working. The case was investigated by W. G. Roll. Even though the young man was closely watched, items kept flying off the storeroom shelves. Roll had the youth clinically examined by Dr. Randall Harper, a professional psychologist. After working with him, Harper wrote in his report that the young man harbored ". . . aggressive feelings which are disturbing and unacceptable to him." The psychologist also found that the youth psychologically diverted any open display of his inner feelings.

Another poltergeist case was investigated by Roll where the center of the attack was a young and very unhappy boy. Here is an extract from the psychologist's report on him:

"Throughout the three interviews the most striking feature was the degree to which he uses denial and repression as defenses. There was considerable evidence of an intense, underlying anger towards his grandmother, but he was never able to verbalize this."

W. G. Roll has not been the only U.S. parapsychologist who has isolated this pattern. Dr. John Palmer, a psychologist who was then working at the University of Virginia's division of parapsychology at the time, ran into a poltergeist which was rampaging in a rural Southern town in 1972. It was a typical object thrower. A teenage boy was the likely PK candidate, and Palmer had him clinically evaluated by a psychologist who knew nothing about poltergeists. After concluding her examination the psychologist reported back to Palmer that the boy's ". . . general approach to life situations is passive and submissive; he tends to deny, to avoid, and to withdraw."

All of these cases support my opinion that the actual poltergeist antics are literal representations of the acts the agent would like to perform consciously. Even the more bizarre aspects of the poltergeist can be explained this way. Take fire poltergeists, for example. I do not know of any child who does not have a strange fascination for fire. Children are constantly playing with matches and will secretly steal outside with them in order to set something on fire just to watch it burn. Probably everyone reading this book can remember how as children they took great delight in filching matches and attempting to light them when their parents weren't looking. Fire poltergeist attacks may be a psychic version of this same common fascination. Water poltergeists threw me for a while until I realized that it was quite likely that the water jettings have a symbolic meaning. If anything, the poltergeist is a means of unconscious protest. Another, albeit more normal, means of psychological protest is bed-wetting. Many parents have learned the sad fact that their child will resort to enuresis when he is disturbed. Most often children turn to bed-wetting when they feel they are not getting enough attention. For example, the arrival of a new baby into the family can ignite an episode. Perhaps water poltergeists are a form of psychic enuresis, a means of protest and attention getting.

A different interpretation of the psychological *meaning* behind the poltergeist's repertoire of tricks, however, has been recently offered by Dr. Joel Whitton. Dr. Whitton is a Canadian psychologist who believes that the form poltergeistic PK takes represents a much more complicated psychological process. Since poltergeists do follow a set pattern of phenomena, asks Whitton, what serves as the model for these phenomena? Where has the child unconsciously learned what PK effects the poltergeist should precipitate? Dr. Whitton's answer is a little more complex than my own view:

> In the first few years of life before the capacity for abstract and rational thought develops, many experiences happen to us that are realized as having an unexplained or magical quality. Noises or

sounds may be heard and objects may be seen to move or disappear and magically reappear. Sensory experiences of touch or smell which have happened to us before we have developed the ability to think about them may be strange, unexplained, and possibly frightening. For example, a baby may hear the footsteps of someone walking on a bare floor above his head. Looking toward the sound, nothing is to be seen. Not able to conceptualize the fact that the sound is simply due to someone's footsteps on the floor above the ceiling, or to someone moving furniture around, the memory remains in the baby as a strange, unexplained experience. Fear could be associated with this experience, if the noises were particularly loud or startling, or if the baby was alone and already anxious about something else, such as the absence of its mother. In the previous example, if anxiety or fear is associated with this memory—this memory of a strange, unexplained sound that the baby hears—the entire conflict complex, the strange noise and the concomitant anxious experience of separation from its mother; the whole thing may be forgotten and repressed and may lie dormant in the unconscious for years. Years later, the adolescent or the adult may experience an anxious separation which may then reenact the early memory of the associated strange noises. The hypothesis that I'm presenting is that in those individuals who have the psychic ability to produce poltergeist activity, the reexperiencing of early sensory memories, because they are associated with a certain fear, leads to those memories being relived or acted out, or externalized in the physical world.

Of course, either Dr. Whitton's or my own views can explain the meaning of the poltergeist, but we are still faced with a huge question mark even if we can solve the psychological enigma of the poltergeist. We have to admit, quite frankly, that we still have not even begun to fathom the mystery behind the physical force which the poltergeist exerts. How the poltergeist can carry out seemingly "impossible acts" is just as great a mystery as ever. As John Beloff, one of Great Britain's leading psychologists and parapsychologists has quipped, "We are really no closer to solving the poltergeist mystery than we were when society believed that the outbreaks were caused by spirits or demons."

Nonetheless, some new light has recently been shed on the mystery which *might* (and I say this guardedly) be the next step in our understanding of the syndrome. Some recent findings by W. G. Roll suggest a whole new approach to the poltergeist. Even though his research has done a great deal to substantiate the "unhappy adolescent theory," Roll has now come to believe that there may be a peculiar link between poltergeist outbreaks and epilepsy. In reviewing some three hundred years of poltergeist history, he discovered that a disproportionately large number of agents had medical histories which suggested epilepsy. But what really got Roll interested in this aspect came in 1975 when he and his associate, Gerald Solfvin, were called in to investigate a poltergeist in the Midwest.

The poltergeist was certainly versatile. Its chief phenomena consisted of raps which were so loud that a demolitions expert stated that they sounded like TNT blasts. Objects were thrown about and finally a series of fires gutted the house. The focus of the outbreak was a frustrated, twenty-one-year-old epileptic youth. Solfvin and Roll discovered that there was an unusual correlation between the PK outbreaks and his medical history. No poundings were heard in the house at the onset of the epileptic seizures, but as his medical history and prognosis worsened, the PK steadily increased correspondingly.

Within recent years several epileptic poltergeist agents have come to light. This has prompted Roll and Solfvin to conclude:

"In many respects, the classic poltergeist agent begins to look like an ideopathic epileptic whose massive discharges in the brain are now somehow transformed into RSPK [spontaneous recurrent psychokinesis]. Stress seems to be the key, for stress can cause both epileptic seizures and poltergeist manifestations."

There is, however, another way of looking at the relationship between epilepsy and poltergeist phenomena which I think Roll and Solfvin have overlooked. O.K., let's admit that a suspiciously high number of poltergeist agents have histories of epileptic seizures. There may be a perfectly normal reason for this. We know that people are afraid to report poltergeist disturbances because they feel that no one will believe them and that they will be ridiculed. However, a household which contains an epileptic member might be more willing to report the disturbances for several reasons. First, the family might think that the disturbances are related somehow to the epilepsy. Second, a qualified doctor might witness the PK and realize that there should be an investigation. Trained professional people, such as a doctor or nurse, might be less reticent about calling in a parapsychologist than the bewildered family itself. So, there may be no real relationship between poltergeists and epilepsy, but just that more of these cases get publicly reported.

As you can see, there are many ways of approaching and studying the poltergeist. This great phenomenon is probably the most dramatic form of PK in the whole realm of psychic phenomena. I encountered my first active poltergeist in 1974 after six years of searching and waiting. I will never forget the awe and excitement I felt. Here it was, PK in action. Afterward, I read everything in my library on the subject. Today, I have come to feel that we have still not answered even the most superficial questions about the nature of the phenomenon. Why, for instance, does it resort to fire setting in one case and object throwing in another? What are the individual psychodynamics which dictate the form the poltergeist will take? The answer must lie in the mind of the agents. Will we eventually find predictable psychological reasons which dictate which effects will be used in each individual case? I would like to see if the agents in rock-throwing cases, for example, have different personality patterns than agents of fire-igniting ones.

However, I am chiefly fascinated by the intelligence behind the poltergeist. As I have studied countless records of historical cases, I have gradually come to believe that poltergeist disturbances are not only outbreaks. They are virtual attacks! I believe this because poltergeist outbreaks often seem to reveal an underlying strategy or even battle plan. In many instances the poltergeist will begin with raps. More complex PK tasks usually occur later, just as though the poltergeist were growing in force and power. Sometimes it will even change strategy in midstream. It will rely on one effect predominately and then shift focus, forsaking the old antics and concentrating on new and even more spectacular and persecuting PK displays.

All this indicates to me that there is an actual sophisticated intelligence behind the poltergeist. It is true that we cannot deny the fact that most of them are somehow created by human agents. But this tells us virtually nothing and has led to a misconception about the poltergeist. It is rather easy to think that a poltergeist merely consists of an agent who goes around "zapping" things unconsciously through PK. But, does the unconscious mind of the agent really decide when and how the PK will manifest? I cannot help but wonder if we really have that much control over the poltergeist during more complex outbreaks. Poltergeists can be extraordinarily vicious, even evil. One poltergeist investigator I know gave up parapsychology after an encounter he had, for he felt that what he had confronted was so malignant that he never wanted to face it again. Often the poltergeist will get out of control and even the agent will be tormented by the PK. Despite what is commonly believed, poltergeists have done bodily harm to witnesses in a few cases, and thousands of dollars in property damage in others. It is certainly not the "noisy, playful ghost" it is often played up to be.

The theory I'm leading up to is one which few poltergeist experts have confronted. I believe that, at least in some cases, the force which masterminds the poltergeist has only a tenuous connection with the agent's mind and body. The agents let loose the poltergeist all right. There can be no doubt about that. But when the poltergeist is unleashed, does the agent's mind still direct and control it? Or does the poltergeist force develop a mind, intelligence, and motivation of its own? I think there is good evidence to support the theory that, at least in a few cases, the poltergeist eventually becomes independent of the mind which has given it birth. Once the poltergeist is unleashed, it develops its own personality. This new personality directs the attacks and manipulates the PK. The agent does not even control it unconsciously at this point.

To me, the poltergeist represents an even greater mystery than we have generally considered it to be. It represents a doorway into the hidden recesses of the mind and its powers. A doorway, I am afraid to say, we may not be prepared to open.

4

Scientists, Mediums, and PK

PK, IT WOULD seem, has two contradictory facets. On one hand it seems to be a capricious and marginal force which dissipates almost as soon as it precipitates. Yet, if we take even a casual look at poltergeist cases, it appears that PK is a force of incredible magnitude and longevity. So, comparing laboratory PK effects to spontaneous PK might be like comparing the finger paintings of a kindergarten child to a Renoir or a Gainsborough.

Is PK a force which is almost hopelessly locked within the organism? Is it a mental force or a biological one? Why does it apparently perform so poorly when we will it, yet so viciously when we employ it unconsciously? Only more research will answer these questions. However, a few possible answers become evident when we start taking a detailed look at the research which has been carried out with those rare individuals who seem phenomenally gifted with PK. Accounts of people with miraculous powers pervade the entire history of both psychical research and religion, and by the nineteenth century a few bold scientists were beginning to question these accounts.

So let's take a retrospective look at a few of the great mediums of the nineteenth and early twentieth centuries. It was their feats of astounding PK—from levitating tables to materializing phantom forms in darkened seances—which awakened some members of the scientific establishment to the importance of studying PK. In fact, the scientific study of PK made some of its greatest strides in these years.

While Western culture has long played host to tales of hauntings and poltergeists, scientists took little interest in PK phenomena until 1848 when a mild poltergeist infestation began to plague a little cottage in Hydesville, New York. Owing to the vast amount of publicity the case received, scientists, news reporters and townsfolk were soon on the scene trying to figure out what force lay behind the "Hydesville rappings," as the disturbances eventually became known.

The cottage was owned by J. D. Fox, who had moved to Hydesville with his wife and two daughters, Margarette (age 14) and Catherine (age 12) in December 1847. Although the cottage had somewhat of a reputation for being haunted, it is doubtful if the Foxes knew (or much cared) about the home's background. However, in March of 1848 the Foxes began to hear weird knocking sounds in the house and these disturbances went on nightly. What was even more frightening, these knockings seemed to be endowed with some sort of intelligence. As Mrs. Fox testified in a written deposition dated April 11, 1848:

> My husband had not gone to bed when we first heard the noise on this evening. I had just laid down. It commenced as usual. I knew it from all other noises I had ever heard in the house. The girls, who slept in the other bed in the room, heard the noise, and tried to make a similar noise by snapping their fingers. The youngest girl is about 12 years old; she is the one who made her hand go. As fast as she made the noise with her hands or fingers, the sound was followed up in the room. It did not sound any different at that time, only it made the same number of noises that the girl did. When she stopped, the sound itself stopped for a short time.
>
> The other girl, who is in her 15th year, then spoke in sport and said, "Now do this just as I do. Count 1, 2, 3, 4 &" striking one hand in the other at the same time. The blows which she made were repeated as before. It appeared to answer her by repeating every blow that she made. She only did so once. She then began to be startled; and then I spoke and said to the noise, "Count ten," and it made ten stokes or noises. Then I asked the ages of the different children successively, and it gave a number of raps, corresponding to the ages of my children.

Prodded by this discovery, Mrs. Fox went on to ask the "entity" if he were the spirit of a living or a dead person. The raps replied to her question immediately:

I then asked if it was a human being that was making the noise? and if it was, to manifest it by the same noise. There was no noise. I then asked if it was a spirit? and if it was, to manifest it by two sounds. I heard two sounds as soon as the words were spoken. I then asked if it was an injured spirt? to give me the sound, and I heard the rapping distinctly. I asked if it was injured in this house? and it manifested it by the noise. If the person was living that injured it? and got the same answer. I then ascertained by the same method that its remains were buried under the dwelling, and how old it was. When I asked how old it was? it rapped 31 times; that it was a male; that it had left a family of five children; that it had two sons and three daughters all living. I asked if it left a wife? and it rapped. If its wife was then living? no rapping; if she was dead? and the rapping was distinctly heard. How long had she been dead and it rapped twice.

The upshot of the Hydesville episode is history. Soon the Foxes invited their neighbors over to witness and question the rapping themselves. The disturbances soon gained nationwide newspaper coverage and even scientists from Harvard traveled to Hydesville to see the phenomena. No one, though, could come up with a normal solution to the mystery.

By this time, it had become clear that the raps were somehow linked to the Fox sisters, Kate and Margarette. The raps could answer their questions immediately, focused on them, and the girls seemed to have a curious rapport with the "ghost." Even after the Hydesville poltergeist had ended its siege in November, the girls discovered that by sitting at a table in a darkened room they could produce similar raps and even table levitations and other PK manifestations. Soon after, Kate and Margarette became the first "physical (or PK) mediums" and toured the country giving séances and demonstrations of their powers.

But, just what force was causing these phenomena?

The townsfolk of the 1840s knew little of the secret energies housed within man's mind and body. (Remember, at this time even the notion of an "unconscious" mind was a pretty radical idea.) So they naturally assumed that these raps and levitations were caused, as the girls claimed, by spirits of the dead. The Fox sisters subsequently claimed that since their powers came from the dead, they were the harbingers of a new religion, which they called Spiritualism. This new movement (which, by the way, was only one of many which began in New York State during the social chaos of the mid-1800s) asserted that anyone could prove the sacred Christian concept of immortality by directly communicating with the dead through mediums. And, indeed, mediums were soon popping up all over the U.S. by the dozens.

The spread of Spiritualism led to the beginnings of scientific interest in the paranormal. In England especially, many philosophers, scientists, and savants began wondering how much truth lay behind Spiritualism and its phenomena. So in 1882, some thirty years after Spiritualism spread to Great Britain, the Society for Psychical Research was founded by these intellectuals to impartially and critically study reports of psychic phenomena and the people who claimed psychic abilities. The founders of the SPR consisted of a wide assortment of people. Several Spiritualist leaders interested in a critical appraisal of psychic phenomena made up one element. The other main constituency was a group of Cambridge scholars who felt that through the study of psychic phenomena they might answer many philosophical questions about the nature of man. However, the Spiritualist element of the SPR began to fall away when it became apparent that the dominant Cambridge group had little interest in the purely cultist aspects of psychic phenomena. An American SPR was founded soon after. The Societies for Psychical Research in Great Britain and in the United States carried out most of the important scientific and scholarly parapsychological work throughout the world until the 1930s when the universities began taking over psychical research after Rhine began his experiments at Duke.

Probably the greatest of the early physical mediums to emerge from the Spiritualist camp was Daniel Dunglas Home, who was born near Edinburgh, Scotland, in 1833. However, when he was nine, he emigrated to the United States, along with his aunt, with whom he lived.

Even at so young an age, Home seemed to possess some mighty unusual psychic abilities, and as a teenager he often became the focus of mild poltergeist-like antics. Objects would move about in his presence, and his relatives, who were of staunchly religious stock, turned him out. They feared that he was inspired by the devil! Soon after, Home took up mediumship and became one of the most celebrated—and widely tested—mediums of his day. Everyone from Harvard scientists to the crowned heads of Europe sought to witness and explore the secret of his powers. Even today, books are still being written about him.

In a typical séance, Home and his experimenters would sit around a table in fairly strong light. Unlike most mediums he rarely conducted his séances in darkness. He would go into trance and then the PK would begin. His PK phenomena were varied. Besides the ability to levitate tables and move objects about paranormally, he could materialize apparitional forms in the séance room, create psychic lights, become immune to fire (one of his most spectacular feats), levitate himself, and bring through messages which purportedly came from the dead.

One of Home's most ardent supporters was a young British nobleman, Lord Adare, who was also the medium's close companion between 1867–1869, during which time he made detailed records of their séances together. His detailed report, *Experiences in Spiritualism with D. D. Home,* is one of the most significant volumes on PK ever written.

The following extract from Adare's book is just a portion of one séance he attended. For the experiment, all the guests sat around a cloth-covered table. Props such as an accordion were kept at hand so that the PK (or the "spirits") would have some handy objects to manipulate:

> The door had hardly closed when there were cold currents, vibrations and raps. I returned, and was scarcely seated, when the alphabet was called for, and this message given: "We love Freddy, but he is not in a state of mind or body conducive to manifestations." [The sitters would call out the alphabet and a rap would resound at the appropriate letter, or the table would tilt a certain number of times in order to designate a certain letter.] Wynne fetched the accordion. Mrs. Blackburn was very soon after touched on the dress, and something became plainly visible moving under the table cloth, along the edge of the table, raising up the cloth several inches, as would be done were a hand and arm [underneath it.] The hand was visible on the cloth to Mr. Home, and I once faintly perceived it. It touched Mrs. Blackburn's hand. This manifestation was repeated different times. I was touched on the ankle and several times on the knee. Miss Wynne's dress was strongly pulled. The table was beautifully raised in the air, by three successive lifts, to the height of eighteen inches or two feet.

Scientists, Mediums, and PK

Later at the séance, the accordion, which had been brought to the table, played by itself. As Adare continues:

> I expressed a wish that it might be played without being held by Mr. Home, upon which he withdrew his hand, placing it on the table; the instrument was just touching the under edge of the table, where it remained, as it were, suspended. It began playing very gently. He clapped his hands several times to shew that he was not touching it. The playing soon ceased, and he took it again.
>
> . . . Soon after this we all heard strong sounds which proceeded seemingly from a large oblong writing table, which stood several feet from us; we could perceive it moving; it stopped within a foot of our table, which then moved up to it. We heard first one and then another drawer opened, on the side of the table farthest from us, and a rustling sound as if stirring papers . . .

PK did not only occur when Home was giving a séance, but seemed to linger on afterward as well. In other words, Home's PK would continue to manifest even after a séance was over and done with, sometimes against his will.

Adare recounts several examples of spontaneous linger effects in his book. For example, on one occasion he attended a particularly impressive séance with Home. No sooner had the group seated itself than cold breezes gusted through the room, the séance table hoisted into the air, raps broke out over the entire room, and Home's trance became agitated and even violent. After this rather trying ordeal, Adare and Home returned to their apartment, but the PK kept right on plaguing them. Raps broke out in their rooms, doors opened by themselves, and phantom footsteps paraded about.

As indicated above, raps and table levitations were not the only phenomena which would highlight Home's séances. Oftentimes Home himself would levitate in full light, and this feat was observed several times during his career by many independent and thoroughly scientific researchers. One of his more bizarre PK effects was the materialization of phantom forms which would precipitate right in the séance room. They were usually vague, apparitional forms, and sometimes only part of the figure would be visible. It looks as though Home had the rare ability to make the PK force become visible by molding it into a humanoid shape. In other words, Home's PK could become a physical substance.

Another one of Home's rather astounding abilities was fire immunity. Somehow during his trances he would become immune to fire and heat, and could even transfer this ability to other people present at his demonstrations. Lord Adare was able to observe many instances of this phenomenon, for which Home became understandably famous. In one case, he watched Home harmlessly place a red-hot coal in the hand of one of the experimenters. At other times he would even place his whole face in a pit of burning embers.

Home was more than willing to be tested by scientists and participated in several experiments conducted by William Crookes, one of the greatest scientists in Great Britain during this golden age. He was the founder of the *Chemical News*, was a fellow of the Royal Society, and had developed several scientific inventions. He was extremely skeptical about Spiritualism and its mediums, and entered into psychical research more to expose it than for any other reason. Then he met Home! Crookes's experiments, which began in 1871, still stand, even today, as some of the most ingenious PK studies ever undertaken. Unlike the Spiritualists, though, Crookes did not believe that discarnate intelligences had anything to do with Home's powers. He theorized instead that the human body somehow housed a force which had previously evaded the notice of science. So he set about to measure and investigate the force carefully, using Home as his principal subject, and reported on his experiments in the July 1871 issue of the *Quarterly Journal of Science*.

Since one of Home's most famous PK abilities was activating an accordion without touching it, this was a natural place for Crookes to begin his tests, so he built a special cage to guard the instrument. This cage was constructed from two wooden hoops, approximately two feet in diameter, around which insulated copper wire was strung, making a drum-shaped cylinder. The whole apparatus was especially designed so it could be slipped snugly under a table in such a way that no one could sneak a hand between the drum top and the underside of the table. However, one hand could be placed in the cage if it were pulled out a few inches from under the table.

The actual tests were run in Crookes's laboratory, and Home was immediately successful with the accordion experiment. At Crookes's urging, the medium picked up the instrument with one hand and dipped it into the basket. Crookes watched the accordion contort about by itself in the psychic's hand. The instrument emitted several notes even though the accordion's keyboard was opposite to the side held by Home. Most astounding of all, the accordion continued to play while floating in the cage after Home removed his hand completely from the basket. Crookes also tried passing an electrical current through the mesh, but it had little appreciable effect on the accordion.

In order to measure Home's psychic force, Crookes also built a peculiar weighing apparatus which consisted of a thirty-six-inch mahogany board. The very end of one side of the board was bolted to a table. The rest of the board extended out and away from the table about twenty-four inches, and its end was hooked to a cable running to an overhead spring balance. If any pressure were exerted on the side of the board extending away from the table, the number of ounces or pounds would be recorded by the spring balance. If one pushed on the end of the board connected to the table, no pressure would be recorded since the subject would be pressing fruitlessly onto the table.

The design of the board was ingenious and Crookes developed it just to test Home's PK. He had the medium place the tips of his fingers on the inch or so of the board bolted to the table. Home was then instructed to exert PK on the opposite end of the board, thereby activating the spring balance and recorder. Home was able to do this with ease and was able to make the board bend down by exerting a PK pressure of between three and a half to six pounds on it. In order to test the apparatus for malfunction, Crookes went so far as to stand with his full weight on the table end of the board but could only exert a pound or two of pressure on it. During the tests, Home was sitting in an easy chair, merely touching the board lightly.

While Crookes was convinced of the existence of PK by these tests, he certainly was not through with Home. In October 1871 he published a confirmatory report in the *Quarterly Journal of Science* in which he answered several criticisms which his first report had prompted. However, he also took the opportunity to report other tests with Home which had been carried out under even more stringent conditions.

After his pilot studies were concluded, Crookes's plan was to rerun the balance scale apparatus but revise the general design so that Home had as little contact with the apparatus as possible. In his previous experiments he had allowed Home to place his hands on the mahogany board. Even though Home could not have exerted any pressure on the board from the way in which he positioned his hands, Crookes wanted to isolate him even further from the balance, and he set about to develop a new device. The new apparatus was a little more complex than its predecessor, but was still only a modification of the mahogany-board setup. Using the same basic apparatus, Crookes placed a vessel of water on the part of the board which had originally been bolted to the table. Home would not have any contact with the board itself. He would, instead, dip his hands into the water and try to use PK on the opposite end of the wood. Even with only this tenuous connection to the apparatus, Home was still able to exercise a great deal of PK on the mechanism. As Crookes reports:

> The apparatus having been properly adjusted before Mr. Home entered the room, he was brought in, and asked to place his fingers in the water in the copper vessel . . . He stood up and dipped the tips of his fingers of his right hand in the water, his other hand and feet being held. When he said he felt a power, force, or influence, proceeding from his hand, I set the clock going, and almost immediately the end . . . of the board was seen to descend slowly and remain down for about 10 seconds; it then descended a little further, and afterwards rose to its normal height. It then descended again, rose suddenly, gradually sunk for 17 seconds, and finally rose to its normal height, where it remained till the experiment was concluded. The lowest point marked on the glass was equivalent to a direct pull of about 5,000 grains.

Ultimately, Crookes was able to remove Home entirely from any contact with the scale. But Home was still able to deflect the board even when standing three feet away from it.

Crookes published his final report on his psychic studies in the January 1874 issue of the *Quarterly Journal of Science*. He devoted this paper mainly to a brief description of some of the more provocative PK he had witnessed with Home between 1870 and 1873. The chemist described seeing the telekinetic movement of large objects, raps, the levitation of the medium, materializations, the appearance of phantom limbs, and other complex PK phenomena.

After his experiments with Crookes, Home gradually retired from public life and died in 1886 from tuberculosis.

Although tales of mediums and levitating tables were rife during the Victorian era, organized science still took little interest in PK despite the work of Crookes and others. However, the tide soon changed and even the most disinterested scientists could not help but be titillated by tales of a new wonder-worker which began to spread throughout Europe in the late 1880s. The critical year was 1888 when some of the greatest scientific minds of Italy, Germany, France, and Poland would begin studying one of the most gifted mediums ever discovered. She was a squatty, half-illiterate Italian woman named Eusapia Palladino.

Despite the fact that Eusapia Palladino was to become the greatest medium of her day, we know relatively little about her background. She was born near Bari, Italy, in 1854 where her mother died in childbirth. Her father was murdered by thieves in 1866. Even as a child, raps and spontaneous telekinesis was observed in her presence. According to one account of her discovery, the wife of a prominent Italian Spiritualist, Signor Damiani, was attending a séance in London when she received communications about a wonderful medium in Italy. Mme. Damiani was given an address in Naples and was led to a middle-class home where Eusapia was employed as a nursemaid.

For the next six years Palladino developed her psychic abilities under Damiani's tutelage. At first her main forte was telekinesis; however her range of phenomena soon soared to over three dozen different types of PK effects. These included table movements, raps, levitations, spontaneous telekinesis, the paranormal swelling of the medium's clothing or curtains in the séance room, the telekinetic playing of musical instruments, levitation of the medium's body, cold winds, the lowering of the séance room's temperature, voices, apports, the materialization of semiphysical but solid phantom forms or body parts, lights, luminous mists, and so forth. In fact, Palladino could apparently produce every type of PK effect imaginable. Usually, though, she worked in the dark or in dimmed light.

Although Palladino was not a professional medium at this point in her career, Dr. Ercole Chiaia, an amateur psychical investigator, witnessed her demonstrations in 1888 and issued a challenge to the Italian scientific community. On August 9, 1888, he published an open letter about Palladino in a Rome newspaper in which he challenged Cesare Lombroso, a prominent psychiatrist and anthropologist, to test Palladino for himself.

Cesare Lombroso was a leading scientific figure in Italy during the 1880s, and his word and testimony pulled considerable weight within Italian scientific circles. At the young age of thirty-two he had become professor of psychiatry at Pavia, then director of the insane asylum at Pesaro, and finally took over a professorship at Turin University where he founded the science of criminology. Lombroso had become a rather outspoken critic of psychical research, so Chiaia's blow was well aimed.

Cesare Lombroso investigated Palladino and reported his formal "conversion" to psychical research in 1891. After witnessing a series of séances with Palladino, he admitted that he had been impressed by her telekinesis. Although the séances had been replete with a variety of PK phenomena, one incident, the levitation of a little bell, struck him as the most striking thing he had observed. The amazed psychiatrist wrote:

> The light was extinguished, and the experiments began again. While, in response to the unanimous wish, a little bell was beginning again its tinklings, and its mysterious aerial circuits, M. Ascensi, taking his cue unknown to us from M. Tamburini (unperceived owing to the darkness) and stood at the right of the medium, and at once, with a single scratch, lighted a match, so successfully, as he declared that he could see the little bell *while it was vibrating in the air* and suddenly fall upon a bed about six feet and a half behind Mme. Palladino.

In 1892, as a result of Lombroso's enthusiastic report, a team of savants gathered in Milan to investigate Palladino impartially. The Milan commission was an ideal one. It included topnotch scientists and intellects of the day who were all well aware of the problems they would confront as investigators. Among the committee members were Charles Richet, a physiologist from the Sorbonne who would later receive a Nobel Prize for his scientific work; the noted philosopher, Carl du Prel; a physicist; and an astronomer. The PK witnessed during the Milan experiments was not great. It consisted mostly of touches, and the curtains of the séance room often billowed out mysteriously. However, the commission did witness one of Palladino's more spectacular achievements . . . her partial materializations. Even when she was tightly held, phantom hands would materialize and touch and even caress the sitters. So just like Home, whatever lay behind Palladino's PK powers was able to take on material shape. The commission was so impressed by these disembodied, materialized hands which soared about the séance room that they concluded in their report:

"It is impossible to count the number of times that a hand appeared and was touched by one of us. Suffice it to say that doubt was no longer possible. It was indeed a living, human hand which we saw and touched, while at the same time the bust and arms of the medium remained visible and her hands were held by those on either side of her."

However, Professor Richet left the séance with lingering doubts about what he had witnessed and called for even more investigations of the medium.

The Milan commission report prompted scientists throughout Europe to study the Italian wonder. Professor Wagner, a zoology professor from St. Petersburg, Russia, traveled to Naples to study her; she was shipped off to Poland for more tests. Some of the séance records of these sittings are spectacular.

For example, Camille Flammarion reported a series of séances he had with Palladino during these years in his book, *Mysterious Psychic Forces*. Here is a part of a typical Palladino séance:

> The candles are blown out, the lamp turned down, but the light is strong enough for us to see very distinctly everything that takes place in the salon. The round table which I had lifted and set aside, approaches the table and tries several times to climb up on it. I lean upon it, in order to keep it down, but I experience an elastic resistance and am unable to do so. The free edge of the round table places itself on the edge of the rectangular table, but hindered by its triangular foot, it does not succeed in clearing itself sufficiently to climb upon it. Since I am holding the medium I ascertain that she makes no effort of the kind that would be needed for this style of performance.

But the séance was just getting going! After even more telekinesis, Palladino began producing materializations in the séance room, quasi-physical phantoms which seemed created from some psychic-biological force exuded by the medium and often molded into everything from disembodied hands to full-form figures. As Flammarion records:

> I feel several touches on the back and on the side. M. de Fontenay receives a sharp slap on the back that everybody hears. A hand passes through my hair. The chair of M. de Fontenay is violently pulled, and a few moments afterwards he cries, "I see the silhouette of a man passing between M. Flammarion and me, above the table, shutting out the red light!"
>
> This thing is repeated several times. I do not myself succeed in seeing this silhouette. I then propose to M. de Fontenay that I take his place, for, in that case, I should be likely to see it also. I soon distinctly perceive a dim silhouette passing before the red lantern, but I do not recognize any precise form. It is only an opaque shadow (the profile of a man) which advances as far as the light and retires.

And later, during the séance, Flammarion was witness to even more impressive PK:

> The little round table, placed outside the cabinet, at the left of the medium, approaches the table, climbs clear up on it and lies across it. The guitar in the cabinet is heard moving about and giving out sounds. The curtain is puffed out, and the guitar is brought upon the table, resting upon the shoulder of M. de Fontenay. It is then laid upon the table, the large end toward the medium. Then it rises and moves over the heads of the company without touching them. It gives forth several sounds. The phenomenon lasts about fifteen seconds. It can readily be seen that the guitar is floating in the air, and the reflection of the red lamp glides over its shining surface. A rather bright gleam, pear-shaped, is seen on the ceiling of the other corner of the room.

In 1894 Charles Richet brought Palladino to his private island, Île Roubaud, in order to test her further, and to allow officials from the SPR in Great Britain to observe her phenomena. The SPR was, at the time, the most important investigative body of psychic phenomena in the world. However, the SPR leaders had had a fair share of merry-go-rounds with fraudulent Spiritualist mediums in their home country and were extremely skeptical about PK and especially about Palladino. Many of them, while admitting the existence of telepathy and even hauntings, just couldn't believe that the mind could directly influence matter. Some of them publicly stated that all physical phenomena, including poltergeist displays, were fake. Nevertheless, Richet invited two well-known English investigators, F. W. H. Myers and Sir Oliver Lodge, to France to experiment with Palladino. Both were impressed by what they were able to observe and shortly after invited the medium to England to be tested by other SPR officials at Cambridge.

The results of the Cambridge sittings have become known as the "Cambridge Fiasco," and for good reason. Analyzing these experiments today, we can easily see why they were such a disaster . . . a disaster which unfairly ruined Palladino's reputation in England, and which probably set back the ultimate recognition of PK by fifty years.

The Cambridge sittings of 1895 were the "official" SPR experiments with Eusapia Palladino, and many of the SPR leaders who had very little experience in working with physical mediums were invited. The experimenters included Alice Johnson; Professor and Mrs. Henry Sidgwick, who had done much of the groundwork for the SPR; a well-known conjuror; F. W. H. Myers; and the SPR's American representative, Richard Hodgson.

As usual, the séances were held in semidarkness while the medium's limbs were held by the investigators. The experimenters were inept and Palladino knew it. So she started outmaneuvering their control in order to use her hands and feet to fake PK demonstrations. Hodgson, who from the start felt the whole thing to be nonsense, deliberately slackened his control of the medium to see if she would fake if and when given the opportunity. Palladino took full advantage of the situation. She was easily detected in the fraud and the SPR leaders branded her a cheap fake and shipped her back to the Continent with the attitude, "Oh, well, we knew it all along."

The SPR report infuriated several continental researchers who had worked successfully with Palladino, since they had warned their British confreres that she would cheat if allowed to do so. They felt that the SPR had merely "baited" Palladino and had suffered the consequences.

Most continental investigators merely ignored the Cambridge affair and continued on with new and novel tests for her. Some of this work was extremely ingenious. By the close of the Victorian era, science was rapidly developing a new technology, and a few scientists adopted it in order to study Palladino. One experimenter found, for instance, that Palladino could discharge an electroscope while standing a good distance away from it. (An electroscope is an instrument which detects an electrical charge.)

Another technological approach to Palladino's mediumship was the brainchild of Professor Philippe Bottazzi, director of the Physiological Institute of the University of Naples. His experiments, conducted in 1907, were run in a laboratory room at his own university. Bottazzi wanted to record mechanically the results of Palladino's PK, so he attached devices to all the séance objects which were, in turn, hooked to smoke paper cylinders. Whenever an object moved, a tracing would be made on the paper. After the séance, Bottazzi could calculate how far and for what duration objects had been moved. The tracings on the cylinders would also reveal the amount of force used or required to move any object.

Professor Bottazzi also set up devices such as a telegraph key unit and metronomes in the hope that Eusapia would use PK to set them in motion. He could then calculate how much force was used to initiate the movement by analyzing the tracings on the smoke cylinders.

Although these experiments were highly successful and interesting, Bottazzi's own personal interest began to focus more and more on the medium's materialization phenomena as the sittings proceeded and Palladino's PK grew stronger. During his sessions, the physiologist was able to examine several hands and forms, and often felt invisible hands poking and touching him. Some of his observations of these forms are fascinating:

> I felt an open hand seize me behind, gently, by the neck. Instinctively I let go of Dr. Poso's right hand with my left and I carried it where I clearly felt this sensation of contact, and I found the hand which was touching me; a left hand, neither cold nor hot, with rough bony fingers which dissolved under pressure; they did not retire by producing a sensation of withdrawal, but they *dissolved, "dematerialised," melted.*
>
> Shortly afterwards the same hand was laid on my head; I carried mine quickly to the spot, I felt it, I grasped it; *it was obliterated and again disappeared in my grasp.*
>
> Another time, later on, the same hand was placed on my right fore-arm without squeezing it. On this occasion I not only carried my left hand to the spot but I looked, so that I could see and feel at the same time; I saw a human hand, of natural colour, and I felt with mine the fingers and back of a luke-warm hand, rough and nervous. *The hand dissolved and (I saw it with my eyes) retreated as if into Mme. Palladino's body, describing a curve.* I confess that I felt some doubt

as to whether Eusapia's left hand had freed itself from my right hand, to reach my fore-arm; but at the same instant I was able to prove to myself that the doubt was groundless, because our two hands were still in contact in the ordinary way. If all the observed phenomena of the seven séances were to disappear from my memory, this one I could never forget! . . .

With reports such as these emanating almost monthly from continental Europe, the SPR was forced to come to grips with Palladino once again, and in 1908 a new committee was sent to Italy to evaluate the psychic. The team was well chosen. It consisted of one of the SPR's shrewdest investigators, Everard Feilding; W. W. Baggally, an accomplished investigator and conjuror; and Hereward Carrington, who had written an encyclopedic book on fraud, *The Physical Phenomena of Spiritualism,* the year before (a book which is still a classic on fraudulent psychic effects). The three men had several things in common. They were all intensely devoted to the cause of psychical research, yet none of them had encountered any genuine physical mediums and were therefore extremely skeptical of Palladino and her claims. The choice of these three investigators by the SPR was not by chance. A more qualified and skeptical committee could not possibly have been formed. The SPR wanted this committee to be as tough and skeptical as possible, and Carrington, before his death in 1958, even admitted that he and his colleagues were sent to Italy more to expose Palladino deliberately than for any other reason.

Before heading for Italy, Feilding, Carrington, and Baggally carefully evaluated all the earlier work that had been published on the medium, noting the strengths and weaknesses of each report. Then they planned, well in advance, the exact procedures they would use to test her. If any PK occurred, they decided, each of them would have to call out his exact position, as well as that of the medium, to prove at all times that Palladino's arms and legs were being properly held. They would keep a stenographic record of all the séances as well. Having carefully architectured their battle plan, the commission held a total of eleven séances with Palladino in Naples, the records of which are still the best and most detailed account of her phenomena ever made.

A hotel room was especially rented for the experiments. As usual, Palladino sat before a cabinet and in front of a table, with her arms and feet held by the experimenters. A minute-by-minute stenographic record was kept for each session. Despite the fact that the three investigators came well prepared for their task and not really expecting Palladino to perform well, the PK came fast and furious. There were breezes, curtain billowings, telekinesis both in the dark and in the light, table levitations galore, and some attempts at partial materialization. The SPR investigators were jolted by the experiences, and after the series was over, all three openly admitted in their final report that they had witnessed indisputable PK. They had been especially impressed by her table levitations which had occurred when all her limbs had been tightly held. Like Home, Palladino's PK also often lingered on after the séances were over and the SPR team was able to witness some spectacular PK, such as objects moving by themselves in full light. Palladino had been vindicated, but the controversy about her abilities was to rage anew when Carrington decided to bring her to the United States for further tests. These tests were not very successful and Palladino returned to Italy shortly after and died in 1918.

Despite the fierce controversies which the Palladino investigations ignited, there were several beneficial outcomes from the affair. Not only had the case for PK been aptly proved, but psychical researchers, probably for the first time in history, began wondering about the nature of the PK process and what mechanics lay behind it. In D. D. Home's day, for example, there were only three explanations for PK. Either spirits did it, or Home used some psychic force to carry out the manifestations, while a few diehards felt that somehow electricity was linked to the whole thing. But these theories explained little, if anything, about the *modus operandi* of PK. However, after years of studying Palladino, psychical investigators began trying to figure out exactly what this force was that could lift up tables and produce phantom limbs and faces.

There were two basic questions which Palladino's investigators kept asking themselves. First, they wanted to know what relationship existed between the psychic force and the medium's organism. Second, they wondered about the nature of the intelligence that manipulated the phenomena.

Although Palladino ascribed her abilities to discarnate intelligences working through her, even her earliest investigators were less sure. They noted that there seemed to be a peculiar relationship between Palladino's own body and the PK. They noted that she lost several pounds in weight during the course of a séance, sometimes the PK would occur only after she had suffered severe muscle spasms, and often the PK would imitate Palladino's physical movements. If, say, she struck the air with her hand three times, three raps would often resound in answer. A striking example of this phenomenon occurred at her Warsaw experiments of 1893–1894. For this series of experiments, Palladino sat without a table in front of her. This allowed the experimenters to watch her more carefully. Almost as if in protest, the entranced medium placed her feet over the legs of one of the sitters. Then she violently kicked the sitter's legs. At that very moment, loud raps reverberated in the room.

Several investigators did, however, adopt the spiritualistic theory. In other words, they believed, along with Palladino, that the spirits of the dead actually manipulated the phenomena. One supporter of this theory was Professor Joseph Venzano, who wrote a lengthy report on Palladino for the *Annals of Psychical Science* in 1907. In the course of his sittings, Venzano had seen several materializations, at least two of which represented the forms of deceased persons known to him. He theorized, quite logically, that in all probability it was the postmortem intelligences of these friends who were directing the phenomena.

It was Hereward Carrington, however, who rightly pointed out that the spiritualistic explanation could not account for many of Palladino's phenomena. For example, many times, while in trance, she would proclaim in a loud voice just what phenomena *she* was about to produce. Sometimes movements or spasmodic jerks of the medium's body would be accompanied by raps or other telekinetic displays. Palladino was also able to produce willful PK effects, such as discharging an electroscope or depressing a scale at a distance, which would indicate that no external agency was involved in her mediumship.

A somewhat novel approach to Palladino's PK was made by Albert de Rochas, a French psychical investigator of some note. De Rochas believed that within the human organism was a "psychic fluid" which could build itself up into the form of the human body. This fluidic phantom could leave the medium's body and carry out the PK and even become visible. De Rochas's theory has had a renaissance over the last decade.

Some of Palladino's phenomena can be easily explained as a product of some sort of fluidic exteriorization. This theory could account for the materializations so often seen at her séances, the phantom limbs which were seen floating about or even emanating from her own body, and could explain how Palladino was able to impress molds of the side of her head into putty kept several feet away from her.

A rather different approach to Palladino's PK was made by the Italian psychiatrist, Professor Enrico Morselli, and the French physician Joseph Maxwell. Morselli believed that somehow Palladino's unconscious mind directed a sort of semimaterial substance within the medium's organism. This element of Palladino's mind, according to Morselli, also had extrasensory abilities. By employing ESP, Palladino could unconsciously produce manifestations which catered to the sitters' unverbalized wishes and desires. For instance, Palladino would have learned about Venzano's friends telepathically and then used the information to create phantoms to resemble them. Dr. Maxwell extended this type of theory. He felt that during Palladino's séances the medium and sitters created a "group mind" which represented the collective will of the entire group. This would eventually become endowed with a semi-independent intelligence which directed the PK by withdrawing some sort of power from the medium's body.

Hereward Carrington was not impressed by any of the theories his predecessors had proffered. To him, there was no doubt that some of Palladino's phenomena were controlled by her own will, consciously or unconsciously. However, he had enough insight to realize that at times it was quite clear that another will was directing the phenomena. As he wrote in his encyclopedic book, *Eusapia Palladino and Her Phenomena:*

> . . . there are many phenomena which do not seem to be controlled by her will, but on the contrary occur in direct opposition to it. An instance of this occurred in our own sittings, when Eusapia said she was tired and asked John [her "spirit" control] if the séance might end. John replied by rapping twice for "No" and the séance was resumed. Soon after we obtained four complete levitations of the table, in rapid succession, and under excellent test conditions, and John then permitted the séance to terminate. Here, then we have evidence of an external intelligence, differing from that of Eusapia, and expressing wishes in direct opposition to her own.

Carrington himself tried to amalgamate several of the above theories which he remolded into one general theory. He believed that within the body is a force, which he called the "vital force," whose job it is to regulate the body's internal functions. However, on rare occasions this force might externalize from the body. Once the force has been temporarily liberated, either the psychic's mind or a discarnate intelligence could manipulate it. (It should be noted that years later, when PK was a little better understood, Carrington began to abandon the spiritistic element of his theory altogether. But he still supported it fervently in his 1946 book, *The Invisible World.*)

Although none of these various theories can explain all aspects of Palladino's multiple talents, there is one common element that pervades all of them which should be kept in mind by modern students of parapsychology. Ever since the work of J. B. Rhine and the emergence of our modern concept of PK, we hear so much talk about "the powers of the mind" or the "mysteries of the mind." Yet, not one intellect who studied Palladino *ever conceptualized PK as a mental force.* They all perceived it as a biological entity and more of a physiological mystery than a psychological one. The fact that Palladino lost weight during her séances, became nauseous as a result of them, that her body emitted vapors and glows, that she became right-handed when in trance when she was left-handed when awake, that when the table levitated her body weight increased proportionately, and that she even underwent sexual orgasm during the production of telekinesis all indicate that the psychic force was a power which pervaded Palladino's entire body. To call this force "psychokinesis"—to move by the mind—is blatantly ludicrous.

One must keep in mind, too, that the term "psychokinesis" is only a description of a phenomenon. It is not an explanation for it. To say that PK comes out of the mind is only a theory and one that is most likely premature. After all, we don't really know where PK comes from. Continental European psychical researchers made a clear distinction on this point. They called any unexplained physical manifestation "telekinesis" (to move at a distance), a term which does not imply any theory about the nature of the force behind the phenomenon. When the force became a material substance, it was called "ectoplasm." But again, this is only a term and not an explanation. Modern Soviet parapsychologists have also realized that PK may be just as much a biological force as a mental energy, and they have hypothesized the existence of a new biological hypersubstance they call "bioplasma." Some Soviet scientists believe that this substance can leave the body and carry out any number of telekinetic effects, or that it can form a duplicate body within the physical organism which they call the "bioplasmic body." "Bioplasma," "ectoplasm," and "PK" are all terms of convenience, and as such have their uses and misuses. So, we must keep in mind that PK may not be some form of "mind energy" but an even greater mystery. It could well be a force which permeates the entire physical organism. So, although I shall keep using the term PK purely out of convention during the course of this book, one must remember at all times that PK is a very poor term for whatever it is we are confronting.

In addition to the discoveries that Palladino's investigators made about PK, there were two cases of physical mediumship which came to parapsychology's attention between the two world wars which shed even more light on the phenomenon. Although good PK mediums abounded in Europe, few of them were ever rigorously investigated in such a manner as to rule out fraud definitely. And psychical researchers had continually to confront the embarrassing problem that many genuine mediums also fake quite cold-bloodedly if given the chance. However, two cases during this era of European psychical research were so striking that they have become classics in the literature on PK.

Both of these psychics, Rudi Schneider and Stella Cranshaw (called Stella C. in all contemporary reports on her), were investigated by Harry Price, a British ghost-hunter and entrepreneur of all things psychic, who also directed his own National Laboratory for Psychical Research in London. Price also tested Willi Schneider, Rudi's older brother, who was also a gifted medium, with astounding results. The NLPR was probably the most advanced parapsychology laboratory of its day and was the perfect battlefield over which the case for PK could be fought. Price was also an outstanding expert on stage magic, conjuring, and mediumistic fraud.

Price met Stella C. quite by accident. Each day he commuted back and forth between London and his country home near Pulborough. One day in 1923 Price found himself sharing a train compartment with a pretty young woman. Their conversation soon drifted to psychical research. The young woman undoubtedly did not realize that she was talking to one of England's top psychical investigators when she mentioned that spontaneous PK often occurred around her. Price's excitement grew and grew as the lady described a gamut of raps, cold breezes, and telekinesis which had plagued her over the preceding few years.

It didn't take him long to recruit Stella Cranshaw for his laboratory. Although she was at first reticent and had a very matter-of-fact disposition toward her own PK, she agreed to a short series of experiments. I don't think she ever realized that her name was about to go down in psychic history. Nor do I believe that Price realized that he was about to discover one of the most gifted mediums of all times.

The tests were run in Price's laboratory which had been especially prepared for the séances. Since Stella claimed that she could produce "cold breezes," Price placed thermistors in the séance room and monitored them by camera. Any change in temperature would be registered and the thermometers photographed. As with most mediums, Stella and her sitters seated themselves around a table after the doors to the séance room were locked.

In order to make the experiments as novel as possible, Price also set about inventing fraud-proof gadgets with which to test Stella's PK. If you recall, the experimenters who worked with Palladino, Home, and others usually placed assorted objects on top of the séance table. Each time an object moved, the investigators would check the position of the medium's hands and feet. This procedure was certainly unwieldy and Price found it rather unsatisfactory. So, for his experiments with Stella C., he invented his own special séance table which would alleviate the problem of fraud altogether. He took a small table and cut a trapdoor into the top. The trap lay flat down, so it could not be opened from the top. It could only be opened by pushing it up from the underside of the tabletop. Price then placed wire gauze around the legs of the table, extending the gauze about halfway to the floor. By placing another board under the table and connecting it to the gauze, the underside was completely sealed and formed a large compartment. Price placed musical instruments in the compartment, hoping that Stella's PK could move or play them.

Price also developed what he called the "telekinetoscope," one of the most ingenious devices ever invented for PK research. The telekinetoscope consisted of a bell jar fixed on a metal base. Inside the jar was placed a telegraph-type key which, when depressed, would signal the experimenters by setting off a light or bell. The key was protected by a bubble blown around it (formed in the stable environment of the jar, a bubble will remain intact for several hours without popping), and tiny holes were drilled in the base unit. To activate the scope, Stella's PK would have to enter the jar, go through the bubble without popping it, and then generate enough force to depress the key. It was impossible to activate the scope any other way.

The series of thirteen séances was held in dim light, although the experimenters were able to observe everything distinctly. The first séance was held on March 22, but the phenomena were meager, although Stella did produce three full table levitations. Unlike most mediums, Stella at first did not go into trance; this was a later development in her mediumship which came when her PK became stronger. Things began to pick up the second séance. Stella seemed to fall into a mild trance, the entire séance room dropped in temperature by some 11 ½ degrees, and the séance table levitated six times.

The odd temperature fluctuations of the séance room were probably the most notable feature of the sittings. Thanks to Price's foresight in rigging the séance room with thermisters, no one can argue that the feeling of cold which permeated the room was a hallucination. Price kept detailed records of the temperature changes and photographed the thermistors. During the Stella C. séances, the room temperature would cool from 3½ to 21½ degrees.

The third séance produced the most spectacular PK. While on previous occasions the séance table had been levitated, the PK thoroughly demolished it at this sitting. Here is part of Price's account:

> The sitters and medium having formed themselves into a circle around the table with only the tips of their fingers touching the table top, great power was quickly developed, and movements of the table rapidly followed. The table was then completely levitated several times, remaining in the air for several seconds upon each occasion. Once the table rose completely above the heads of the sitters, some of whom had to rise in order to keep contact with it. During this levitation, the lower platform of the table struck the chin of Mr. Price

(who had remained seated, and had lost contact), and came to rest on his chest. The sitters then removed their hands from the table, only the finger-tips of the medium remaining upon it. Movements of the table still continued. The sitters again placed their fingers on the table top, when still further power was developed with increasing violence, two of the legs breaking away from the table with a percussion-like noise as the fracture occurred. At this juncture (12-27) Mr. Pugh excused himself and the séance continued without him. Colonel Hardwick, Mrs. Pratt, and Mr. Price still retained their fingers upon the top of the table, which was resting on the remaining leg. Suddenly, without warning, and with a violent snap, the table top broke into two pieces; at the same time the remaining leg and other supports of the table crumpled up, *the whole being reduced to what is little more than matchwood.* The sitting then concluded.

By the fourth séance, it was quite clear that Stella was entering a deep trance in order to facilitate the PK. She even developed a spirit control. It was also during this fourth séance that Stella began exhibiting ESP powers as well as PK. During her trance, she began spontaneously to describe a vision she saw of the May 19, 1923, issue of the London *Daily Mail*. Since the sitting was being held on April 5, Stella was apparently describing a newspaper issue which would not be published for over a month. The medium told the sitters that she saw the name "Andrew Salt," and had the sensation, as she described her feeling, of a falling boy, with a man or doctor standing over him pouring out a white powder from a tin. Thirty-seven days later, on May 19, the front page of the *Daily Mail* carried an ad for "Andrews Liver Salt," which showed a boy who had just spilled a tin of salt. There can be little doubt that Stella had made a startlingly accurate prediction. Why her ESP should have focused on that particular newspaper issue is one of those mysteries which continuously baffle parapsychologists.

As the sitting proceeded, Stella's phenomena became bolder. Lights started appearing, the table would veer up and remain pivoted on two legs so securely that no one at the séance could push it back down to the floor, and masses of materialized matter would appear on the floor. On one occasion a large sprig of lilac, 16½ inches long and in full bloom, fell right into the locked séance room.

It was while the sittings were well in progress that Price

introduced his trick devices. Stella's PK had no difficulty moving the instruments in the gauze cage and playing upon them as well. The telekinetoscope was no challenge either. The PK activated the key with little difficulty.

After thirteen séances Stella announced that she was through with them. They were becoming tiring and were disrupting her life, she complained. Later she did give another series of sittings for Price, but then withdrew from psychical research altogether. Now in her seventies, Stella C. lives a quiet, uneventful life in London. She has little interest in the developments of contemporary parapsychology and rarely discusses her landmark experiments with Price. Someday, it is hoped, Stella Cranshaw might write her own reminiscences about her mediumship.

Even though Stella worked with only one committee of investigators, and her total career spanned only two meager series of experiments, her mediumship ranks as one of the most important in the annals of psychical research. There are several reasons for this.

To begin with, the Stella C. sittings precluded fraud. Certainly, it should be the prime responsibility of the investigator to set up fraud-proof conditions at the start of any investigation. Price met this responsibility courageously, and did it in a way very different from any other investigators before him. During the experiments with Home, Palladino, and others, the investigators focused their attention on carefully controlling the psychic. Now, this left a loophole that the skeptics could always fall back on. They merely had to argue that the psychic was, in most cases, shrewder than the scientists and could evade their controls. For example, Palladino certainly had the very clever ability to remove one of her hands from a novice experimenter's grasp when she wanted to cheat. Price was aware of this, so he decided to assault the fraud problem from a different perspective. He did not institute fraud-proof controls, *he developed fraud-proof tests*. By instituting tests which were in themselves fake-proof, physical control of the medium became a matter of convention, not necessity. Indeed, Stella could have used a leg to kick the table about or flashed magnesium powder about to produce little lights. But she succeeded at PK tasks which were totally impossible to carry out in any normal way. There was no way she could activate the telekinetoscope fraudulently. The device just couldn't be beat, and Stella C. proved her

PK ability when she first activated the bubble-guarded key. Neither was there any way Stella could have manipulated the objects in Price's special trick table. Lastly, how are we to account for the mysterious temperature drops in the experimental room of up to twenty or so degrees? No one has ever attempted to explain away this phenomenon, nor offer a way the effect could have been fraudulently produced.

This fluctuation phenomenon is also a possible key to understanding the force behind PK. Similar "cold breezes" were noted during both Palladino's and Home's séances. If you recall, in the Ingo Swann experiment run at City College of the City University of New York, Swann was able to make a piece of Bakelite or graphite alter in temperature; other pieces of the same substance in the experimental area altered temperature in the opposite direction. Is there some law indicated here? Could it be that temperature fluctuations are intricately related to the PK process?

A good case could be made for such a theory. It is hard to believe that the body itself houses a force of such magnitude that it could teleport objects or move extremely heavy furniture with such obvious ease as the poltergeist displays. But, what if the psychic actually draws energy from another source? The atmosphere in the room is rich with energy. If you cool one cubic foot of air only one degree, it will release fifteen foot-pounds of energy. (In other words, the energy released could move a fifteen-pound object one foot.) So, an enormous amount of energy is given off when a room's temperature dips by even a few degrees. Stella was able to change room temperature by some three to twenty degrees. So, it seems likely that Stella C., Palladino, and Swann were all using their initial PK somehow to draw energy from the atmosphere in order to redirect it into further PK.

The dual cases of Willi and Rudi Schneider of Bramau, Austria, also came to Price's attention in the 1920s. Both boys had shown remarkable PK ability while still adolescents. Luckily, the case came to the notice of the famous German pathologist, the Baron Dr. Albert von Schrenck-Notzing. He sensed that Willi, the older brother, could be developed into a gifted physical medium and took him under his wing, acted as his mentor, and groomed him for scientific testing. Later, he did the same for Rudi.

The Schneider brothers at first gave séances only for their family. The sitters and medium sat around a table in a circle while target objects were placed strategically throughout the room. Willi was the main medium and only later did Rudi even begin to attend the séances. The control of Willi was not solely by hand and foot, but, in addition, luminous pins and bracelets were placed over his entire body so that his outline could be observed at all times during the darkened séances. Despite the severity of the controls, he was still able to produce telekinesis and materialization phenomena. Very often objects placed in a completely enclosed gauze cage were moved.

In 1922 the wondrous tales about young Willi's mediumship prompted Harry Price and Dr. Eric Dingwall, then the SPR's research officer, to travel to Germany to test Willi themselves. After only three séances Price was able to conclude:

> These séances were, to all intents and purposes, under our own control. We examined everything, affixed our own seals to the séance room door, etc., etc. After the séances Dingwall and I signed statements to the effect that we had witnessed genuine phenomena, which included many telekinetic movements—starting and stopping of a musical box in a gauze case—to order. The box also wound itself up. A pseudopod of handlike form picked up my handkerchief several times. Loud raps inside the cabinet were heard, the "hand" or pseudopod showed itself against a luminous plaque, etc., etc. And all these phenomena occurred at a distance of some feet from the medium, who was controlled by two persons. At the forecontrol Willi was searched and put into black tights, which were outlined with luminous bands and buttons. It was a wonderful display of phenomena, produced in really excellent red light . . ."

Despite his PK abilities Willi soon lost interest in his own mediumship and retired from the psychic scene. He devoted the rest of his life to dental work and died just a few years ago.

Price had his first séance with Rudi in April 1926 and witnessed telekinesis, cool breezes, materialized hands, and a variety of raps. He had taken all precautions to ensure that Rudi could not fake the PK, and as a result of his initial experiments issued an enthusiastic endorsement of the young medium. Several subsequent investigators successfully tested Rudi, who was quickly outshining his brother's fame, and he soon became one of the most controversial mediums in Europe. On one hand, such highly respected investigators as Price and Schrenck-Notzing were declaring Rudi to be the greatest medium in Europe. Yet other investigators were simultaneously accusing the entire Schneider family of being in cahoots and systematically defrauding the investigators.

This controversy over Rudi's mediumship prompted several investigators—notably Price, Schrenck-Notzing, Karl Krall, Fritz Grunewald, and others—to wonder whether or not a new means of control could be developed which would once and for all outlaw any possibility of fraud. Procedures such as hand control or outlining the medium's body with luminous pins had been tried, but for some reason did not seem to satisfy the skeptics. They still insisted on believing that the experimenters had been duped.

It was Price who finally perfected the ultimate control system, and he eagerly invited Rudi to his London laboratory to test it out. Rudi arrived late in 1929 and the experiments were soon under way.

Price's device consisted of several electrical circuits to which the medium would be connected. His hands were locked in special gloves and his feet were placed on metal inductors. All of the circuits led to a display board consisting of several lights, each indicating one of the circuits. The medium could not escape control after being hooked up to the circuits, since if he broke control by moving a hand or foot, one of the signal lights on the panel would go out. The investigators would immediately know that the psychic had evaded control.

In order to maintain complete control over the séances, Price made every sitter hook up to the display panel. When the sittings with Rudi finally took place, every single person present was perfectly monitored. As was his usual custom, Rudi sat in front of a partitioned-off cabinet while the experimenters sat in a circle. A table with objects placed upon it, such as a luminous wastepaper basket and musical toys, was also left in the room and a red light permeated the area.

This mechanical control was instituted for each of the 1929-1930 séances. Rudi would enter the séance room dressed in a special pajama outfit developed by Price, was attached to the conductors, and would enter trance. After achieving this, Rudi's mind would give way to a new personality named Olga who, of course, claimed to be a spirit and who would act as mistress of ceremonies for the sittings. For example, she would ask that music be played or ask the sitters to sing to help the PK get rolling. Despite the controls Price instituted, some of Rudi's London demonstrations were stunning.

For instance, at one séance the PK came so fast and furious that hardly a minute or so went by without some sort of PK amazing the sitters. The curtains moved by themselves, a bell laid on the séance room table was moved about, phantom materialized hands were seen. This last-mentioned phenomenon was particularly impressive. As Price recorded in his notes:

> Lord Charles Hope asks if Olga would be so good as to show herself to the sitters. She says it shall be done. Immediately the waste-paper basket lifts, the sitters distinctly seeing the pseudopod supporting it. Some sitters saw the fingers, three in number, and part of an arm. [From my angle I distinctly saw a white or semi-luminous 'paw' which appeared to have a large thumb and two thick fingers.] This 'teleplasm' lifted the waste-paper basket, moved it round in a circle very gently, lifted it above the red light outside the cabinet curtains, and then dropped it. Mr. Sutton says he saw the pseudopod disappear *before* the basket dropped. Red light is slightly raised in wattage by Miss Kaye. Mr. Sutton is asked to place the waste-paper basket on the table in front of the opening of the curtains. Again the waste-paper basket gently lifts, moves around in a circle, and is thrown towards the sitters. Both curtains suddenly and violently blow out, shaking the red light hanging in front of them. The table goes over with a crash. Lord Charles Hope asks if Olga would show herself just a little better. She says it shall be done.
>
> Olga says she would like the sitter at the end to place a handkerchief on the floor for her. Mr. Sutton does this and immediately joins up again. [Mr. Sutton says he feels an extremely cold breeze at his end of the circle.] The sitters all see a white seemingly shapeless mass form between the opening of the curtains.

The next triumph in Rudi's career came shortly after his London adventure. In November 1930 he underwent a number of ingenious tests designed by Dr. Eugene Osty of the Paris-based Institute Metapsychique. Osty, too, was preoccupied with finding a way to preclude any possibility of fraud. His plan was just as unique as Price's and led to a curious discovery about PK. Working with his son Marcel, Osty set up a device in the experimental room which would project an infrared beam. The beam acted as a guard, separating Rudi from the objects he was supposed to manipulate by PK. If Rudi were, for instance, to grab an object and throw it, the fraud would be instantly detected. As soon as his hand penetrated the beam as he made the grab, the disruption would cause a camera to go off. The flash would notify the experimenters of fraud and a photograph would be taken of the medium *in flagrante delicto*.

Osty, no doubt, expected that Rudi would be able to move the séance objects without disrupting the beam. But the French physician was in for a surprise. Osty had seen some good PK with Schneider during his pilot tests. Under good conditions he had seen a gray fog appear which pushed and moved the séance table about. It was at the fourteenth experiment that Osty introduced the infrared control and on two occasions the cameras did flash, indicating that something had penetrated the beam. Yet, when the plates were developed, Rudi could be clearly seen with his hands controlled by the experimenters. Osty realized that somehow a force was leaving Rudi's body which, while normally invisible to the eye, had enough substance to absorb about 30 percent of the beam and set off the cameras.

For his next test, Osty hooked a bell device to the infrared setup instead of the cameras in order to see how long the substance would manipulate the bell. While manually controlled by the experimenters, Rudi's PK consistently rang the bell for periods up to and over one minute. Spurred on by this new discovery, Osty decided to revise the infrared projection so that a record could be made of the exact oscillations of the beam as Rudi's PK penetrated it. By using this complicated design he could gauge not only the duration of the PK effect, but also record its level of density and volume as it interrupted the beam.

Osty did discover that Rudi's PK oscillated while it interacted with the beam. However, the investigator made one further discovery which is of even greater importance. Rudi always hyperventilated during his sittings. Sometimes he would breathe 120 to 300 times a minute, and the PK oscillations were always found to be exactly double that of his respiration rate. A definite tie-up between the PK and the medium's organism seemed proved.

In 1932 Price was able to secure Rudi's services for another series of séances at his laboratory. By that time, though, the relationship between them was extremely strained since Price was jealous of the fact that his star medium was working with other investigators. It was this factor which probably led to the odd outcome of the tests. For this series of experiments Price reverted back to hand control. The goal was to photograph the materializations and telekinetic displays. Although the séances were successful, months later Price announced to his stunned colleagues that one of the photographs showed Rudi moving an object with a hand he had tricked the experimenters into releasing, and publicly accused the medium of fraud. Rudi denied the charge angrily and with considerable consternation. He gave up his mediumship soon after, since he had begun to lose interest in psychical research anyway, and became an auto mechanic in his hometown where he died in 1957.

It wasn't until thirty years later that Rudi was finally vindicated. Many years after Price's death, Anita Gregory, an English parapsychologist began reanalyzing Rudi's career. Among other things, she wanted to resolve the mystery of Rudi's exposure. Price had willed his archives to the University of London, and Mrs. Gregory discovered this famous photograph among his papers only after a hard and diligent search. It had been mysteriously hidden by Price in his own files and sealed over with paper. The reason for this camouflage was obvious. When the original photograph was examined, Mrs. Gregory was able to prove that it was a carefully doctored and deliberately contrived double exposure. There could be little doubt but that Price had deliberately set up Rudi in order to get even for what he felt to be the psychic's disloyalty.

D. D. Home, Eusapia Palladino, Stella Cranshaw, and Rudi Schneider were only four mediums who emerged during parapsychology's years of maturation. There were many more However, studying the careers of just these four psychics is not merely a matter of historicity. I have presented the facts about their careers in order to pose a very important question: What do these old studies tell us about PK?

We can learn several lessons from the study of physical mediumship. If anything, whatever force lay behind Palladino's or Rudi Schneider's ability was not some vague mind-over-matter energy, but a very real physical force and substance emanating from the medium's body. These older tests all but prove that our modern conception of PK as a purely mental force is false. It is just too hard to dismiss the probability that PK, whatever its nature, can transmute itself into a tangible substance. These old accounts of mists, phantom limbs, and materialized faces cannot be dismissed. We cannot, as much as we might like to, close our eyes to Dr. Joseph Venzano's accounts or ignore all those experimenters who watched Rudi Schneider's phantom creations. Whatever PK is, it travels along an infinite boundary between mind *and* matter.

Second, all of the psychics we have been discussing usually became physically agitated during the production of PK. Palladino would lose several pounds and become hysterical during and after séances, Rudi Schneider breathed frantically, while Home would usually end up exhausted after a sitting. So, we are entitled to ask, could there be a relationship between PK and physical stress? In fact, one famous pioneer of psychical research, Dr. Gustave Geley, compared a medium producing PK to a woman in childbirth. But we find no evidence of stress or strain in poltergeistic and death-coincidence PK. Poltergeist victims are obviously psychologically agitated when the PK erupts, but there is little evidence that they are physically vigilant at the time of the outbreak. Likewise, the agent in death-coincidence cases is more than likely preparing for bed, sleeping, or doing the dishes than running around uptight when the PK strikes.

Why should this contradiction exist?

One key may be the subject's mental attitude toward PK. In poltergeist and death-coincidence cases the PK is utilized unconsciously. The great physical mediums produced their feats willfully, even if they had to enter trance first. Even though they all believed that they were controlled by discarnate beings, these mediums all knew that they were the source of the raw PK and therefore had to do "something" in order to eject it from the body. It could be that willfully exercising PK is a more stressful process than using it unconsciously.

There is even some strong laboratory evidence that mental attitudes can have a drastic effect on PK. Charles Honorton, while working at the Maimonides Medical Center's Division of Parapsychology and Psychophysics in the early 1970s, was well aware that many star PK subjects went through physical ordeals as they exerted their PK. So he theorized that muscular tension might be a key to the phenomenon. Honorton and his associate, Warren Barksdale, tested several subjects for PK with a Schmidt generator. He found that subjects were more successful when tensed than relaxed. However, he found one subject who scored very well when tensed, but did just as well but negatively when relaxed. (For example, he made the generator land in the wrong position more times than chance would allow.) In other words, this subject was able to use PK under both physical conditions, but his mental attitude drastically affected the way the PK would actually manifest.

Nonetheless, poltergeist and death-coincidence PK do indicate that PK is basically an unconscious process. Although mediums have a willful *volition* to produce PK, the unconscious nature of PK is also suggested by the careers of the great mediums. All four of the mediums I have focused on in this chapter would enter trance before exhibiting complex PK phenomena. So we cannot really say that they consciously controlled their PK, although Home and Palladino could produce some minor PK when in a normal state of consciousness. In fact, quite to the contrary, it looks as though these mediums could not produce strong or complex PK until they had relinquished consciousness altogether. Even Stella C., who was not a professional medium, soon developed a trance as she began giving PK performances.

Another question contemporary parapsychologists are asking is: how come there are no mediums of Palladino's or Home's caliber around today? I think that this is one question about PK we can answer for a change.

With the exception of Stella C., all the mediums discussed in this chapter were products of the Spiritualist movement, and this setting, no doubt, molded how their PK manifested. After the decline of Spiritualism between the two world wars, news about great physical mediums seemed to dwindle. European investigators began wondering why new Palladinos did not appear on the scene, and physical mediums virtually became an extinct race after the Second World War.

In a way this decline could have been predicted. The great physical mediums were carefully trained by the Spiritualists before they embarked on their professional careers. Home, Palladino, and Schneider were all taken under wing by Spiritualist mentors or sympathetic scientists who worked with them and helped develop them by guarding them from misusing their talents and, quite literally, burning themselves out. They made sure their young talents did not misuse their abilities by demonstrating them too soon or by sitting too frequently. As Spiritualism declined, this rich breeding ground also diminished. Remember, Palladino was developed for six years by M. Damiani before she became a public medium. Even young Rudi was trained by a Spiritualist friend, Captain Fritz Kogelnik, before he further developed under Schrenck-Notzing.

I like to compare the decline of mediumship to what opera devotees call "three-year wonders." Every so often a great young vocal talent will appear on the opera scene. The singer has of yet only a vestige of greatness, but the potential is there crying for development. But instead of carefully training the voice and learning how to use it, manage it, and save it, the singer goes stage crazy. Using raw talent, the singer starts performing at every opportunity. What happens is a tragedy. The voice is wrecked before it ever really blossomed. Many mediums do the same thing. They don't take time to develop their gifts. As soon as they realize that they have any PK ability, they begin giving demonstrations and sittings, never taking time really to develop their talent. They never develop their potential, they stifle it. They need training. The Spiritualist mentors were the "vocal coaches" of the psychic scene and as they disappeared so did the development of topnotch PK mediums.

Stella C. represents an enigma, though. She was not a Spiritualist and had no personal exposure to the religion when Price met her. She was only a very young woman puzzled by some mysterious things she had witnessed about her. Yet, as soon as she began her sittings with Price, she developed a trance, a spirit control, and all the other trappings of the traditional Spiritualist medium. Why? Was it only to imitate the mediums she had heard about? I think that the trance state and the emergence of a "control" who takes responsibility for the séance must be intrinsic steps to producing volitional PK of a major magnitude. I think Schrenck-Notzing realized this also. The baron was so sure that Rudi's control Olga was nothing but a splinter of the young medium's own psyche that he hypnotized and conditioned Rudi to reject and stop manifesting the Olga control. He was successful. But Rudi could produce no PK until Olga was conjured back by the understandably baffled physician!

These issues raise a more intriguing question. How good a case for survival after death does physical mediumship suggest? There certainly is some evidence that would support the spiritistic theory. Once again my own mind is brought back to Venzano's experiences with Palladino. Home, as well, would often receive telepathic messages which seemed to emanate from the dead. Were these mediums channels between two worlds, or were the types of phenomena they produced molded by the culture in which they developed? If a D. D. Home were to develop today, would he become a Spiritualist medium or a Space Age psychic like Uri Geller who ascribes his powers to space intelligences working through him? If a Palladino appeared on the scene, would she go into trance or exhibit PK from a normal state of consciousness? There are no easy answers to questions such as these.

However, it is very curious that as Spiritualism and the nineteenth-century culture which gave it birth faded into history, few new physical mediums appeared on the scene. The psychic drought became so bad that English and American parapsychologists began to wonder if perhaps the investigators and not the mediums were the ones really entranced during these historical séances. Were earlier investigators duped? Did they hallucinate? Lie? Or just report things that never happened?

There was another reason for this great drought as well. Isn't it odd that most of the great physical mediums came from continental Europe and not Great Britain or the United States? If you listed all the great mediums of psychical research's golden years, only two—Kathleen Goligher, who will be discussed in a later chapter, and D. D. Home—came from the British Isles. It is also a most curious coincidence that the English investigators were not interested in PK very much. They were more interested in trance mediums who could bring psychic messages from the purported dead, or exhibit other clairvoyant powers. Continental parapsychologists were of a different ilk. Remember, Osty, Schrenck-Notzing, Morselli, Richet and others were biologically oriented. They were exceedingly interested in PK. So it looks as though the parapsychological atmosphere in these different countries actually influenced the very types of powers their psychics developed. Great physical mediums did not flourish in a parapsychological culture which had utter disdain for PK. Frankly, too, the English researchers weren't looking for great physical mediums. In countries where the dominant parapsychological tradition actively encouraged PK, physical mediums abounded.

This theory becomes more plausible when we realize that there is an intrinsic relationship between ESP and PK. Palladino, Home, Stella C., and company, all had both ESP and PK gifts. Yet, which ability became dominant was dictated by the demand characteristics of the people about them. Most psychics deliberately concentrated on only one aspect of psi to the exclusion of the other. Only a few, such as D. D. Home, had equal versatility with both. Likewise, most of the famous mental mediums and psychics of this era also had PK abilities which faded out as they developed their ESP into optimal working order. Stories of strong PK phenomena abound from the early careers of such great psychics as Mrs. Gladys Leonard, Gerard Croiset, Eileen Garrett, Stefan Ossowiecki, and others.

After the Second World War, the dominant parapsychological climate throughout the world was radically different from that of the Victorian Age. Experimentation was the password. Everyone was testing for ESP in themselves, in their families, and even in their pets. The climate was no longer conducive to darkened séance rooms and floating tables. Parapsychology became a psychological discipline, physical mediumship became a thing of the past, and for thirty years experimenters had to throw dice and roll little balls or cubes in order to prove PK. Then, in the 1960s a bomb fell on parapsychology. News started leaking out of the Soviet Union about a psychic who, in the tradition of Palladino and Schneider, could actually move stationary objects by PK. The age of the PK medium was about to stage a comeback. But, this was a new type of psychic. No darkness, no séances, no spirits, no materializations, and no trance. A new variety of physical medium was developing in the Soviet Union: psychics who knew that they possessed a psychic force that could shove little objects across tables and deflect compasses. A new chapter in the PK story was about to open. . . .

5

Nina Kulagina: The Soviet PK Breakthrough

ALTHOUGH TO ALL appearances Nina Kulagina looks just like a typical Russian housewife, she is probably the most celebrated PK subject in the world today. Not only have scientists in the Soviet Union been studying her for several years, but scientists from the United States, England, Finland, and even Australia have ventured behind the Iron Curtain to observe Kulagina's demonstrations. These scientists have watched the Russian housewife slide objects across tabletops, gyrate suspended Ping-Pong balls in Plexiglas cubes, create burn marks by merely touching an onlooker's arm, or any of many other feats. These demonstrations may seem almost like child's play in comparison to the levitating tables of Palladino, or the materialized hands of Rudi Schneider, or the fire-immunity exhibitions of D. D. Home. Yet, Nina Kulagina is unquestionably one of the most important PK subjects in contemporary parapsychology. She has certainly been the most tested PK subject in recent decades and almost single-handedly proved that PK on "stable systems" could be scientifically studied and examined in bright light and with none of the seance room theatrics which so hindered the parapsychologists of yesteryear.

Nina Kulagina (whose maiden names was Nelya Mikhailova which is sometimes used in the reports) was born in 1928. She survived the German siege of Leningrad, having herself borne arms against the invaders as a teenager. Now a married woman with children and even grandchildren, Kulagina is devoting most of her time to scientific experimentation.

Just how Kulagina discovered her PK abilities is a bit puzzling since the psychic herself has offered two different stories. She told one version to Sheila Ostrander and Lynn Schroeder, who interviewed her in the Soviet Union while collecting material for their *Psychic Discoveries Behind the Iron Curtain*. According to this account, Kulagina first became aware of the existence of her PK when spontaneous telekinesis started to occur in her presence. But at that time she had no idea that she had any control over the PK or could learn to induce it.

"I didn't know until a few years ago that I could move things at a distance," she told the writers. "I was very upset and angry that day. I was walking toward a cupboard in my apartment when suddenly a pitcher in the cupboard moved to the edge of the shelf, fell, and smashed to bits." This was only the beginning though, and PK soon became a common occurrence in the Kulagin home.

Kulagina gave a different version of how she discovered her PK gift to Dr. Thelma Moss, an associate professor of psychology at the UCLA Neuropsychiatric Institute. During her interview with Moss, Kulagina flatly denied the "pitcher" story and claimed that her PK was an outgrowth of some ESP tests in which she had been engaged.

Soviet scientists have long been interested in a phenomenon called "dermo-optical perception," sometimes more loosely called "skin vision." They were discovering that many people have the ability to distinguish colors by touch. Some subjects with whom the Soviets were working had developed a remarkable control over the ability, though it is a debatable point whether skin vision is actually a form of ESP, hypersensitivity of touch, or subliminal perception.

The dean of Soviet parapsychologists during these years was L. L. Vasiliev, a physiologist at the Leningrad-based Bechterev Institute for Brain Research and later a professor at Leningrad University. At one time in his career, he, too, had eagerly studied skin vision. Before his death in the 1960s, Vasiliev had made several notable contributions to parapsychology, one of which was the discovery of Nina Kulagina.

Kulagina was originally one of Vasiliev's skin-vision subjects, and it was during their sessions together that she thought she noticed that the objects she was "sensing" moved about slightly under her fingertips. Intrigued with her observation, Kulagina began practicing PK on her own and eventually succeeded in moving small objects such as matches, vials, and other light items. However, there was one flaw in her PK during these early years. She had a difficult time demonstrating it for observers.

Professor Vasiliev enthusiastically encouraged Kulagina to develop her PK further and introduced what was eventually to become one of her standard displays. He suggested that she try to deflect a compass needle by PK, and Kulagina was immediately successful at this new task. To this day, she often warms up with a compass before graduating to more complex demonstrations.

It is rather curious that, to all appearances, Kulagina herself has given two different stories about the discovery of her gift. To be sure, there may not be a real contradiction between the stories. It could well be that Kulagina encountered PK before she developed it consciously, but rationalized the incidents away as just odd accidents. It could have been in retrospect that she realized that she had encountered PK before her actual tests with Vasiliev. If this were the case, then the Ostrander-Schroeder story could be an account of how Kulagina discovered the *phenomenon* of PK, while the Moss story would more specifically represent an account of how she discovered that she was herself the source of the PK.

However, this confusion does point out a very important problem that we will continually confront as we try to evaluate Soviet parapsychology: There is so much contradiction and confusion about what Soviet scientists claim for their work, and about what Western visitors have been told, that it is extremely hard to gain a fair picture of what exactly is going on there.

The discovery of Kulagina only became known to the West a few years after she began her PK work with Vasiliev. Western scientists first began focusing their envious eyes on the Russian psychic in the late 1960s when films of her PK began to show up in Europe. Some of these films had been smuggled out of the Soviet Union, and some of them were just short of sensational. They first made their appearance in England where they came to the attention of Mr. Benson Herbert, a physicist who directs the Paraphysical Laboratory in Dowton, Wiltshire, and whose publication, the *Journal of Paraphysics,* was the first to begin publishing translations of Soviet papers on parapsychology. Herbert made the first detailed analysis of the Kulagina films in 1968–1970.

One of the films was taken by Dr. Zdenek Rejdak, a Czech

scientist at the Prague Military Institute. Rejdak visited Kulagina in 1968 in order to test her and photograph the PK. These tests were carried out only after the psychic had been searched for magnets, strings, and other props which she could conceivably employ to fake the PK. This is what Rejdak reported:

> . . . After we sat down around the table, I required Mrs. Kulagina to leave the position at which she had decided to sit, and to sit at the opposite side of the table. The first test was to endeavor to turn a compass needle first to the right and then to the left. Mrs. Kulagina held her hands approximately 5-10 cm over the compass during the experiment, as well as during the following ones. After an interval of concentration, the compass-needle turned more than ten times. Thereafter, the entire compass turned on the table, then a matchbox, some separate matches, and a group of about 20 matches at once.
>
> I placed my gold ring on the table: it moved faster than all the other objects . . . I chose some glass and china objects from the buffet, weighing from 10 to 20 dg., and Mrs. Kulagina made them move as well. On request, she could induce motion in the objects, while they were on a seat or on the floor. All this was performed in full light. The gold ring which she had made move was taken by me from my finger and put on the table. She passed her hands over it and the ring moved toward her. Threads or other attachments were out of the question.
>
> The matches we used had not been examined because they belonged to us, as also did the match-box, and so could not have been prepared by her. Fraud was impossible, as she was sitting in a fully illuminated room controlled by Prof. Sergeyev, Dr. Zvenev, Mr. Blazek, and myself. Other objects . . . were selected by myself and so she had no opportunity of preparing them.

During the entire series of tests, Kulagina's body had been monitored to see what was happening to it physiologically. After the experiments were over, it was clear that she had lost weight, her heart beat erratically, her blood sugar increased, and her muscles ached. In general, this all indicates a "stress-alarm" adaptation.

Mme. Kulagina's physical reactions to her PK are very similar to the ones about which Palladino would complain at the end of one of her séances. She, too, was a physical wreck at the completion of a trying set of tests. She lost weight, cramped up, and would even vomit. There is little doubt, to my mind at least, that both Kulagina's and Palladino's PK represents virtually the same process at work and has (or had) the same relationship to their organisms. Once again it looks as though stress is the key to volitional PK. But why? Why should PK be related to a stress reaction? Why can't it be exercised with ease a la the poltergeist?

There is obviously a delicate balance that must be reached between psychological readiness, conscious volition, and physical readiness before PK can manifest. It could be that if there is no psychological readiness to exhibit PK (as, for example, the psychological frustrations which provoke the poltergeist), then physical volition must compensate for it. Obviously, subjects like Kulagina are always physically ready to produce PK, but they are not always psychologically prepared. If, however, the subject can manifest the requisite psychological conditions to produce PK, then the physical factors can take second place. For instance, Kulagina did not at first produce PK with any strain. Objects apparently just moved under her fingertips. At this point, she had a psychological readiness to produce PK. Since she also had an innate physical readiness to perform, the PK could manifest easily. Later as she tried consciously to produce and control the PK, she had to use physical stress to compensate for what might be considered a psychological resistance to producing the phenomena. Great psychics may not always be prepared—consciously or unconsciously—to exert PK. This is where the strain comes in . . . working with the physical body to eject the PK against mental resistance. Since PK is usually an unconscious process, we are probably always mentally resisting it, consciously or unconsciously, even if we *believe* we are trying to produce it. Very few poltergeist agents, for instance, are good experimental PK subjects.

The films made and collected by Dr. Rejdak and his colleagues are fascinating and were shown in England to members of the Society for Psychical Research on March 14, 1969. The films depict objects moving while sealed in a transparent box, a cigarette balanced on end moving along a tabletop without rolling, and other items either moving, sliding, revolving, or contorting under the psychic's hands. One film shows an even more astounding feat. A cigar case is balanced upright on top of a playing card and is placed in a box. As Kulagina concentrates, the card and case slide across the box together, the case remaining upright at all times.

At Dr. Rejdak's urging, a conference on parapsychology was

held in Prague on September 25-26, 1968. At that meeting Kulagina's husband, who has carried out much of the pilot work with his wife, listed the following psychic abilities as ones he has observed with her: telekinesis on stationary objects, levitations of objects, deflection of compass needles, the ability to impress letters or numerals onto photographic paper, the inexplicable production of cold light on photographic emulsion and PK on living organisms. (Kulagina has been known to speed up and slow down the heartbeat of a frog by PK.) According to Mr. Kulagin, his wife has also been able to demonstrate telepathy and clairvoyance.

However, not all of the experiments with Kulagina have been conducted by newswriters and relatives. Soviet scientists have studied her as well. Chief among these has been Dr. Grenady Sergeyev of the Leningrad-based A. A. Uktomskii Physiological Institute. Sergeyev feels that PK is most likely a biological-type field. During his tests with Kulagina, he determined that her body radiates much more electromagnetic radiation while she is performing than when she is at rest. Much of this radiation is generated from the back of her head, Sergeyev claims.

Soviet scientists have also discovered several other factors which contribute to or seem to guide Kulagina's PK. First, despite their rather physicalistic approach to parapsychology, the Soviets have isolated several psychological factors which seem to contribute to the PK process. A good, friendly, and informal atmosphere helps Kulagina. Also, new tests take more "energy" out of her, and she has to rest frequently during them. On the other hand, she can manipulate material of any physical constitution; metals, plastics, fabrics, and organic materials have all been successfully used. This is an interesting point, since some of the great mediums, notably Eusapia Palladino, adamantly refused to work with certain materials. Palladino had an aversion to metal and even her wooden séance table was pieced together with wooden pegs. Was Palladino's inhibition psychically or psychologically motivated? The results of the Kulagina work would suggest the latter. Kulagina herself, according to Dr. Rejdak, prefers and feels that she can best work with gold.

Even the very movements of the PK-affected objects appear to be governed by a few rigid principles: (1) It is easier for Kulagina to roll objects such as cigarette or cigar containers than to shift them from an upright position. (2) When Kulagina is working with new objects, they always move away from her; only after practice can she attract them. (3) However, objects that are attracted to the psychic's body move faster and more energetically. (4) It takes greater energy for Kulagina to move objects farther away from her than ones close at hand. (5) Often the objects begin their motion as though imitating the psychic's own bodily movements. When she swings and contorts her body as she strains to exert the PK, the objects might begin to move in similar fashion. (6) Even after a test is over, an object might continue to move although Kulagina is no longer attempting to induce PK.

Soviet scientsits have also studied how screening affects the objects Kulagina tries to influence by PK. They have found that screening the target objects with lead-impregnated glass, paper, metal plates, wood, and so forth has no effect on the PK. Shielding will not affect the PK even if a screen is placed around the objects while they are in motion. Yet, on the other hand, Kulagina cannot move objects placed in a vacuum. Unlike Palladino, though, Kulagina cannot discharge an electroscope, nor has any electrical charge ever been detected around her moving objects.

It wasn't long before Western scientists began traveling to the Soviet Union to see for themselves. One of the first American parapsychologists to make the journey was Dr. J. Gaither Pratt, a researcher from the University of Virginia's division of parapsychology. Pratt has long been interested in PK. He was one of J. B. Rhine's original co-workers at the Duke University Parapsychology Laboratory and was one of the first Duke workers to reanalyze the early dice-rolling experiment and to investigate poltergeist cases for the lab.

Pratt first heard about Kulagina at a Soviet-sponsored symposium on parapsychology which he attended in June 1968. It took Pratt two years to get back to the Soviet Union, and he arrived in Leningrad in June 1970, accompanied by Dr. Jürgen Keil, a psychologist from the University of Tasmania. Unfortunately Pratt only conferred with Sergeyev on this trip and did not get to work directly with Kulagina. However, he returned in September with an assistant, Champe Ransom, and got down to business. The initial tests were carried out in Pratt's own hotel room.

The first test to which Pratt and Ransom subjected Kulagina was an attempt at psychic photography. Pratt had brought along an old Polaroid camera, but Kulagina could not impress anything on the film. Pratt and Ransom then turned to testing her telekinesis. In order not to make the psychic nervous, the investigators (who included two Soviet scientists) moved to an adjoining hallway while she warmed up in private. From this surreptitious position, Pratt was secretly able to watch the psychic at her exercises. In his *ESP Research Today*, Pratt wrote:

> . . . I could see Kulagina through the open door; she was sitting on the far side of a small round table facing me and the matchbox and compass were lying in front of her on the table. After a time I noticed that the matchbox, while she held her hands stretched out toward it and appeared to be concentrating very hard, moved several inches across the table in her direction. She put the box back near the center of the table and it moved again in the same way.

Champe Ransom took over Pratt's vantage point and he, too, watched the matchbox move. As it approached a compass which also rested on the table, the two objects began to move cojointly. This is a phenomenon that investigators have also noted with the psychic.

Since Kulagina now seemed warmed up and ready to go, the experimenters resumed their tests with the Polaroid film. However Pratt and Ransom were in for a little surprise. They placed the film atop a nonmagnetic metal cylinder, supported at one end by a small block of wood. From where she was seated, Kulagina could only see the film and block, not the cylinder, although she knew of its presence. Pratt was instituting the test to replicate some Soviet work which indicated that film will be uncannily exposed if objects near it are moved by Kulagina's PK. Pratt and Ransom expected Kulagina merely to concentrate on the cylinder; they did not expect her to move it. Yet, as Kulagina focused her attention on the film, Pratt clearly saw the cylinder move. The film, though, was in no way affected and it showed no odd markings or exposures when finally developed.

Pratt and Jürgen Keil paid another visit to the Soviet Union in February 1971, but the trip was a disappointment. From what Pratt was able to surmise, Soviet officials had heard about a review of the now-published *Psychic Discoveries Behind the Iron Curtain* and were apparently so flabbergasted by the claims made in the book that they had put Kulagina strictly off limits to foreign investigators.

But Pratt was persistent. In September 1971 he and Keil paid one further visit to the Soviet Union. On this trip they struck pay dirt, although the trip was not without its headaches. Six scientists from four different countries had tried to prompt Soviet officials into inviting them, in an official capacity, to work with Kulagina. The appeal was denied, so Pratt and Keil had to work unofficially. When they arrived in the Soviet Union, they immediately contacted Kulagina. That very evening, although they only expected to pay the celebrated psychic a social visit, Kulagina gave them a private performance par excellence. She moved several objects for the visitors, even though she apologized as she explained that it had been a year since she last employed her ability.

The most striking thing about these impromptu experiments was that Kulagina did not seem to have very much control over her PK. She kept displacing it. (Displacement in ESP and PK testing means that the subject has psychically responded to the wrong target.) For example, during her demonstrations for Pratt and Keil, Kulagina tried to move a cup. Yet, as Pratt explains, "The empty cup between Kulagina's hands remained stationary, but a small wooden cube we had placed on the table and that was four inches further back on the book moved two times." This displacement continued right on throughout the demonstration. For the next test, Kulagina tried to move two dice which were resting on a gravel bed inside a plastic cube. However, the whole cube moved instead of just the dice.

These PK "accidents," if we can call them that, do tell us a bit about Kulagina's PK. Pratt noted, as have most other observers, that Kulagina had to strain to induce the PK. Yet, an object she was *not* paying special attention to moved instead of the target item. I think that this phenomenon exemplifies the psychophysiological, yet unconsciously directed nature of PK. It is clear to me that the energy needed to move the objects emanates from Kulagina's entire physical system, but it seems directed by psychological factors. It could be that the psychic was unconsciously more intrigued with the box and plastic cube than with the actual target object. Her unconscious fixation may have overridden her conscious desires and volition.

There are many other oddities about Kulagina's PK which pop up now and then in the written accounts about her. Some of these have been mentioned earlier. First of all, Kulagina, like Palladino, will often produce linger effects. Second, an object being moved by PK will sometimes "infect" nearby objects and they will be carried along with it as though the PK were affecting an area rather than an object. To me, these two factors indicate that Kulagina is generating a PK field which exists in a localized physical area, affecting everything in its range, and which, like any physical field, dissipates gradually. It is true that Kulagina has been able to use PK consciously on only one matchstick within a cluster of them, but this phenomenon may represent her ability to minimize willfully the PK's sphere of influence. Right now, I'll only offer this theory as a possibility. But we must keep in mind that PK sometimes acts like a field, not like an all-or-nothing, beamlike mental projection.

Pratt's and Keil's investigations were basically observational. None of their tests were in any way designed to discover anything novel about Kulagina's powers. However, one Western scientist who has studied Kulagina in order to explore the mechanics and range of her abilities is Benson Herbert.

Herbert and his associate, Manfred Cassirer, visited the Soviet Union in July 1972 to attend meetings with Soviet colleagues as representatives of the paraphysical laboratory which Herbert directs. In many respects, these British investigations are much more provocative than Pratt's since Herbert wished to explore an entire range of Kulagina's PK and not just to observe her influence over small objects.

Herbert, Cassirer, and Kulagina all met at a Leningrad hotel. Unfortunately, Kulagina was not in any mood to offer a demonstration. She was prostrated by a heat wave which was engulfing the city and had been ill the day before. The skies were threatening a thunderstorm to boot, and Kulagina, like many other psychics, does not like to perform if the atmosphere is electrified.

The trip was not a complete failure though, for before she left, Kulagina did demonstrate for Herbert one of her more peculiar phenomena. As Herbert recalled:

> Kulagina gripped my left arm about two inches above the wrist—in this tropical heat wave my shirt sleeves were rolled up—and I waited, not quite knowing what to expect. If anything, I thought I may feel some beneficial or soothing influence, but for two minutes, I felt nothing whatever, save only a natural increase of warmth under her hands. Then, quite abruptly, I experienced a new sensation,

which I described at the time as a kind of "heat" but which now, after much reflection, I believe to be more akin to a mild electric shock.

It was however enough to be quite unpleasant; my arm writhed and my face grimaced, to the amusement of the onlookers. After perhaps two minutes, I came to the conclusion that I could not endure the sensation a moment longer, and disengaged my arm from Kulagina's formidable handclasp. One interesting feature was that throughout these two minutes, the sensation as far as I could judge remained quite constant; and it began suddenly as if with the turning on of a switch. There was no gradual build-up of sensation and discomfort such as might have been expected through some one gripping one's arm too tightly.

Kulagina attempted to replicate the demonstration on Cassirer's arm, but failed. Then she turned her almost sadistic attention on the investigators' translator. She gripped the translator's arm and soon this new victim was grimacing with pain.

Since Herbert was specifically interested in psychic healing, he asked the psychic if she had any healing ability. Certainly the heat experiment had proved that Kulagina could use PK on living organisms.

"I can induce a feeling of heat," responded the psychic in Russian, "such as you have just experienced, on my own hands, whenever I wish, either the left or right hand as I decide. I seem particularly able to heal infected wounds rapidly, and to do this, I hold the area in the neighborhood of the wound. For cases such as pneumonia, I place my hands over the sides of the patients. Dr. Sergeyev, who carries out experiments with me, will only consent to deal with patients who have been abandoned by medical doctors as incurable. . . . The patients must sign papers to testify that they agree to the experiments. We do not treat broken bones or fevers. One man age 26 came with partially paralyzed legs, and after three months treatment was able to walk perfectly again."

In fact, Kulagina continued, experiments in healing came before she turned her attention to PK under Vasiliev's tutelage, but after they had begun their dermo-optical perception experiments in 1961.

Herbert continued to ply Kulagina with questions. How does she implement her healing? Is it true that she can move gold objects easier than other materials?

Kulagina denied that she has any affinity for gold and told the visiting Englishmen that she can move all objects just as easily. This, I am sorry to say, is a flat contradiction of some of her previous statements. Dr. Rejdak, who has personally worked with her, has made special comment of this fact in his reports. I think this all tends to illustrate that Mme. Kulagina may not be the most reliable source of information about her own abilities.

Nevertheless, Kulagina adamantly believes that she possesses healing powers and claims the ability to direct her PK onto organic materials. There is one report on record that Kulagina used PK to accelerate a skeptical onlooker's heartbeat to a dangerous degree, which thoroughly terrified the would-be detractor.

Kulagina even gave Herbert a demonstration of this unique ability. According to the physicist:

". . . she clenched her right hand, palm upwards, we watched her arm, and within a minute or so, a circular mark appeared two inches above the wrist. This slowly began to fade during the remainder of the interview. But she showed us a more pronounced burn on the other arm which had remained unchanged for two days."

Before concluding her interview with the visiting parapsychologists, Kulagina did consent to one brief experiment. Herbert handed the psychic a packet of photographic enlargement paper which she held in her hand for a few minutes. When developed, two of the sheets in the packet showed peculiar gray markings and fogging effects. Psychic photography? Coincidence? Developing error? Or what?

Herbert was able to make a more detailed study of Kulagina in April 1973 at the Hotel d'Europe in Leningrad. For these tests the physicist brought several devices with which he hoped to measure Kulagina's PK. One of them was a floating hydrometer. The hydrometer (a tube which scales the gravity or density of any liquid in which it sits by the level to which it sinks) was placed in a saline solution and was protected by an earthed screen and an electrostatic probe. Herbert hoped that Kulagina could depress the hydrometer. From its readings, he could then calculate the amount of force Kulagina had exerted.

When Kulagina finally arrived for the tests with Dr. Sergeyev, Herbert's face dropped. She had been ill again and it looked momentarily as if the tests would be a washout. Even Herbert wasn't ready for what was to come:

Suddenly Kulagina startled us by walking over to the table and placing her hands in various positions near the rim of the metal cylinder (6″ diameter, 5″ high) that encased the glass vessel in which floated the hydrometer. At her sudden decision to overcome her indisposition and make an attempt at a demonstration, we were electrified into activity. I hastily switched on the equipment and all of us formed a circle around the table, with a battery of cameras poised.

As her hand approached the probe, I noticed with surprise that she evidenced much less electrostatic activity than I had expected (later we found that the field strength surrounding her body was only about three-quarters that surrounding the others present, at equal distances.) The hydrometer began to move slowly through the saline solution. This movement was repeated several times. However, her hands sometimes contacted the apparatus, and I thought it likely that the motion was due to vibration, but later all of us tried for the same effect, without success. Then Kulagina returned to her chair, three to four feet from the apparatus, and sat down as if exhausted.

In view of subsequent events, it is important to stress the fact that now a clear space existed between her and the table. Through this space, several of us walked during the next few minutes, as we talked and moved slowly around discussing other apparatus we had brought. Any fine wires or fibers that a critic may have supposed Kulagina had laid, connecting her to the hydrometer, must have been broken, or dislodged during this period.

Suddenly we fell silent, having noticed that Kulagina, after moving her chair only a few inches nearer to the table, had apparently fallen into a state of concentration (Not, I think, a trance), and was gazing intently at the hydrometer. Kulagina slowly moved her arms, raising them so that the palms of the hands faced toward the instrument. Shortly after, the hydrometer began to move away from her in a straight line across the full diameter of the vessel, a distance of 2½″, and came to rest at the opposite side, the transit occupying some 90 seconds. She then lowered her arms and remained quite still. The hydrometer remained stationary for two minutes, then commenced to move again, at the same speed as before, retracing its path until stopped by the edge of the glass nearest to her.

Throughout these two movements, the highly sensitive electrostatic meter had shown no response. Her success stimulated her, and she walked across the room to another table upon which stood two Crookes' radiometers, one containing air at atmospheric pressure, the other rarefied. I stood right beside her and watched closely. She placed one hand on each radiometer and after several attempts, in which she swung her head in circular fashion counterclockwise, she succeeded in causing both to turn counterclockwise (normally heat from the hand would turn the rarefied instrument clockwise.) However, I felt that the hand contact, slight muscular trembling may have produced the result, though on placing my hand on the table, I could feel no vibration. In view of the hand contact however, I would not like to affirm that the motion did not have a normal cause.

At this moment, Sergeyev engaged me in conversation, and for a few seconds I looked away from Kulagina. But Mr. Cassirer, who was also standing very close to her and had kept her under continuous observation, nudged me, and I hastily looked around. Mr. Cassirer and myself formed as it were a barrier between Kulagina and the others. I observed that Cassirer had placed his own compass case on the table in front of Kulagina. She was at once intrigued as the compass is her favorite instrument for "warming up", and she passed both hands over the compass, at a height of about 10 cm. in circular sweeping movements as seen on her films.

It is true that the needle swung to and fro but I felt there was too much vibration from the floorboards—as the spectators shuffled around to get a good view over our shoulders—to be sure what was causing the motion. She fell back in her chair to rest. By this time everyone was still, and the compass needle swung gently from side to side about 5° to either side of magnetic north, indicating that only the earth's field was operating. I bent down closely to the compass and realized I had a clear view of the edge of the table right down to the floor; the nearest part of Kulagina's body, her knees, were clearly separated from the table by a space approximately one foot; her feet were together; the hem of her skirt, short by Soviet standards, was about 2 inches above her knees. I was able to take in the entire scene while keeping the compass itself in view, and was very startled to see the entire compass case, right under my nose, turn round about 45° counterclockwise. Shortly after it slid bodily across the table, moving in peculiar and irregular zigzag fashion, in short jerks, each jerk carrying it 2 to 2.5 cm., the first movement slightly away from Kulagina to her left, then to the right rather more toward her, coming to rest after a total of 4 or 5 jerks some 4 inches nearer to Kulagina than its starting point. Each individual movement lasted between one and two seconds. The total movement occupied about one minute. This may seem a short time in the telling, but I was in a condition of extreme alertness, my brain worked at lightning speed and I was able to make a number of important observations and tests.

After this dramatic exhibition, Kulagina turned her talents to other types of PK displays. Manfred Cassirer noticed that the psychic was still scarred by the burn mark on her arm which the two investigators had seen on their previous visit. Their comment about this to Kulagina acted like a posthypnotic suggestion and soon she was enthusiastically trying to replicate her "shock" effect on Herbert's arm. Herbert was ready and willing and . . . in true scientific fashion . . . instructed the psychic not to let go of his arm no matter how distressed he seemed to be.

All the guests present at the demonstration huddled around Herbert while the psychic rubbed a little vodka over her hands to sterilize them. She gripped Herbert's arm snugly. Immediately he felt what he could only describe as "acute physical pain." The ache was so intense that he soon found himself clenching his teeth and stomping on the ground in order to endure it. Finally, after four or five minutes Herbert collapsed. He was totally drained by the experience and a reddish, burnlike area prominently discolored his arm where the psychic had gripped it.

Herbert was roused, though, by the groans of Mr. Cassirer. Looking up, he saw that Kulagina was pressing a camera against his companion's arm and was transferring her PK heat *through* the object. After only a few seconds, Cassirer asked Kulagina to stop. Although he had felt intense heat, the camera was not even warm. It took Herbert's burn mark eight days to heal. (As a postscript to this experiment, I should add that Kulagina has also demonstrated this heat effect to Jarl Fahler, a prominent Finnish parapsychologist. Kulagina produced the heat while holding her hands several inches away from, but over, Fahler's arm. Although she was able to produce a marked heat on the arm, a thermistor placed between Fahler's arm and the psychic's hand showed no temperature change.)

At present there is little information about any new work with Kulagina. There were some reports a few years ago which claimed that Kulagina's whole system was being torn apart by the PK. We do know that she is under a great deal of physical strain during her performances which adversely affect her blood-sugar level, portions of her brain, several internal organs, and there are probably side effects that we don't even know about. But whether or not Kulagina is literally "tearing herself apart" by her constant PK demonstrations is a debatable point. The reports could be true, or they could be typical Soviet maneuvers to keep Kulagina under close guard.

There are so many different aspects to Kulagina's PK that it is hard to do justice to her in this brief discussion. However, in order to collate much of the work that has been done with the Russian psychic, a joint report has been prepared by Dr. Jürgen Keil, Benson Herbert, Dr. J. G. Pratt, and Dr. Montague Ullman. This joint analysis, "Directly Observable Voluntary PK Effects" was issued by the Society for Psychical Research in January 1976. By reanalyzing all the extant literature on Kulagina, these four parapsychologists found that certain definite statements could be made about her PK. Here are some of their conclusions: (1) Many of the early tests with Kulagina were carried out in a manner which seems to have excluded the possibility of fraud. (2) Objects will often move after Kulagina has ended her demonstration. (3) Objects often move in circular trajectories as well as toward and away from her. (4) Sometimes items other than the specifically designated target will be affected by the PK. (5) More than one object will sometimes move when Kulagina is demonstrating her PK, usually in a uniform direction. (6) Kulagina can move a group of objects simultaneously in several different directions. (7) She can use PK to disturb the movements of objects already in motion and can even make them change direction. (8) She can exert PK on living material such as slowing down and stopping a frog's heart. (10) There is some evidence that during her concentration, Kulagina discharges energy from her head. (11) There is no evidence that electrical fields come into play during her performances. (12) Screening has little appreciable effect on Kulagina's PK but (13) storms do inhibit it. (14) Kulagina loses weight during her PK exhibitions, suffers loss of motor coordination, and shows signs of physical stress.

6

The PK Epidemic

As with most inquiries into PK, the Kulagina work poses as many questions as it offers answers about the PK force. However, some possible solutions to these new puzzles about the PK mystery have begun to become clearer as scientists, both in the Soviet Union and in the West, have proceeded to work with new and even more provocative PK subjects.

One of these gifted subjects is a young, dark-haired, and pretty educational psychologist named Alla Vinogradova. Vinogradova certainly comes from a scientific family: her husband is Dr. Victor Adamenko, a talented young Soviet physicist. Vinogradova first became intrigued with PK through watching films of Kulagina in action. Soon she began practicing, too, imitating the older woman, and eventually became rather proficient at producing a weak semblance of Kulagina's displays. However, there is considerable debate going on in parapsychological circles whether or not Vinogradova is employing PK or has really learned some curious method of manipulating electrostatic forces. If the latter is the true explanation for her abilities, then she is really not a PK subject at all. For her demonstrations, the young psychologist usually makes cigar cones or paper cylinders move as she waves her hand back and forth over them. Although this *looks* like PK, electrostatic fields can also account for this phenomenon equally well.

Alla Vinogradova was introduced to the parapsychological community at large during the XXth International Congress of Psychology held in Tokyo, Japan, in August 1972, during which Victor Adamenko presented films of his wife's PK along with a formal presentation about her. The films show Vinogradova seated before a dielectric table. A paper cylinder is placed before her. As she rolls her hand over the object, it rolls as if connected to the hand by an invisible string. At other times, her hand acts to repulse the movement of the cylinder, reminiscent of the way similar poles of two magnets will repel each other.

In a somewhat critical review of these films published in the September–October 1972 issue of the *Parapsychology Review*, Benson Herbert has aptly pointed out that Vinogradova's demonstrations are not unequivocally PK displays. As the physicist points out, anyone sitting on a rubber insulating mat and charged up with a Wimshurst machine (a device which discharges static electricity) can move objects under his hands. This is a natural property of static electricity. As Herbert also noted, "It is true that a girl wearing fashionable synthetic underwear does not need a Wimshurst to be 'turned on.'" The friction between the skin and the material is enough to produce an electrostatic charge.

Nonetheless, many features of Vinogradova's phenomena are slightly different from how static electricity usually acts. For instance, a human hand, charged with static electricity, will usually only *attract* objects, yet Vinogradova can clearly repel them as well. Second, she can produce an enormously high-voltage gradient of some 10,000 volts per cm. and has extraordinary control over the field she is creating, whatever its nature may be. Also, Vinogradova can selectively manipulate this force. She can, among other things, move one of two objects placed side by side. Further, she can produce her effects while standing barefoot on a metal floor and when wearing a grounded metal bracelet. These guards should ground any electrical buildup the subject might be producing.

One witness who believes that the mystery behind Vinogradova's powers is far from understood is Pamela Painter de Maigret, an American writer who visited the Adamenkos in Moscow in 1973 and watched the psychologist move cylinders back and forth across a tabletop. It took immense effort and strain for Vinogradova to produce the effects, but once she was warmed up she could move the objects with ease. As Mrs. de Maigret describes it:

> "[The cigar tube] . . . rocked back and forth several times, then slowly began to roll across the plastic table top away from her hand.

When the cylinder neared the outer edge, Alla quickly reached over the table and put her hand on the far side to it. It stopped abruptly six or eight inches from her hand, rocked a few times and then started to roll in the opposite direction. She continued while the tube rolled across the table several times. Each pass seemed to become easier for her. The strain and tension left her face; her body became more relaxed; the cylinder moved with greater ease . . .

As Mrs. de Maigret noted, Vinogradova seems to have complete control over the cylinder. She can make it change direction, spin it, and so forth.

Mrs. de Maigret was in for a surprise, though, when Vinogradova stepped up to her and suggested that *she* could roll the cigar case. Vinogradova took the writer's hands and rubbed them briskly. Hand in hand they jointly pushed the tube back and forth. "I thought I could feel a faint repulsive energy between the cylinder and my hands," writes Mrs. de Maigret; "it was rather like the feeling of trying to force similar poles of two magnets together."

What Mrs. de Maigret has really given us is a perfect description of what a static charge feels like. For instance, on a windy day rub your feet on a thick carpet and bring your finger near metal. Do not touch it, since that will, of course, merely produce a static shock. But bring your finger near to the metal to about a half inch, and you will feel the type of elastic resistance Mrs. de Maigret describes.

After Vinogradova finished "helping" out Mrs. de Maigret, the writer could produce the movements independently. Her power soon petered out, so Vinogradova had to recharge her, and immediately Mrs. de Maigret found her quasi-PK ability reborn!

Not all of Vinogradova's demonstrations can be easily explained as some sort of electrostatic-field manipulation, though. Some of her powers smack of true PK. For example, Mrs. de Maigret witnessed a few incidents which looked more like genuine PK than an electrostatic discharge when she and some other visitors placed pen caps, some matches, a Ping-Pong ball, and other objects on a table for Vinogradova to move.

> . . . She could roll the pen caps in bumpy fashion due to their pocket clips or could make them skip without rolling. She could push them over from a standing point but could not raise them upright

from a prone position. The Ping-Pong ball could be made to skid across the table or to roll or bounce. To bounce it Alla quickly raised and lowered her hand about six inches above the ball. The ball started to shake, then bounced a bit and with each bounce went higher. This was the only time I saw Alla appear to draw something toward her hand rather than push it away.

The matches, which were emptied out of their box in a jumbled heap on the table, reacted in even stranger fashion. At first the jumbled mass did not move as a whole. As Alla pushed at them from about a foot away individual matches suddenly jumped, scattering the other matches around them. A momentum appeared to be building up that reminded me of popcorn held over a fire. The wooden matches "popped" in all directions. Only after several minutes did Alla get the whole mass to move away from her across the table; individual matches still popped around. I thought that chemicals in the match heads might have affected the movement but when we snapped the heads off a dozen or so they still reacted in the same way.

The strange powers of Alla Vinogradova must remain a mystery since one can offer several arguments for and against a physical explanation for her abilities. But there is another possibility we must contend with as well. Could it be that Vinogradova at first discharges an electrostatic field which gradually or sporadically changes over to PK? This is a theory which I find attractive. It also suggests that PK may have some peculiar link with electricity. Let's take a look at this idea, for the moment.

While I adamantly do not believe that PK is in any way electrical in nature, there is some evidence which suggests that PK and electricity might have some affinity for each other. For one thing, some psychics have an odd attitude toward thunderstorms. Nina Kulagina, Mary Wimberley, and Blue Harary are all gifted psychics, yet all of them prefer not to work if an electrical storm is brewing. When I was studying out-of-the-body-experience accounts at the Psychical Research Foundation in 1973, I came across two independent accounts by people who claimed that they had left their bodies but had become "glued" to electrical power lines and had to travel down them before finally breaking loose. However, there are other points of similarity between PK and electricity. Here are three of them:

1. Kulagina, as well as Palladino, often create(d) electrical-like sparks during their performances.

2. Palladino, but not Kulagina, could discharge an electro-

scope, which would indicate that she was somehow creating a field with electrical properties.

3. French, German, and Polish psychical investigators often noted at the onset of sittings with the great physical mediums that the smell of ozone pervaded the room. (See Professor Gustave Geley's *Clairvoyance and Materialization* [New York: Doran, 1927] p. 213.) The odor of ozone (a pungent smell like that of chlorine which results when electricity passes through the air) would indicate that electrical activity was present in the room before the start of the PK manifestations. This may relate to the "cold breeze" effect, that is, that the psychic in order to produce PK must somehow manipulate the atmosphere in the room. Could the subject be manipulating O_2 molecules, charging them electrically to O_3 molecules for some unfathomable reason?

Of course, none of these three points in any way demonstrates that PK is electrical in nature. From what we know about PK, such an explanation would be ridiculous. But somehow PK may manipulate electricity or imitate its properties.

Yes, imitate. If anything, our PK power is a born mimic. If a sensitive should appear on the psychic horizon who claims a curious form of PK gift, imitators with similar gifts will soon abound. Even Kulagina did not develop her PK abilities out of the blue. She developed them as she tried to imitate and emulate two psychics of yesteryear, Stanislawa Tomczyk in Poland and Cleio in Greece, who also used PK to move small objects about. (I will discuss both these psychics in more depth at the end of the chapter.) And we know that Alla Vinogradova used Kulagina's performances as her psychic model.

Now, going on with this same argument, PK will sometimes initially imitate electrical disturbances as well, or will seek out electrical gadgets to disrupt. A perfect example of this peculiar property of PK was quite obvious during the Rosenheim poltergeist of 1967–1968.

This poltergeist, which struck a law office in Rosenheim, was one of the best observed cases on record. Not only did several witnesses observe the PK, but investigators from the University of Freiburg studied it as well. One of the most outstanding features of the Rosenheim poltergeist was how it imitated electrical phenomena as though trying to conceal its true psychic nature. The poltergeist began its siege by manipulating lights, exploding light bulbs, and disrupting office telephones. When a voltage amplifier was attached to the building's voltage main, it, too, began fluctuating inexplicably. It was only after a parapsychologist was called in that the disturbances were finally diagnosed as a poltergeist. As though unveiled, the PK soon gave up its mimicry and starting acting like a conventional poltergeist.

It seems highly likely to me that Vinogradova can actually exert both an odd electrostatic field and PK. One may literally hide behind the other. Why? Perhaps the notion of electrostatic discharge is less psychologically threatening to Vinogradova than PK. Since PK is basically an unconscious process, it likes to work undercover so to speak. And what better way of doing so than by hiding behind static electricity? It may also be that whatever Vinogradova does physically to create this static field, also helps implement PK in some unknown way.

Another possible PK subject who is making quite a sensation in Eastern Europe is Dr. Julius Krmessky, a seventy-six-year-old Czech physicist who was at one time a lecturer at the State Pedagogical Institute in Bratislava. However, the case for Dr. Krmessky's PK is weaker than Vinogradova's.

Dr. Krmessky believes that he has discovered a new energy which is molded by the will. He came to this conclusion when he discovered that he could gyrate little paper mobiles hung by threads or balanced on pins by bringing his hand close to them. While Krmessky is very intrigued by the possibility that these effects are caused by some form of new energy, there are many normal factors that can account for the movements. Krmessky's demonstrations will commonly begin with his trying to manipulate these mobiles. He usually cups his hands around, but not touching, the object, and sure enough it will begin to move after a short interval. This movement, however, could easily be the result of tiny wind currents. By placing the hand around the object, a miniature wind-tunnel is produced. And the very motion of moving the arm into that position will cause air currents to be set up around the mobile. In a room with any ventilation at all, air currents will abound. Heat and static electricity can also make the objects turn or gyrate. I can get this myself by rubbing my hands against my trousers and then bringing them close to the mobile. I can spin them slowly even if I am grounded. Even back in the 1930s, the *Journal of the American Society for Psychical Research* issued a warning against this type of psuedotelekinesis explaining the true causes of the movements. But Dr. Krmessky fell right into the trap.

However, Dr. Krmessky may be very similar to Alla Vinogradova in one respect. It is possible that PK will, on occasion, interplay with the normal forces which usually affect the target systems.

Benson Herbert visited Krmessky in October 1971 and witnessed several performances by the physicist. Herbert soon realized that what he was seeing was hardly evidence of PK or of a new energy. So Krmessky, at Herbert's insistence, participated in another series of tests in which the target objects were shielded. Some of these demonstrations were more impressive. As Herbert reported:

> . . . in some experiments under total shielding conditions, the systems certainly appear to obey Dr. Krmessky's commands . . . Thus, a vane, floating upon water in a wine glass and completely covered by a glass vessel, remained quite stationary for ten minutes; then Dr. Krmessky began his experiments. He stared with quiet concentration on the vane from a distance of four feet; no one moved; doors and windows remained shut. Within four minutes, the vane was rotated 45° in the desired direction, then a further 90°, only coming to rest when Dr. Krmessky retired to an armchair about ten feet away, and ceased to look at the vane. This struck me as either paranormal or an improbable coincidence.

During this same series of tests, Herbert also saw Krmessky move a paper cylinder resting on a needle point and shielded inside a tin can. Despite these impressive displays, it is still very hard to determine whether the "Krmessky effect" is genuinely paranormal, or a normal reaction to air currents, static, or heat. Certainly air currents could explain most, but not all, of Krmessky's demonstrations. Static fields represent an enigma in themselves, and are a harder possibility to rule out. It certainly looks as though Vinogradova and Krmessky somehow manipulate static fields, but electrostatic fields and phenomena are just not very well understood by physicists. Frankly speaking, we do not know the range, power, or all the properties of electrostatic fields, so we don't know what they can or cannot account for. Of course, this doesn't make PK research very easy.

There is another possibility we cannot totally dismiss. While studying reports on Dr. Krmessky's powers (and there aren't very many available to us), I have failed to find any accounts in which onlookers brought along or constructed their own systems for Krmessky to influence. In every case, the physicist supplied his own. This certainly does not necessarily indicate a hoax, but it certainly doesn't help make a case against it either.

Dr. Krmessky's work certainly cannot be ignored. But, based on the few reports on him which have found their way to the West, it is nearly impossible to make any decisive judgment on his claims. However, the Soviet Union and its satellite nations are not the only countries to boast of potential PK subjects.

In 1971 one of the films of Kulagina at work was shown at the Maimonides Medical Center where the audience consisted mostly of the staff and volunteer helpers at the hospital's dream laboratory. In the audience that day was a young hematologist, Felicia Parise, a red-haired and vivacious girl who seems much younger than she really is. She had been one of the lab's best ESP subjects. Miss Parise was peculiarly affected by Kulagina's performance. She couldn't wait to get home and try to imitate her; she intuitively knew she could do the same thing. Felicia kept up her enthusiasm for several months. Each day she would take out the same plastic eyelash container and concentrate on moving it. But nothing happened.

These months were trying ones for Felicia. Her grandmother, to whom she was deeply attached, was dying in a hospital and the PK self-development was going nowhere. But, Felicia admitted, ". . . I could hardly wait each night to get home for a quiet period with my plastic bottle. That was the only time I could stop thinking about the heartbreak and tragedy that was coming on at the time. It became such an obsession that I took my plastic bottle to work and tried to move it during lunch hours and coffee breaks."

This ritual went on for several months. But when Felicia finally did move the bottle, it was under very different circumstances. She had come home from work one evening and was taking off her artificial eyelashes in order to put them away for the night in the little vial of alcohol. Just then the phone rang—it was her mother who hurriedly told Felicia that her grandmother had taken a turn for the worse. Felicia tried to compose herself and prepared to rush back to the hospital. She ran to get her eyelashes when . . . the little vial slid away from her hands as she reached for it.

Felicia's grandmother died shortly after the incident, and several weeks later Felicia discovered that she could now move her vial willfully by exerting a tremendous amount of effort. At first she kept her talent private and would not demonstrate it for anyone. During this period of self-development she also expanded her repertoire of PK effects and gradually learned to deflect a compass needle and rock pieces of aluminum foil back and forth.

Charles Honorton, who was then a senior research associate at the Maimonides lab, was probably the first to witness Felicia's PK. Felicia had a close bond with Honorton since she had been one of his most successful ESP subjects. As Honorton reported to the 1973 convention of the Parapsychological Association held in Charlottesville, Virginia:

> Late in the summer of 1971, while in Durham, North Carolina, I received a letter from Parise in which she reported success in displacing a small alcohol bottle, presumably by PK. When I returned to New York I was invited to her home for a demonstration. The alcohol bottle was actually a small clear plastic medicine bottle (59 mm. high and 34 mm. in diameter), filled approximately one-fourth with denatured alcohol. Parise used this bottle to preserve her cosmetic eyelashes. As we arrived in the kitchen, she placed the bottle on the formica countertop, approximately one foot back from the edge of the counter. She placed her hands on the edge of the counter, then silently looked at the bottle for two to three minutes. At that point she exclaimed that the bottle had moved. I did not see any movement. Parise was silent for another minute or two. Then the bottle moved one and one-half to two inches to my right and away from her. I then picked up the bottle and examined it carefully to be sure there was no moisture present and nothing attached to it, then replaced it on the counter to see if it would slide by itself. The bottle did not move. Later, Parise again placed her fingers on the edge of the counter. This time the bottle began slowly to move forward and to my right, in a curved trajectory. It stopped and started again three times and finally (after reaching a distance of approximately four and one-half inches from its starting position) reversed direction, returning toward me, and then stopped.

After watching Felicia's demonstrations, Honorton did all he could to determine if trickery could account for the movements of the vial. He examined the counter, tried manipulating it to see if he could move the vial any way normally, and even took a carpenter's level to it in order to make sure it wasn't grossly inclined. As he goes on to say in his report:

> During the following months I had occasion to repeat these observations, under the same conditions, a number of times. Parise became successful at deflecting the needle of a small pocket compass. In working with the compass, she would frequently place her hands, cupped slightly, à la Kulagina, around the periphery of the compass, about six inches over its surface. Often I would unexpectedly pass her hands directly over the face of the compass to insure against concealed metallic shavings, etc. In no case did similar movements occur when I did this.

In order to produce her PK, Felicia strains violently. It could be that she is merely imitating Kulagina, who first inspired her to try her hand at PK. However, the vial first moved totally spontaneously, so we know that strain is not necessary per se in order for Felicia to induce the phenomenon. I think that this contradiction further supports my view that PK will occur easily when there is psychological readiness as well as a physical readiness within the subject to induce the force. There can be little doubt that Felicia was physically ready to produce PK all the time she was practicing. However, the phenomenon first manifested during a period of extreme stress. The PK practices were Felicia's only escape from her grandmother's agony. And it was right at the very time her grandmother reached her crisis that the bottle finally moved. It was as though the PK were trying to console Felicia . . . a substitute for the ultimate loss of her grandmother. Many people turn to the study of psychic phenomena at a time of crisis, though Felicia went so far as to produce the phenomena herself.

Even during the height of her career, Felicia did not always have to strain to induce the PK. Sometimes it would occur spontaneously, Honorton reported:

> PK attempts in the laboratory were always a strain for Parise, and she was not as confident there. While she never succeeded in moving the bottle in the laboratory, she did succeed on a number of occasions in producing good compass deflections. On one occasion, while she was in my office, I tried to coax her to "zap" my own compass. She was in a hurry to leave, and did not want to get "worked up" for PK. However, I prodded her, and as she stood about 18 inches from the

desk on which the compass lay, she waved her arm in the direction of the compass and jokingly said "Abracadabra"! The compass needle immediately deflected 90 degrees.

There were two other investigations made of Parise. The first was by Honorton himself when he decided to film the PK at Felicia's apartment. The cameraman he brought along was an amateur magician who was duly impressed. Honorton was able to film Felicia moving her vial, deflecting a compass needle, as well as moving a piece of foil and deflecting the compass needle while they were both covered by bell jars.

After substantiating Felicia's claims to his own satisfaction, Honorton took her down to the Institute for Parapsychology of the Foundation for Research on the Nature of Man in Durham, North Carolina. There further tests were designed and executed by Graham Watkins and his wife, Anita, who were both research associates at the institute. Their tests turned up some interesting surprises.

For their first test, the Watkinses asked Felicia to move a bottle that was situated behind a glass window and which sat on the coil of a metal detector. Packets of film were set around the bottle at varying distances. Felicia couldn't move the bottle, so a compass was substituted. She failed at that task also. Finally she asked if the glass could be removed, and the Watkinses brought out the entire setup, film and all, and placed it directly in front of Felicia. The psychic concentrated, her body jerked and trembled, and the compass needle began to deflect. "When the movement of the compass needle was finally accomplished," Watkins reported, "it was accompanied by a change in the sound frequency produced by the metal detector, whereupon a total shatter of the tone occurred; this could be artifically simulated only by placing a very large metal mass (a two-pound roll of solder) in the field coil."

The compass needle had deflected by about 15 degrees and seemed lodged there. The Watkinses at first thought that the compass was broken. However, as soon as they took it away from the immediate experimental area, it returned to normal. The needle deflected again automatically when it was brought back into the specific area of the room where Felicia had worked her PK. It took twenty-five minutes for the PK influence to dissipate. Furthermore, the film packets around the compass were all exposed, the degree of exposure increasing in proportion to each packet's proximity to the compass.

This finding is a perfect example of a linger effect. The Watkinses' experiments with Felicia also substantiate my view that whatever its nature, PK actually sets up a field. The Watkinses were even able to discover the perimeters of Felicia's PK field; it radiated about four feet from the target area. The proportional fogging of the film in direct relation to its distance from the compass also indicated the presence of a field with definable limits. The linger effect likewise indicated the existence of a field. If an energy field is set up and its power cut off, the field doesn't suddenly become inert. It dissipates gradually by using up its residual energy. This property of energy fields probably accounts for these linger effects.

There are also other aspects of Parise's and Kulagina's PK which indicate a field function. Felicia cannot move objects in any direction she wishes. They always move away from her. This would indicate that every time Felicia exhibits PK she is initiating the same process. If PK were *not* a field with mechanics of its own, she should have been able to change the motion of the objects willfully. Instead, it looks as if Felicia could only set up the PK field, while it was the field which actively governed the direction and mechanics of the phenomena. Many observers of Kulagina's PK performances have noticed that when one moving object bypasses a fellow object, both items will often move together as though magnetized. This tends to indicate that Kulagina's PK affects an area rather than an object.

Felicia doesn't practice her PK anymore; she gave it up about two years after she started, and has given two explanations for why she put a stop to it. First, it was a drain on her. "In order to maintain a high order of success with PK, I have to devote all my time to it, and I mean all my time," she would say. "I have tried to maintain a normal life-style continuous with PK and found it impossible to do so." The PK also became both psychologically and emotionally trying for her. She just couldn't handle the fact that her close friends and associates were eyeing her suspiciously and with skepticism. She couldn't stand the alienation she knew she would have to face if she continued on with her psychic development.

However, there are two other factors which could have influenced Felicia to give up her PK work. Felicia still works at the Maimonides Medical Center where I first met her and is a constant visitor to the center's division of parapsychology and psychophysics (which was expanded from the original dream laboratory). We soon became friends and Felicia turned into one of my most enthusiastic and successful ESP subjects. One day I asked her point-blank if, during her PK career, she had been plagued by *spontaneous* PK outbreaks around her. Indeed there had been. Felicia began to realize that she had to force this newly liberated PK of hers back into dormancy. Another reason for her giving up PK work is probably psychological in nature. Felicia turned to PK in order to escape from the ordeal her grandmother was going through. I cannot help but wonder if eventually she lost interest in PK because, as she got over her grandmother's death, it lost its emotional appeal and comfort.

As the years roll on, no doubt more PK subjects will emerge. Many of them will not be as powerful as Kulagina or Parise, but hopefully some of them will be stronger. But, volitional PK of the order which Kulagina produces is not a new development in parapsychology's search for PK, and there are two kindred cases in our history which are very similar.

The first case is one about which we know very little. The subject was a Greek psychic who was given the pseudonym Cleio, and was discovered by A. Tanagras, a Greek amateur psychical researcher who died a few years ago. We only know about Cleio at all because Tanagras made a presentation about her at an international congress on psychic research which was held in Oslo, Norway, in 1935. Films of her PK were also shown. According to his report, Cleio had been plagued by haunting-type manifestations in her home after her father's death. Tanagras convinced her that it was her own PK at work and pressed her to develop her talents. At first she was reticent, and to make his subject less inhibited Tanagras began hypnotizing her, so as a result she usually performed while under hypnosis or following a posthypnotic suggestion.

Cleio's main feat was deflecting a compass needle, and films were made of her moving the needle while the compass was shielded by glass. The most memorable sequence of the film comes toward the end, as Cleio jumps up and down with delight when she realizes that she has been successful!

Our other historical case comes from Poland. The subject was a young woman named Stanislawa Tomczyk; the investigator was Dr. Julien Ochorowicz, who was a lecturer in psychology at the University of Lemberg and from 1907 onward was codirector of the Institute General Psychologique of Paris. His fascinating reports on her were published in the *Annals of Psychical Science* in 1909.

Tomczyk might be called a super-Kulagina. She, too, had the ability to move small objects by PK, and she could also levitate them by placing her hands on either side of the objects but not touching them. The object would rise as she raised her hands, and several photographs were taken of her.demonstrations at extremely close range. Tomczyk could also deflect compass needles and spontaneous apports would often fall into the room in the course of the experiments. The sessions were always carried out in full light. Tomczyk was first placed in trance by Ochorowicz, and then a new personality, named "Little Stasia," would take over the psychic's body, talk with the professor, and help precipitate the PK.

There were many enigmas about Tomczyk's PK. During her trances, "Little Stasia" would direct the phenomena and would become a real intelligence, totally independent of the psychic's. And it was not only a psychological presence either, as Ochorowicz soon learned. The Tomczyk work was full of surprises, and one of them came on January 17, 1909, when the psychologist was testing to see if Tomczyk could make a pendulum swing without touching it. The psychic could do this easily. But later in the tests, Tomczyk announced that "Little Stasia" was right in the room with them and sitting in a nearby armchair. At that moment Ochorowicz turned around to see his dog staring at that very chair and growling repeatedly at some invisible presence.

Professor Ochorowicz came to believe that Tomczyk exteriorized a "fluidic double" during her performances and that this psychic projection took on the personality of Little Stasia. His theory was virtually the same as that of de Rochas, who also suggested that Palladino could exteriorize a phantom of herself composed of some psychic substance. (No doubt Ochorowicz's theory would delight our Soviet confrères with their concept of the "bioplasmic body.") However, Ochorowicz also came to believe that, although engendered by the psychic's own mind, Little Stasia could manifest a will and personality of her own. This would, in fact, be very similar to the theory which I have formulated to account for some poltergeist outbreaks.

Tomczyk was best known for her levitation performances, and the most notable aspect of these levitations was a discovery that was made by Ochorowicz. As he worked with Tomczyk, the psychologist gradually began to see tiny spiderweb-like threads emanating from her hands and connecting to the objects as she levitated them. One could easily jump to the conclusion that these threads were merely strings fraudulently manipulated by the psychic, but this could hardly have been the case since these threads had mighty strange properties. Ochorowicz could pass his hands through them, cut them, or do anything he liked to them. The rays would immediately resume their continuity when he was through disrupting them.

Sometimes Tomczyk would levitate small objects which were enclosed in cups or funnels. She would move her hands alongside the shields, and the object inside the container would float up synchronously.

Two other psychical investigators also worked with Tomczyk successfully. The first was the Baron von Schrenck-Notzing who replicated Ochorowicz's work. The second was Everard Feilding, still somewhat fresh from his Palladino investigations. Feilding must have been impressed by what he saw, for within a matter of months he and the psychic were married!

Stanislawa Tomczyk, now Mme. Feilding, is today an elderly lady living in seclusion in England. She can't tell us much about her PK, I am sorry to say. If asked, she will immediately remind you that she was in trance most of the time.

Mme. Tomczyk is not the only psychic to have produced "rigid rays," as Ochorowicz called them. I saw something which looked almost identical on a still photograph which showed Kulagina levitating a ball. (It is the only picture I know of which depicts her fully levitating an object.) If you look closely, you can see a tiny thread leading from the ball to her hand. Is this a physical thread? Was Kulagina caught in a sham? Or did the camera just happen to catch Kulagina exteriorizing the same psychic substance which

Tomczyk employed to levitate her little balls, pencils, and other items?

Even though many contemporary parapyschologists like to compare Kulagina and Tomczyk, there are many differences between them. Most notably, a session with Tomczyk was replete with many totally spontaneous PK phenomena. Clumps of snow would fall into the experimental room, small objects would apport in as well, and sometimes objects would levitate unexpectedly. Once Ochorowicz watched a burning-hot frying pan pick itself up from a stove and hoist into the air where it remained suspended for several moments. We hear virtually nothing about spontaneous PK with Kulagina. Tomczyk was also much more proficient at psychic photography than Kulagina. Ochorowicz's crowning achievement was prodding Tomczyk to imprint psychically an outline of her own hand, ring and all, on a piece of photographic paper sealed in a bottle. Nor does Kulagina have to be hypnotized in order to produce PK.

When I outlined the careers of the great mediums earlier, I argued that these studies are of more than purely historical or pedagogical interest. They tell us quite a bit about the nature of PK. In this same vein, one might ask, what are these new PK mediums telling us about psi?

Soviet scientists have probably been the world's leading theorists on PK. In fact, theories about psi are exported out of the U.S.S.R. like vodka—crates upon crates of them are shipped out annually. Many of these theories have been outlined to account for the type of PK effects Kulagina, Vinogradova, and others have been demonstrating.

One of the most provocative of these theories is Professor V. Inyushin's concept of "bioplasma." Professor Inyushin and his colleagues believe that all living things generate an atomic structure of "counter energy" which builds up into a duplicate physical system within the organism. This substance can act selectively within the body and outside it, or can build up into a duplicate of the human body which Inyushin calls the "bioplasmic body." Inyushin's theories are in part based on research into Kirlian photography, a process by which objects are photographed in a high-voltage electrical field. The result is a striking aura effect around the material photographed. According to the original

Soviet work in Kirlian photography, dying material radiates no aura. Thus, the Soviets believe that this aura is some sort of life field which permeates all living matter. Nevertheless, much contemporary work into the Kirlian process has tended to indicate that the effects are most likely perfectly normal electrical effects. Most of the talk about "auras" and "life fields" was really premature, and most of it was offered before the parameters of radiation field photography were understood.

Even though the Kirlian effect probably has no bearing on psychic phenomena, Professor Inyushin's theory deserves to be taken seriously. For one thing, the concept of a double which is locked in the human organism and which is responsible for PK is a very old parapsychological theory. Inyushin also claims that this bioplasmic body radiates energy and creates life fields, and he believes that this bioplasmic structure consists mainly of free charged particles which create uniform energy networks.

Inyushin himself makes the following points about the nature and properties of bioplasma: (1) It is not a chaotic field, but a complex organization. (2) It can be a discrete system or systems acting as constellations within the organism, but all bioplasma may represent a uniform structure. (3) Bioplasma "drifts" throughout the organism, and propagates electromagnetic energy within the system. (4) This field regulates the interactions among the cells of the body.

Professor Inyushin's concept certainly has all the trappings of a scientific theory, but none of the hard evidence for one. Admittedly, he does not specifically try to apply this theory to account for PK, and I cannot see how his concept could apply to the types of phenomena which have been observed with the great psychics. For example, Inyushin insists that the plasma is charged electromagnetically. But we know that PK cannot be electromagnetic in nature since it is not barred by distance or barriers.

Actually, though, I have nothing against the basic idea behind Inyushin's theories. On reading them it is very clear that he has stumbled upon many ideas which the early parapsychologists hinted at independently. For one thing, biological plasma is little different from the "psychic fluid" the French researchers believed existed. Inyushin's belief that bioplasma helps to regulate organic systems internally is almost identical to Hereward Carrington's concept of a "vital force." Even J. B. Rhine has suggested that PK's true function within the body is to act as a nexus between the mind, the brain, and the body.

There is a further aspect of Inyushin's theory which I find particularly attractive. By defining bioplasma as both an energy field and as a substance, his model explains why PK can function sometimes as an energy pushing objects about or levitating tables, and at other times as a material substance as exemplified by Palladino's materializations and Tomczyk's "rigid rays."

Nonetheless, Inyushin's theory cannot account for many types of PK activity. How could this quasi-biological field act over distances, travel through physical barriers, apport material, dematerialize matter and rematerialize it later? How could a biological field develop a personality as some poltergeist phenomena seem to indicate? Inyushin severely restricts what bioplasma can account for by endowing it with electromagnetic properties. Yet, even if we strip his concept of its electromagnetic aura, it still can't explain much PK phenomena.

There is also one final objection to this theory. For a theory to be scientific, it must be testable. I fail to see how Inyushin's concept can be put to a critical test, nor have I read anything by Professor Inyushin in which he has tried to demonstrate experimentally the specific, not inferential, existence of bioplasma.

So, in summing it all up, how germane is Inyushin's bioplasma model to the field of parapsychology? I think his general concept may be very helpful. I think he has outlined a good *conceptual model* for the force behind PK. However, his theory, as of now, can't explain the range of PK. As Inyushin refines his theory and studies more about PK, his concept may develop into a good working hypothesis to guide research in PK. Hopefully, he will redefine bioplasma in a way that would predict how PK would be expected to function under certain set circumstances. Then contemporary parapsychologists can test his theory experimentally and either verify or nullify it.

G. A. Sergeyev, Kulagina's chief investigator, has also come up with a theory about PK. He argues that PK can be explained on the basis of resonating bioelectric and magnetic fields. He also believes that ultrasonic radiation comes into play during Kulagina's performances. However, this theory fails to explain most types of PK effects. The theory also fails to recognize the basically unconscious nature of PK. For example, Sergeyev argues that "neural cerebral oscillations" are projected by the subject to induce PK. These oscillations are set into being by concentration while the brain acts as a lens, projecting them in the direction of the subject's gaze. Yet, this argument cannot explain even the mildest poltergeist case or most death coincidences. As any veteran parapsychologist will tell you, rarely will the poltergeist move an object which is being stared at attentively. It usually waits for all backs to be turned.

Dr. Victor Adamenko, Alla Vinogradova's husband, is one of the few Soviet thinkers who realizes that PK is not a force which is analogous to physical energy. His belief is that PK represents an X energy within the organism. It is neither electromagnetic nor organic, and Adamenko is a very verbal critic of Inyushin and his theories. Adamenko also believes that this energy may saturate an object which will then become charged with it. His theory does make one strong point: PK is not like any normal force. But actually, the young physicist's theory really tells us more about what PK isn't than what it is, so we are right back where we started from. Dr. Adamenko has, however, realized that though PK is not akin to physical radiation, it may take on the properties of a field. If Adamenko's X energy is independent of space and time, then it can explain distance effects and linger effects. But this purely energy-type concept cannot account for materialization phenomena.

These are just three of the different theories which have been offered by Soviet scientists to account for psychic phenomena. They remind me of something Gerald Blum once wrote about psychological theories of personality. He complained that they ". . . are multiplying like a plague, the disease can take the form of types or traits, factors or fields, canalizations or cathexes. Unlike most epidemics, however, this one is allowed to rage unchecked. It almost seems to be more fun for the doctor to get the bug himself than to try to discover what caused the last victim to die."

These same sentiments could easily apply to Soviet theories about PK. It doesn't take any great insight to realize that most of these Soviet thinkers have attempted to account for physical psychic effects on the basis of a physicalistic theory. But, are we entitled to do so? The fact that none of these theories can account for the total range of PK manifestations speaks for itself. Benson

The PK Epidemic

Herbert has hit the proverbial nail right on the head when he writes:

> The attempts to describe psi phenomena within the framework of physics is, strictly speaking, illegal. Physicists are concerned with phenomena of inanimate matter. However, in spite of its complex problems biophysics has made many important contributions. PK consists of a peculiar interaction between man as a biological system and the physical environment. Consequently it is not surprising that a confusing variety of phenomena occur which seem to defy physcial explanations. It is not to be expected that the contemporary framework of physics can now completely enclose and describe psi phenomena. Physics as a relatively late structure created by human experience is limited to some extent to the outer layers of appearances and does not take into account deeper associations which are likely to exist between its own structure on the one hand and life and human consciousness on the other.

But when all is said and done, we still have to admit that the PK manifestations produced by Kulagina, Parise, and crew are still weak beer in comparison to those of Home, Palladino, Schneider, and Stella C. So we are still confronted by that nettling question: Where have the *really* great mediums gone? Even Tomczyk, who superficially resembles Palladino, had a much vaster range of PK. Certainly the parapsychological climate in both the United States and the U.S.S.R. is encouraging PK subjects and research. But we still have no Homes or Palladinos.

I think the reason for this is two-fold. As I have already suggested, PK subjects today are not trained and developed. They are just subjected to tests and more tests! We don't know what potential Felicia Parise may have had, since she developed herself.

Second, I cannot help but believe that somehow the mediumistic trance markedly facilitates PK. Tomczyk, Palladino, even Cleio, all went into some sort of trance and I don't think this was merely out of convention. Could it be a way to get the inhibitions of consciousness out of the way? Could trance allow some independent substratum of the personality to arise which has the power to manipulate PK more effectively than our conscious mind? And could this substratum account for Little Stasia, Olga, and other mediumistic controls who seem to have personalities all their own? We tend to think that our conscious minds direct PK, but more and more evidence indicates that it is really the unconscious which directs the phenomena. But what is the unconscious?

Many of the early pioneers of psychology believed that the unconscious is a series of independent "streams of consciousness," each of which has its own volition, traits, and functions within the personality. Perhaps one of these systems controls PK. If this were so, we should have to dig deeply into the psyche to provoke this portion of the id into showing us its wonders. Trance, dissociation, and meditation might easily allow this substratum of the psyche to work more freely and easily and with greater opportunity for expression. Multiple personality cases such as that of Eve White, who became the pathetic heroine of *The Three Faces of Eve*, would indicate that the psyche is actually composed of various substructures which normally work together creating what we call "personality." But what if this structure becomes shattered? There are cases of multiple personality in which the victim develops two, three, five, ten, or even fifteen separate personalities, each representing a part of the psyche, yet existing independently of it. It seems likely to me that there is some specific "stream of consciousness" deep within the psyche which is endowed with the ability to produce and regulate PK within the system and in the physical environment. This element of the unconscious acts behind the cover of the conscious mind... either working with it, as in Kulagina's case, or independently of it, as in poltergeist cases. We have to make contact with this stream of consciousness within ourselves in order to produce PK. Trance may have been a tool the great psychics used to contact and tap this source.

As Benson Herbert suggests, though, it is plain to see that physics has just not learned enough about the universe to account for PK. I don't think psychology has either. So for now, trying to understand the core nature of PK may not be of uppermost importance to contemporary parapsychologists. First let us study how PK behaves and what principles it follows. In that respect, we owe a great deal of thanks to people such as Nina Kulagina and Felicia Parise who have allowed us to observe PK and study it with the feeble tools of modern science.

7

Examining the Geller Effect

URI GELLER needs no introduction. He is undoubtedly the best known and controversial psychic on the parapsychology scene today. Through his PK and ESP demonstrations he has converted several skeptical scientists to the cause of parapsychology, yet he remains the bête noire of the disbelievers. In fact, talking about Uri Geller is not like talking about science at all, but more like talking about a legend. But a legend that keeps looming before us.

Geller's background is as controversial as his psychic claims. Born in Tel Aviv on December 20, 1946, Geller first noticed his psychic abilities while he was still a youngster. According to his own account, he first learned that he had psychic abilities when his mother gave him a watch for his seventh birthday. "I could see the hands move ten minutes, fifteen minutes. Nobody touched the watch," the psychic told *Time* magazine writer, John Wilhelm. "Always it happened in class. Then I knew things had to happen when people were around, because I'm using their energy." If we are to believe Geller, PK was not his only childhood power. He would often psychically guess how well his mother had done at her frequent card games.

Geller became better known in this country after meeting Dr. Andrija Puharich, an entrepreneur of the psychic field who spends considerable time searching the world for data, and soon astounded the public with a new claim. His psychic gifts were not inborn abilities, he maintained, but were gifts from the space people who were working through him! However, Geller's claims didn't stop there. Both Geller and Puharich also asserted that they had become the emissaries of these space people. (See Puharich's book, *Uri: A Journal of the Mystery of Uri Geller*, I tend to think that these two were carried away by Arthur C. Clarke's *Childhood's End.*)

Despite Geller's and Puharich's rather extravagent personal claims, many notable scientists became interested in Geller and his apparent ability to bend metal psychically, dematerialize and rematerialize objects, and perform just about every other psychic feat under the sun. Although Geller's theatrical background casts a dim light on his psychic claims, some topnotch scientists quickly became converted when they witnessed some of his more startling PK effects. And some of their testimonials are downright dumbfounding.

One of these incidents was reported by Gerald Feinberg, a Columbia University physicist, and one of America's most esteemed scientists. Feinberg was having lunch with Geller, Puharich, ex-astronaut Edgar Mitchell, and Mitchell's secretary one day in August 1972 when Geller suddenly decided to give one of his impromptu but impressive demonstrations. He spontaneously asked Mitchell's secretary to take off her gold ring and clench it in her fist. He waved his hand over hers and then asked her to open her fist.

"She opened it up," recalls Feinberg, "and the ring then appeared with a crack in it, as if it had been cut through with a very sharp instrument. Initially there was a very small space, probably a fraction of an inch. It looked essentially like a whole ring, but with a crack going through it. But even more interesting, he took the ring and put it down on a table where several of us were sitting. Over the period of a couple of hours, the ring twisted. It had originally been a circle with a crack in it, but over the period of two or three hours it twisted so that it went gradually into the shape of an 'S'. It didn't twist fast enough that you could actually see it happen, but if you looked every fifteen or thirty minutes you could see the angle increasing."

"It didn't seem to me that he went near it during that period to do anything to it," Feinberg told John Wilhelm, "but I wasn't trying to monitor him."

This narrative is very typical of the reports which come out about Geller . . . a fascinating anecdote but one which prompts many more questions than it answers. How was everyone seated? Did Geller touch or handle the ring after the young woman had first taken it off? What happened during the fifteen- or thirty-minute segments when no one was watching the ring? Where was it placed down? Near Geller or across the table from him? Why didn't they monitor it or put a glass over it?

As I said, Dr. Feinberg's anecdote is typical of so many which are reported by people who have worked with Geller. They imply everything, yet really tell us nothing.

An even wilder, yet much more impressive anecdote about Geller's powers comes from former Apollo astronaut and moon walker Edgar Mitchell.

Mitchell likes to talk about one incident he witnessed with Geller which is probably the most impressive ever recorded. If Mitchell's memory and reporting are accurate, it is hard to figure out how Geller could have faked this apport.

The incident occured during a lunch break at the Stanford Research Institute cafeteria. Geller was undergoing a series of tests at SRI at the time and was lunching with Mitchell and SRI physicist Harold Puthoff. He was eating his ice-cream dessert when his spoon struck something hard. "We cleaned the ice cream off the metal," declared Geller, "and saw that it's a piece of a broken tie clasp. We all started saying how odd, how many chances that it would get into my ice cream, like a million to one."

Mitchell took the broken tie clasp from Geller and casually examined it. But his nonchalant attitude soon transformed into wild enthusiasm. "My God," exclaimed the startled astronaut, who continued after composing himself, "well, about three years ago I got a present from Bear Archery Company when I did some advertising for them. They gave me a pin exactly like you have in your ice cream."

So far this little incident could have been either a coincidence or, if Geller had staged the affair, a most fortuitous choice of a hoaxed object. However the story doesn't end there.

Mitchell, Geller, and Puthoff, who was carrying out most of the SRI work with Geller, along with his colleague Russell Targ, were walking back to a SRI lab room when—clink!—another little metal object fell to the floor. The scientists picked it up, and Mitchell identified it as the other half of the clasp previously discovered in Geller's ice cream. Mitchell was impressed but, verbally addressing the alleged intelligences behind Geller's powers, made a prophetic remark.

"I wish they could bring something back we could be one hundred percent sure about," he stated in no uncertain terms.

Just at that moment, another metallic clink was heard. There, on the floor between Mitchell and Puthoff, was another tie clasp. This one had a pearl head. Mitchell became tremendously excited, claiming that this clasp matched one which he had lost four years before. It had been a present from his brother, who had purchased it in Japan. And Mitchell could prove that it was the same one. He showed Geller and Puthoff that the tie clasp's clutch pin was an old brass navy pin. Mitchell told the startled onlookers that he himself had substituted the pin for the original one years before.

As I said, these incidents occurred during Geller's 1972 visit to the Stanford Research Institute. These experiments were the most famous ever carried out with the Israeli psychic. So let's examine them in depth.

"This sort of thing is anecdotal material. But to me I *know* it happened. And I know where those things were and weren't," states Mitchell unequivocally when asked about the incident.

Because of the furor Geller had prompted with his PK and ESP feats, a meeting of minds had been called between Mitchell, Judy Skutch of the Foundation for Parasensory Investigation in New York, and others. They decided that the best way to promote parapsychology was to have Geller tested under scientific conditions. Mrs. Skutch's foundation put up the front money, which she delegated to Mitchell's Institute of Noetic Sciences, which in turn funded it out to the two physicists, Russell Targ and Harold Puthoff, who were carrying out parapsychological tests at the Stanford Research Institute in Menlo Park, California. SRI is a private research institute which carries out studies in every conceivable branch of science. Targ and Puthoff were both originally laser physicists who became interested in psychic studies and were spending most of their time studying this challenging new science. So, in November 1972, Geller flew to the United States to participate in what was to be two series of ESP experiments at SRI.

It is really remarkable that Targ and Puthoff were able to get anything at all done with Geller during his SRI stint. Television audiences who have seen Geller during his public ESP and PK performances see only one side of him: a boyish, enthusiastic, almost naive performer who often seems more astounded by what has happened than his wide-eyed hosts. But the true Geller is very different. He insists on his own conditions during tests, and he demands that everything be done his way and his way only. He continually threatens to walk out of experiments—that is, when he shows up for them at all—and is likely to fly into a rage of recriminations. Working with Uri Geller is not easy, by any means.

Targ and Puthoff only tested Geller's PK informally, so their results can only be considered suggestive but by no means proof of his PK powers. First they tried to see if Geller could alter the readings on a magnetometer. (A magnetometer is a device which measures the fluctuations in a magnetic field. It is connected to a strip chart recorder which inks out a continuous record of the fluctuations. Normally a magnetometer is insensitive to jarring, but a magnet or static discharge around it will make the pen wiggle.) Geller was searched for hidden magnets and then asked to concentrate on the magnetometer. The psychic passed his hands over the device and, sure enough, the recorder did show a little "jump." However, Targ and Puthoff could not rule out artifact or a trick as the cause of the odd recording. I might add that to a good sleight-of-hand man, a search is no great challenge. Geller could easily have outmaneuvered a search had he wished or needed to.

Next, Geller tried to offset a one-gram weight balanced on an electric scale. The weight was placed under a metal can which was also balanced on the scale, and the entire system was enclosed by a bell jar. Geller waved his hands over the setup, and the recording pen, which monitored the weight, showed a concurrent deflection. Unfortunately, floor vibrations or a host of other normal factors could cause similar deflections, so this test didn't prove anything either.

While at SRI Geller also demonstrated his metal bending and his ability to deflect a compass needle but, according to Targ and Puthoff, never under conditions which would conclusively outlaw tricks. However, the real substance of the SRI work was a series of ESP experiments designed by Targ and Puthoff. During these tests Geller, who was sealed in an enclosed and grounded chamber, was able to reproduce drawings selected and sketched by the experimenters. Sometimes his successes were astounding. A bunch of grapes chosen for one target was *exactly* reproduced by

Geller. An entire series of these picture-drawing tests were carried out successfully. Geller apparently was also able to guess clairvoyantly the uppermost face of a die shaken in a closed box. After the tests were concluded, Targ and Puthoff felt their experiments with Geller should be brought to the attention of the scientific community in general. So they reported them as part of a paper, "Information Transmission Under Conditions of Sensory Shielding," which was published in the staid British journal, *Nature*, in October 1974. The editors of *Nature* were a bit reluctant about publishing the report and prefaced it with an editorial in which they pointed out several flaws. They argued that: (1) It was vague about many details of the protocols used for the tests. (2) The targets for the picture-drawing trials were not selected truly randomly. (3) Safeguards to prevent fraud were not spelled out. However, *Nature* did decide to present the paper to its readers since, in its view, it represented a valid and scientific approach to the study of the paranormal. Nothing about Geller's PK was included in the brief report.

Publication of the SRI paper caused a near riot in traditional scientific circles. After it was published, a lengthy editorial appeared in *New Scientist,* charging that Targ and Puthoff had been duped by Geller. It also reported gossipy behind-the-scenes comments which pointed out alleged weaknesses in the SRI work and even claimed that Geller had actually been caught in fraud. The issue continued by accusing the SRI scientists of selectively reporting only a few of their tests with Geller and of whitewashing the "circus atmosphere" and lax conditions which had pervaded the tests. The charges went on and on. The most serious charge against the psychic and SRI was that *if* Geller had a miniature radio-receiver implanted in his tooth, a confederate could have relayed descriptions of the target drawings to him. This explanation might seem as if the *New Scientist* reporters were clutching at straws, but they pointed out with relish that Shipi Strang, Geller's constant companion, was always present and "constantly underfoot" during the tests. (This unfortunately had not been mentioned by Targ and Puthoff in their paper.) Even more suspicious was the fact that Puharich had actually invented such a miniature device.

When all was said and done, the SRI report had suffered considerably. Although fraud by Geller or incompetence on Targ's and Puthoff's part had not been proved, the critics had blown enough holes in the *Nature* paper to discredit it as any proof of Geller's abilities. And what was worse, though, was that there did exist some direct evidence of fraud on Geller's part during his SRI stay. This story will serve as an intersting sidelight on the SRI work.

By December 1972 Geller had undergone some five weeks of testing at SRI, and several independent scientists were becoming more and more eager to observe the Israeli wonder-worker for themselves. These included George Lawrence, an official from the U. S. government's Advanced Research Projects Agency; Dr. Robert Van De Castle, a parapsychologist and psychologist from the University of Virginia; and Ray Hyman, an ex-magician turned college psychology professor. All three traveled to SRI as an ad hoc committee to test Geller informally.

Geller received his three prestigious guests graciously, and began his session by telling some stories about his abilities before getting down to business. After becoming more familiar with his guests, Geller asked Lawrence to write a number from one to ten on a paper pad. In the meantime, Geller covered his eyes with his hands and Lawrence wrote down his choice. It wasn't a very novel trick and Hyman easily spied Geller looking through the cracks of his fingers and following the tip of the pencil. By watching the pencil top, Geller could easily ascertain what Lawrence was writing.

After some inconclusive ESP tries, Geller turned to his *pièce de résistance,* his metal bending. The psychic, unfortunately, just couldn't seem to get into the mood for PK, though. He tried to bend Hyman's nail clippers, but couldn't, so he put them aside and then wafted from article to article, trying to bend at least something. It all seemed to no avail. Finally, he took up the nail clippers once again, putting them in Lawrence's clenched hand before the scientists could catch sight of it. The showman passed his hands over Lawrence's and then instructed him to open his fist. The clippers were bent. It is clear that Geller had created confusion by meandering from object to object and had more than enough opportunity to bend the clippers during that time.

Geller was in for a surprise himself, though, before the day was over. In order to impress his visitors, he tried to demonstrate his ability to PK a compass needle by swaying his body and putting pressure on the floor until the needle deflected. But Lawrence was one up on the psychic. He walked up to the compass, imitated Geller's movements, and deflected the compass even further than the psychic had done. Geller grew angry, accused Lawrence of hoaxing him, and threw a tantrum. Lawrence and Hyman left SRI sure that Geller was just another clever fake; but Van De Castle remained agnostic. He didn't feel Geller had been given a fair chance. One day just isn't enough to test a psychic, he justifiably argued.

Nonetheless, there are other cases on record which are curious. For example, Geller bent and broke a spoon when he appeared on Barbara Walters' "Not for Women Only" show. An amazing feat of PK? In his book *The Magic of Uri Geller*, the Amazing Randi, one of this country's leading magicians and critics of parapsychology, reproduced five close-up shots of the spoon from a tape of the program. One can plainly see that the bowl and stem of the spoon Geller holds is actually soldered together. Geller had merely to put pressure on the connection in order to break the spoon. Now, where did this very odd spoon come from? It was obviously a prepared implement.

Geller also met his match in England when he demonstrated his powers for *Daily Mail* columnist Richard Herd, and magician Billy McComb in November 1973. For their session together Geller attempted to bend a fork the magician had brought along. A photographer recorded the whole scene. McComb wasn't impressed by what he witnessed.

"He rolled it about to make it appear as if it was getting soft," McComb explains, "but nothing happened until the photographer began to reload the film. Geller quickly brought the fork down beside him, and it was then lifted up under cover of his hand and shown to be bent."

So Uri Geller proposes an unfathomable enigma to all who have worked with him or observed his demonstrations. Showman or psychic? Or a bit of both? Like Palladino, who was also adept at faking, could it be that Geller freely mixes fakery with genuine psi? It is hard to say. One difficulty we have is that it's very hard to evaluate Geller merely by reading written reports about him. Many of these accounts, while they may seem very impressive, just don't give enough information for us to make a judgment about the genuineness of his performance. Remember the "ring" incident Feinberg talks about and which I quoted earlier? It certainly looks as if Geller produced genuine PK in this instance. Yet, we would have to restage the entire sequence of events carefully to determine what access Geller might have had to the ring. The verbal account we have from the Columbia University physicist is too incomplete to be taken at face value. On the other hand, though, it seems highly unlikely that Geller could have faked the tie-clasp apports at SRI. Sadly, though, most reports on Geller's PK are worthless as scientific evidence.

The first time I witnessed Geller's psychic displays was on June 6, 1975, in Los Angeles when he appeared on the Lou Riggs show over radio station KCRW, a small Santa Monica station. My colleague, Raymond Bayless and I arrived sometime before Geller. Geller was, as usual, late. His tardiness was in one respect opportune, for it gave us time for a little legwork around the station. All the employees were very excited about Geller's appearance and were eager to see his metal bending and telepathic feats. They were all believers, so Geller could be assured of a sympathetic audience. One man had brought along a watch which he claimed had not run for five years. If Geller could get it running, he told me, that would prove his abilities as far as he was concerned. I asked to examine the watch, and was able to get it running twice for several seconds with little difficulty by quickly jabbing the back of the case. I pointed this out to the station employee, but he said nothing and merely put the watch back into his pocket.

For this first feat, Geller announced that he would reproduce any drawing his host could diagram, as long as it was simple. But Geller first instructed Lou Riggs to wait until he turned his back and covered his eyes. Geller proceeded to situate himself at about a 45-degree angle to Riggs's chair, placed his right hand over his eyes, and gave the interviewer an O.K. to draw his target. From where I was standing, I could readily ascertain that Geller could watch Riggs by peaking through the cracks of his fingers. Riggs drew his diagram slowly and deliberately, so Geller could easily have figured out the drawing by watching the interviewer's pencil. Geller had no trouble reproducing the diagram as soon as Riggs was through drawing it.

After this initial warm-up, Geller turned to another one of his stunts. He announced dramatically that he would telepathically impress a diagram of his own onto Riggs's mind. He first drew a brief sketch as Riggs turned his head away, and then instructed him to stare into his (Geller's) eyes and draw the first thing that came to mind. I could see that Geller had drawn a circle within a triangle. This is the figure Geller just about always draws when he attempts this feat. As Riggs stared intently into Geller's eyes, I saw the psychic guiding him by making slight head and eye movements. Geller was, in fact, diagraming his picture subtly with his head, and shortly afterward Riggs drew a circle in a square—a near miss. I certainly don't think that there was any collusion between them, but I do think that Geller artfully guided Riggs without him even knowing it. (Geller is a master at this kind of manipulation which is an old magician's trick.)

Next on the agenda was watch starting. He was approached by the same technician whose watch I had started only shortly before. As Riggs continued to interview him, Geller tapped the watch forcibly, and at one point toyed with the winder. "It's ticking," shouted the psychic enthusiastically. But Geller had done nothing to the watch that I hadn't done earlier in order to get it started.

It was during all the commotion over the watch ticking that the next phenomenon took place. Someone in the booth suddenly cried out that the watch hands had jumped several minutes ahead of where they had been previously set. But I had seen him toy with the watch stem while he was being interviewed, so he had ample opportunity to reset the hands. I also noted that when Geller handed the watch back to Riggs, Uri fumbled and dropped it onto the wooden table between them. This might have been accidental, but such a jar will most assuredly get many run-down watches ticking for a few seconds or longer.

Geller's only other feat during this series of demonstrations was metal bending. This was the thing I had most wanted to see personally. Several small metal objects were laid before Geller, including a few keys. As be began fondling the objects (which had been collected right on the spot), I focused my eyes directly on any item Geller handled, making sure that he did not fraudulently bend it before going on to another item. (I was theorizing that he might bend an object, and then go back to it later, rehandle it, and pretend it bent paranormally at that time.) At no time did I allow my eyes to wander from the objects Geller was playing with, nor become distracted by any superfluous motions he might make with his other hand. After several warm-up moments, Geller finally decided to bend a key. The key was lying flat down on the table and I could see that it was not bent at that time. From that point onward, my eyes never left the key at any moment. Raymond, too, kept his eyes peeled on it. Here is his written account as to what happened next.

> Mr. Geller placed his hands over a key for some minutes but never held his hands in a position which would gain him normal leverage. Frequently he held it between two fingers and periodically stroked it with one finger. He infrequently transferred the key from one hand to the other to "stroke" it but during this transfer no vigorous muscular pressure was seen. The position in which the key was held would only allow very little muscular force to have been used. I watched intently to see if any muscular effort would show and such was not the case.
>
> I saw that the key was bent about 8° as it was held "edge on" to my view. The key was a heavy, standard "front door" specimen and after the interview had ended I examined it and attempted to bend it but could not. Probably, if I had exerted all my strength I could have bent it, but such an effort would have been ridiculously obvious. Further, I would have had to use both hands in such an effort. The key belonged to a member of the station's staff and when I questioned him he identified it as his house key.
>
> At the beginning of the bending of the key I continually watched for the opportunity to "sight" along it and was able to do so more than once. The key was perfectly straight. Further, the key never left Mr. Geller's hands and there was no possibility for a substitution to have taken place; I watched for this possibility in particular.

Indeed, Geller had kept the key in open view at all times. At no time did he "duck" the key under the table or to the side of his chair in order to bend it fraudulently. Substitution could not account for the bend, nor could previous bending, since Raymond was able to see clearly that the key was not bent when Geller began his stroking.

If Geller had fraudulently bent the key, he would have had to do it with manual force. I can't dismiss this possibility, although neither Raymond nor I saw him grip the key in any way which would allow him to get enough leverage to bend it. On the other hand, people do not realize how strong human fingers can be. Bending a key with one hand may seem impossible, but I was rudely awakened to how much force the hand can exert while watching a noted violinist perform at a rehearsal. Apparently his bow strings were loose, so he extended his little finger and tightened the turn screw on the bow. This would take a considerable amount of leverage and strength, but the violinist—through years of practice—could do it easily. Even his own students were amazed. One man I know can physically bend rather thick nails in his hand. So I certainly believe that Geller might have the strength in his hands to bend metal objects. But I must also admit that this is pure speculation and that we saw no evidence of such manual force during his performance.

After the interview was over, I was introduced to another of Geller's formidable powers . . . his incredible sensitivity to the people around him. I tend to think that his conscious mind and senses act like radar. He is incredibly sensitive to the people watching him, and his eyes wander incessantly looking for cues, feedback, or other reactions from his audience. Although there were more than ten people watching the interview, Geller singled me out right after the show and accused me of being a hostile skeptic. This was hardly ESP. I probably stood out in marked contrast to the technicians and other guests who were utterly astounded by the day's demonstrations. I admitted nothing and replied that while his exhibition was "impressive," I just couldn't judge it because of the informal conditions which had existed in the studio during the show. Geller left the room to talk with Shipi and his manager.

A moment later Geller called to Raymond from the back room of the studio, explaining that he wanted to talk to him in private. Raymond then called me in. No one else was with us and the door was shut. Once again Geller accused me of being hostile toward him, while I could only respond by saying that I was "completely open" to the possibility that he possessed psychic powers.

"We'll do an experiment. If I can pick up something from you, that will prove you aren't negative," Geller responded in an instant.

I was a bit surprised. I certainly had not expected the challenge. Here was one opportunity in a million, the chance to test Uri Geller personally! As he had previously done with Riggs, Geller urged me to take a pad of paper, which was lying on a nearby desk, and draw a geometrical design. He would then reproduce it by ESP. I sat at the desk while Geller positioned himself about ten feet in front of me. He instructed Raymond to watch him in order to make sure he couldn't cheat, and invited him to sit anywhere he wished. Naturally, Raymond tried to sit directly between us, thereby blocking the psychic's view of me. But as soon as he began to sit down, Geller immediately repositioned himself in order to maintain a good vantage point. Raymond saw the move and adjusted his chair accordingly, but Geller likewise shifted his position again. Raymond knew that if he kept on trying to block Geller's view, the psychic would get suspicious of us and refuse to go on with the test. So he let Geller have his way.

"I'll turn around and cover my eyes, and you draw something . . . but keep it simple," Geller said.

Geller stationed himself at a 45-degree angle to me, exactly as he had done during his tests with Riggs, and covered his eyes with his hands. Geller could easily see me from where he was sitting, but what he didn't know was that *by the time he had positioned himself, I had already made my diagram.* I had sketched it quickly while Geller and Raymond were playing musical chairs. And I had made the sketch very small so that he wouldn't be able to see me manipulating the pencil.

Geller totally failed to reproduce this picture, so he urged me to try once again. And once more, unbeknown to Geller, I made my drawing before he even resituated himself. Since he couldn't observe my pencil motions to ascertain the figure, he asked me to concentrate on it by drawing it over and over again in my mind. I knew that he would try to pick up cues from the way I moved my eyes and head as I visualized the target, so I closed my eyes. Geller immediately asked me to keep them open! I tried to keep my gaze steadfast and my head stationary as Geller stared into my eyes and tried to draw the figure I had sketched in the air. At one time he actually seemed to be drawing something similar to my sketch (a fishing hook), but gave up and said he couldn't get anything. I, in turn, informed Geller that it did look as if he was beginning to get my picture and encouraged him to go on, but he refused. (Actually, what I think happened was this: Geller made several random movements in the air while watching my reactions closely to see if I would respond to any of them. If I had responded, Geller could then try to get me to follow his strokes and unconsciously guide his hand with my head. He may have seen me give some indication that he was on the right track as he drew a curved, downward line, but lost the cue since I was concentrating very intently on not allowing my head or eyes to move in any way.) We tried a third attempt but this failed also.

Geller blatantly revealed himself on the fourth test. First, he asked to see my three previous diagrams. Then, for this test, he positioned himself in such a way that I thought it better if I moved to a different desk. Unfortunately, by the time I had moved there, Geller was already prepared, seated, and with his hands over his eyes. I was somewhat surprised and amused when he yelled to me, "Draw larger this time." Geller had seen that my pictures for the past three trials had been minuscule. Even if he were watching me now, drawing very small pictures rapidly would not give him a chance to watch my pencil at all well. So, Geller gave himself away by requesting me to draw larger. I drew, very deliberately, a triangle bisected by a line, knowing full well that Geller would follow my pencil.

I was a bit surprised when after the sketch was done Geller still maintained that he could not get an impression of it. I had expected him to read my pencil strokes. But no, Geller admitted he just couldn't get anything from me.

"Let me see your drawing," he bemoaned as though disappointed with himself. I showed him what I had sketched and he became ecstatic.

"That's what I got. Look! I drew that," he kept exclaiming as he turned to a bunch of discarded papers, picked one up, and held it out to me. "There, you see," he said. Indeed, it was a perfect replica of my triangle and line.

I can only describe what happened next as sheer pandemonium. Instantly my mind shot over the entire scene and it dawned on me what *might* have happened. First, he could have seen my pencil strokes but was too unsure of them to produce his drawing until he had seen mine and knew he had successfully reproduced it. Or, more likely, he surreptitiously and quickly drew the replica as he turned to grab his discarded papers and while his back was to me. (The only time during the test that Geller was unobserved was when he turned at this moment.)

To this day, I still remain unimpressed by the tests I carried out with Geller. It was obvious to me that during our ESP tests together, Geller outmaneuvered us as we tried to set up fraud-proof conditions. Had I insisted on *my* conditions for the tests, I am quite sure he would have refused to go on with them. I was

Geller's guest and had to play the scene his way, or no way at all. I had really hoped that he would carry out a PK test for me, and I did ask him to bend one of my own keys, but he refused. The most suspicious part of his performance, to me, was a probable ruse he used, that is, admitting failure at a test in order to see the target, and then reproducing it secretly and claiming success. Uri has done this with others.

For example, the same week that he appeared on Lou Riggs's show, Geller was at the UCLA Neuropsychiatric Institute. (The *National Enquirer* had arranged for him to be tested there by Dr. Thelma Moss.) As Dr. Moss reported about her experiment:

> There were many trials in which Uri tried to receive a number, or a geometric figure, or a letter of the alphabet. He was never successful. On one occasion he reported feeling an "electric" sensation traveling up . . . into his arm. On that trial he had been trying to receive a number, but had felt unsure and did not say the number aloud—although he wrote it on a boxtop, in the dark, and showed it to me after John told us the number was five.

You may have noticed one coincidence between Dr. Moss's and my own accounts. In both cases Geller only pulled the likely fraud after a series of failures. This indicates to me that if tested under controlled conditions, Geller at first actually tries to get an impression of the target by ESP, but failing, resorts to fraud.

Yes, I actually believe that Geller genuinely does try to demonstrate ESP at times. So far, I have not been very kind in my comments about Mr. Geller. Although everything I read about him makes me tend to believe he has genuine powers, everything I have personally seen with him makes me feel the exact opposite. He is certainly the shrewdest performer I have ever encountered. His ability to misdirect attention, pick up cues, gain sympathy, heighten expectancy, and manipulate his onlookers is truly phenomenal. I've never encountered anything equaling his cleverness before or since in the ten years I've been investigating the field. So, it may be a surprise that, despite the fact that he is a talented magician, I also believe that Geller does in fact possess some genuine PK ability. I resisted believing this for two years until several reports began coming out which I feel are reliable. Palladino was certainly an expert at fraud, there is no doubt about it. But she could also produce marvelous PK. Geller may come from similar psychic stock. I don't hold Geller's theatrical background against him as many others do. It may not be unlikely that he went on the stage after discovering his psychic abilities, only to discover, like others, that these talents aren't always very reliable. I see no reason why Geller could not have genuine psi capabilities while also being an accomplished magician. Fraud does not necessarily exclude the genuine; it merely complicates it no end.

Even though Geller has been caught in trickery, there are still several reports on his PK which cannot be easily dismissed. At least one of these reports is, to me, virtual proof of Geller's PK.

One of the more noteworthy investigations into Geller's PK was made by W. E. Cox. Cox is a research associate at F.R.N.M.'s Institute for Parapsychology, has had a long career designing laboratory PK tests, and also has a considerable background in magic. Cox visited Geller at the psychic's New York apartment on April 24, 1974, and during the meeting was able to carry out two especially intriguing PK tests.

During their first experiment, Geller and Cox faced each other over a glass-topped coffee table. Geller suggested that they begin with a key-bending trial, so Cox handed him a flat, ungrooved, blank key. Geller was a bit nonplussed and told the investigator that he preferred to work with a more personal key and inquired whether Cox could supply one. Cox feigned that he only had the one key in order to force Geller into using it. (It was 2¼ inches in length, made of steel, and virtually unbendable by hand.) Geller examined the key and then returned it to Cox, suggesting that he place it flat down on the edge of the coffee table. Cox placed his own finger on one side of the key, while Geller began stroking the rest of it gently. Since the key was lying flat down on a transparent-glass tabletop, Cox could be sure that the key had not been bent in advance of the test. Yet, as Geller continued to stroke the object, it slowly began to bend upward. As Cox explains:

> The key was flat upon the glass table, touching along its length. My right forefinger pressed upon one end of the key with only a normal force, and Geller's right forefinger gently stroked the rest of the key as he stood bending over the coffee table.
>
> I took advantage of the table's transparency to gain a view of the underpart of the key with the aid of a mirror I held in my left hand. Light from a window, at 6:15 p.m. EDT, enabled a relatively clear view. The top of the key, of course, could be seen directly, with

Geller's finger touching it. After making several strokes, he said it was bending, then raised his hand and pressed his end of the key so as to rock it approximately one eighth of an inch. He slid the key from under my finger and again rocked it, expressing some pleasure. I resumed control of my end of the key, bringing the mirror into use at this point. Geller then resumed stroking the key until it bent to an angle of about 12¼ degrees. The entire event, I would judge, took less than a minute.

The temperature of the part of the key under my finger did not appear to change. What is more important is that the position of my end of the key did not change, except when Geller first rocked the key. The distance between my eyes and the key throughout the test was no more than one and a half feet. Intentionally, I had exerted no strong pressure on the key, nor did the normal downward pressure of my finger vary more than it might have if Geller had met with complete failure.

A specially prepared Hamilton pocket watch played the key role in Cox's second and more novel test of Geller's powers. Since many people claim that Geller has been able to start their broken clocks and watches, Cox decided to have a watch rigged so that it couldn't possibly run. In that way, a critic could not argue that the watch had merely been jarred or knocked into running. He had had a piece of aluminum foil placed inside the watchworks, obstructing the balance wheel, which would prevent the watch from operating at all. The foil was placed on the balance wheel and beneath the regulator arm in such a way that even vigorous shaking could not dislodge it or get the watch running. Cox only told Geller that the watch had been specially prepared. The psychic took the timepiece, shook it, and held it to his ear. It wasn't working and Geller expressed his trepidations about the test. But, after another half minute, the watch started ticking! Upon opening the case, Cox discovered that the foil, which had been very securely placed in position, had been mysteriously moved, thereby allowing the watch to operate normally. There seemed no normal way Geller could have manipulated the foil.

While Cox's tests are impressive, an apparently even more startling experiment with Geller was carried out in October 1973 (and later again in 1974) by Eldon Byrd, a scientist with the Naval Surface Weapons Center, White Oak Laboratory, in Silver Springs, Maryland.

When Byrd met with Geller on October 29, 1973, he brought

along two pieces of nitinol wire. Nitinol is a rather curious alloy which was at the time not generally available commercially. Its most peculiar property is that it retains a "memory" of the shape in which it was manufactured. No matter how it is bent, creased, or crumpled, it allegedly always returns to the shape in which it was manufactured when heat is applied to it. Lighting a match under it is enough to do the trick. There is practically no way to deform a piece of nitinol wire permanently once it has been cast. For his test, Byrd handed Geller a piece of the wire and asked him to see what he could do with it.

Geller could not at first succeed at causing the wire to deform at all, so Byrd brought out a small diameter piece of nitinol wire, cut in into three five-inch lengths, and urged Geller to try again with one of them. Reports Byrd:

> Geller asked me to hold the wire. I held it tautly between the thumbs and index fingers of both hands, keeping it very straight. Geller put his thumb and index finger over the wire and started to rub back and forth. After about twenty seconds of rubbing the wire Geller said he felt a lump forming in the wire. When he removed his fingers, the wire had a definite "kink" in it . . .

But what happened next really astounded Byrd:

> I asked that some boiling water be brought in, he continues. "This particular wire was formed, at the time of manufacture, in a straight configuration, and immersion in boiling water should have caused it to spring back vigorously to that shape. *But when I placed it in water, the wire, instead of snapping back with some force into a straight shape, began to form approximately a right angle.* I lit a match and held it over the kink, but still the wire did not straighten out . . .

Later Byrd had the wire X-rayed, but the examination revealed nothing. An X-ray crystallographic analysis was made which uncovered a slight alteration in the structure of the kinked section of wire, but nothing very notable.

A year later Byrd again met with Geller and asked him to try to exert his PK on another piece of nitinol wire. Again the psychic was able to kink it. And once again, too, X-ray analysis showed no notable structural deformation of the wire. As Byrd concludes his report:

> How did Geller achieve such results? At the present I have no scientific explanation for what happened during both testing periods.

I can only say that the possibility of fraud on Geller's part can be virtually ruled out. Because of the unusual properties of nitinol, the scientific controls essential for any investigation are, for the most part, built into the testing material . . .

(New light on these nitinol experiments has been made by parapsychology's archcritic, Martin Gardner, in the April-May issue of *The Humanist*. Gardner points out that Geller may have had access to nitinol wire and smuggled it into the experimental room. He also points out that on occasion one can permanently kink the wire. So the reader will have to judge the merits of Byrd's experiments for himself.)

Another impressive report was made by Arthur Zorka, a magician and member of the Occult Investigations Committee of the Society of American Magicians, Atlanta Chapter. Zorka, along with several colleagues, watched a television performance by Geller in June 1975, during which he demonstrated several of his PK and ESP feats. However, Geller gave a private demonstration for the magicians after his performance which included a metal-bending attempt. According to Zorka,

> The first test involved Uri Geller's attempt to bend a fork that I provided. The fork was made of forged steel, with a nylon-reinforced handle. I specifically selected this fork because of its extreme resistance to physical stress. I placed the fork in Mr. Geller's outstretched hand. His fingers curled around it, and in moments, without the fork's leaving my sight for even an instant, it literally exploded, sending fragments across the room.

A more convincing instance of metal bending has been reported by Dr. Thomas P. Coohill, a physics professor at Western Kentucky University in Bowling Green, Kentucky. The actual incident took place at Dr. Coohill's own home during a social get-together with the psychic. Writes Dr. Coohill:

> We did not ask Geller to bend anything for us at lunch, nor did he suggest that he do so. However, after we had eaten Geller and I went into the living room and began talking about caving . . . After about a minute we both heard a metallic "clink," it sounded as though something metallic was dropped on a solid floor. Looking around, I saw a spoon behind my desk. It was bent . . .

This part of Dr. Coohill's testimony is not very impressive. It is quite conceivable that Geller could have distracted the physicist and thrown the spoon quickly. However, as Dr. Coohill continues:

> As I held it in my hand and called the other people into the room, the spoon suddenly began to bend in another place (at right angles to the handle . . .) It seemed as if the spoon were observed by all present . . . The incident further amazed me since the floor to my living room is thickly carpeted. Where the "clink" came from I cannot imagine.

I don't put much stock in the "clinking" sound Coohill describes. The noise could have easily been caused if Geller had thrown the spoon against the desk behind which it fell. Since the room was thickly carpeted, the spoon would not have made any noise as it fell to the ground after striking the desk. The result would have been a sudden metallic noise and nothing more. Nevertheless, it is hard to dismiss Coohill's testimony that the fork bent right in his own hand and in full view of several independent observers.

A third example of a semispontaneous Geller-effect has been reported by Danish magician Leo Leslie in his book, *Uri Geller*. Leslie had been initially skeptical of Geller's claims, but had the opportunity to meet the psychic in January 1974 when Geller was scheduled to appear on a Danish television program. Leslie had been called in to coach the TV personnel on how to spot trickery if Geller should resort to it. The most surprising upshot of the show, though, was that Leslie himself became one of Geller's most enthusiastic converts. Here is what happened:

During the show, Leslie watched Geller perform his usual program of ESP and PK effects. He was impressed but still skeptical, and told Geller so when the two met after the program was over. Geller always likes a challenge, so he took Leslie to task, asking the magician to test him personally and under his own conditions. Leslie was delighted, but not prepared for the metal-bending feat Geller had in store for him:

> After his demonstration of telepathy Geller tried psychokinesis. A nickel-plated, enameled key was given Geller. He asked the journalist who was present to hold the key between two fingers. Geller then rubbed it a couple of times, very lightly, with his forefinger. "I can't do it," he suddenly said. "You have done something to this key. I cannot get in contact with the metal." I immediately suspected that Geller probably uses a chemical to soften

metal, and that with the coating on the key he felt defeated. I took the key from the journalist and studied it closely. But while I sat looking at the key the enamel suddenly started to crack, and a second later strips of the nickel plating curled up like small banana peels, while the key actually started to bend in my hand. I don't know who was more excited, Geller or the rest of us in the room. I only know we were all thrilled.

Leslie's encounter with Geller is the most impressive I have read. It is clear in this instance that the metal was seen to bend while Leslie held the key. Many witnesses claim that Geller bent metal in their own hands, but rarely have any of them actually seen it in the process of deforming.

Could these metal-bending feats be due to chemical treatment? This theory, however, cannot explain many of his metal-bending accomplishments. While it is true that you can soften metal by soaking it in a solution of metal halide, this causes the metal to become brittle. It will snap if pressure is put on it; it does not bend. In order to pull off this stunt, Geller would have to use a prepared metal object, yet it is certain that many investigators have brought their own keys, forks, and so on, which Geller has successfully deformed. Several other chemicals can be used to weaken metal such as diluted nitrate of mercury or aqua regia. But these are highly corrosive. How could Geller be expected to manipulate these chemicals while being watched by onlookers in a brightly lit room?

In light of Coohill's and Leslie's reports, I think it is firmly established that Geller can bend metal psychokinetically. How often, I don't know, since it is also equally certain that he will bend metal by trickery if he thinks he can get away with it. This is the puzzle that makes Geller the mystery man he has become. How much genuine PK does Geller possess? How often does he cheat? I don't think even Jimmy the Greek could give reliable odds on these questions.

Even since news of Uri Geller's metal-bending powers hit the international press in the early 1970s, metal-bending psychics have cropped up all over the world. For some reason, many of these up-and-coming psychics have been children, and a few of them are creating quite a stir. For example, Geller appeared on German and Swiss television in January 1974. He presented his usual array of demonstrations, and then advised the audience members that they, too, could bend metal. Over one thousand people reported to the station afterward that, at Geller's prompting, they were able to bend metal psychokinetically. Several of these reports were investigated by a team of researchers from Freiburg University, headed by Dr. Hans Bender. If that weren't enough, several children claimed that they had developed continually demonstrable metal-bending PK powers as a result of Geller's appearances. But, "Most of them were tricksters," Bender admits dolorously.

The Freiburg team made a presentation on its field research at the 18th Annual Convention of the Parapsychological Association which was held in August 1975 on the campus of the University of California, Santa Barbara. Although they admitted that most of the claims they investigated were bogus, they also reported that one eleven-year-old boy they discovered had been able to bend spoons in sealed and plugged plastic retorts. Unfortunately, they also admitted, the lad could apparently only bend the metal when alone and unwatched!

Youthful metal benders seem to be flourishing in Great Britain as well. Dr. John Taylor has, by far, been that country's leading investigator of these pint-sized psychics. He has made quite a stir in parapsychological circles by claiming that he has witnessed considerable genuine PK with these children. However, when I read Dr. Taylor's report on these juveniles which he included in his book *Superminds,* I became pretty skeptical.

Most of the children Dr. Taylor tested have worked with spoons, which are easy to bend normally. The professor has also noted that metal objects rarely bend when being watched, but rather in gradual stages when attention is diverted from them. Although Taylor feels that some of these displays are genuine, he does admit in his book that none of his subjects have been able to bend metal strips placed in tubes under controlled conditions in his laboratory. But, he adds, some of them have been encapsulated metal objects which they have been permitted to take home with them.

Unfortunately this does not make a very strong case for PK. First of all, spoons are the easiest sort of metal implements to bend manually. They can be bent by hand, or by pushing them against any hard surface available. Why couldn't Taylor's psychic children bend the metal objects when they were being carefully watched? If a child were using fakery, we would *expect* the implements to bend in gradual stages as the child deforms the object more and more whenever he can divert attention. And this is just what Taylor encountered. I am not surprised that he couldn't find any children who could bend sealed-up objects in his own laboratory nor am I surprised that some of the children could bend them at home. Taylor says that the sealed tubes were designed in such a way as to circumvent fraud. So even if the tubes were taken home, he argues, they could not be opened without detection.

However, the Amazing Randi, one of Dr. Taylor's most verbal critics, doesn't share the professor's confidence. The magician visited the British scientist incognito in 1975 to see for himself how Taylor carried out his work and found that the tube was easily opened.

Another setback in the study of these metal-bending children during the Geller epidemic in England came at the University of Bath. Two investigators invited six children who claimed metal-bending ability to demonstrate their powers at the university. Each one of them was given a spoon and then sent into a lab room accompanied by an observer. This note-taker had been previously instructed to divert his attention from the child every twenty minutes. This was a setup, of course, since other observers were watching the whole experiment through a one-way mirror. The upshot of the session was predictable. The children merely waited until their observers looked away and then bent the spoons by hand or against the furniture.

Ever since 1974 metal bending has been quite the rage in both England and the United States. At least fifteen cases have come to my attention in my home state of California alone. These reports have come from university physicists, baffled parents, skeptics, and believers alike. So, in 1975 I decided to look more closely into these cases. The result was disappointing. Although I was told incredible stories about these children, I have personally observed nothing but out-and-out trickery.

What can be said about all these bright, new, pint-size Gellers who are invading the psychic field? It is probable that a few of them really do possess PK metal-bending ability. Since Geller has this extraordinary ability, some other psychics must have it as well. But, although I am certainly no disbeliever in PK, I have yet to find any reports about these children which impress me.

There is one final aspect of the Geller mystery which I find even more interesting than Geller's eager imitators. Uri Geller often says that when he appears on TV, metal objects will spontaneously bend in the homes of people who are viewing him. This is not a claim that can be taken lightly. Every time Geller appears on television, for instance, the station phones are soon jammed by people calling in to report strange happenings in their homes. Some claim that metal objects have bent in their own hands, others claim that broken clocks have merrily ticked away again, and so on.

In many respects, these spontaneous PK effects are very bit as interesting as Uri Geller himself. Now, many of these cases probably have normal explanations. To be sure, some reporters are people who have merely found bent utensils in their kitchen drawers which they just never noticed before. Many others run to get watches or clocks to place before the TV set when Geller appears. They usually bump them around in their haste to get back to the set, which often gets them running again. Nonetheless, some cases are more interesting. An editor of a medical journal told me over the phone how she ran and got a kitchen knife to place near her TV set when Geller appeared for an interview. Neither she nor her husband touched it during the program. But they discovered that the knife was noticeably bent after the show was over.

Another detailed account of a Geller-type incident is given by Dr. J. G. Pratt and Dr. Ian Stevenson in a report, "An Instance of Possible Metal-Bending Indirectly Related to Uri Geller," which appeared in the January 1976 issue of the *Journal* of the American Society for Psychical Research. In this case, a blade on Pratt's own pocketknife apparently bent while he listened to a record Geller has made. However this case is a weak one, since Pratt admits that the day before another person had handled the knife and sharpened the blade. The blade could have been accidentally bent at that time.

A complete report on a similar rash of Geller effects has been made by Dr. E. Alan Price, a South African parapsychologist. Geller toured South Africa during the summer of 1974 in order to make several media presentations, and an epidemic of Geller effects broke out in the homes of many local people who had watched the Israeli psychic. Price gathered 137 reliable reports of spontaneous Geller effect, from watch startings to metal bendings. In some cases, the viewers discovered that metal had spontaneously bent in their homes during or after Geller's appearances. In other instances, observers willfully tried to bend metal objects themselves, consciously attempting to imitate Geller's performances.

One astounded witness to this type of PK was a forty-five-year-old gynecologist. Although skeptical about Geller and his claims, the doctor himself became the percipient of an especially convincing metal-bending demonstration. Here is his narrative:

> The event took place on the 17th July at approximately 10:00 p.m. during a demonstration by Uri Geller at a charity premiere at the Carlton Hotel Ballroom. I was holding a teaspoon in my right hand; between thumb and middle finger, concentrating on bending the spoon through the medium of Uri Geller's efforts, when I experienced a warm, tingling sensation in the thumb and finger, and the spoon began to bend. As I was skeptical about the "powers" of Geller, I would not believe my eyes and started to shout, "The spoon is bending!" and displayed it to people around me, including my wife and professional colleagues.
>
> The spoon kept on bending, and the more it bent, the more jubilant and excited I became until I reached a stage of almost "hysteria." I kept on shouting, "Look, the spoon is bending more and more!" The "spoon bending" was continuous and lasted about four minutes and at the end the teaspoon was bent into a U shape.

In this case, it looks as though the metal bent right in the doctor's full view. More often, however, the object will bend only after the onlooker has stopped trying to bend the metal consciously. Since PK is a basically unconscious process, it might be more easy for it to operate only when the witness has stopped his conscious attempt, but is probably still motivated unconsciously. The following from Dr. Price's files is a typical example of this phenomenon:

> "Deadline Thursday Night," 11th July, 7:30 p.m. I have a machine key made of steel belonging to my mother. I got the same out and started stroking it as Uri Geller spoke. Nothing happened so I put the key down, switched off the radio, as "Deadline's" singing

irritates me. I went on reading until about 11:30 p.m. I turned to switch off my bedside light when to my utter shock the key had bent nearly double. When I showed it to a locksmith he said the breaking strain was about fifty pounds. To say I was astonished is to put it mildly. I took a long time to fall asleep.

Price has learned from a statistical analysis of his cases that men and women report the phenomenon equally as often. However young and middle-aged adults experience it more often than children or the elderly. Interestingly enough, people who described themselves as "skeptical or doubtful" reported Geller effects as often as the believers did. (Unfortunately, Dr. Price's report does not make it clear whether his percipients were reporting belief or doubt in regard to Geller, in metal bending specifically, or in psychic phenomena in general.) Needless to say, while most spontaneous Geller effects are probably due to malobservation or downright lying, I don't think we can merely dismiss all of these accounts from serious consideration.

What causes these Geller effects to manifest? Most of the percipients I have talked with believe that somehow Geller himself causes the PK right over the TV set or radio. However, it seems more likely that these witnesses had really momentarily unlocked their own PK abilities. Death coincidences and poltergeist cases indicate that we all probably possess an inert PK potential. A person watching Geller perform may become psychologically prepared to unlock this potential. Since the onlooker will consciously attribute any PK which should occur to the power of Uri Geller, the PK can work at an unconscious level. The onlooker will not be inhibited from demonstrating PK since he will usually refuse to believe that he himself is the source of the metal-bending power.

There are three different aspects of the Geller mystery: Geller himself, his imitators, and spontaneous Geller effects. I can only look upon all three of them with a mixture of belief and doubt. But there is one more comment I would like to make.

Even though the phenomenon of PK-mediated metal deformation has become widely known due to Geller's claims and performances, this psychic effect is not a new one in the annals of psychical research. It did seem at first as if Geller were offering parapsychology a brand-new type of PK effect. No other person had ever come onto the psychic scene demonstrating anything like it. However, the first recorded case of metal-bending PK actually occurred nearly one hundred years ago during a poltergeist outbreak.

A report on this poltergeist appeared in the May 13, 1905, issue of the *Nashville Banner*. According to a firsthand account printed as part of the story, the poltergeist plagued the A. P. Surrency family, who lived in a rural southern Georgia town in 1879. The poltergeist was your typical object-thrower. Kitchen objects would fly about, doors would open and close by themselves, and people were often painfully struck by well-aimed missiles. But as one witness claimed, "These were only small beginnings. Frequently during the meal hour, milk, tea, coffee and soup were flung into the faces of those at the table, several times inflicting painful scalds and burns. *Spoons were broken, or suddenly twisted out of shape in their hands.*" (Italics mine.)

An Additional Note on the "Geller Effect"

Though I am not a good PK subject, I have noticed over the years that minor PK effects will sometimes break out around me during times when I am preoccupied with and writing on the subject. For example, on two occasions I have heard raps in my home right as I was writing about paranormal knockings.

The final draft and corrections on this chapter were handed to my typist on the evening of August 19, 1976. While writing this chapter, the thought came to mind that one of my own keys might bend paranormally as I focused my attention on the Geller work. I even checked the seven keys on my key ring on two occasions as I wrote this chapter to check for any bending. All my keys were straight at that time.

On August 20 I had lunch with a friend at a restaurant. Our conversation drifted to the subject of PK. I mentioned to him that I had just completed writing a chapter on Geller, and we soon found ourselves discussing the evidence for paranormal metal bending, especially of keys. I was rather negative about the subject, as this chapter indicates, so took the role of devil's advocate. I took my own keys out of my pocket and jostled them around in order to show my friend how Geller might distract attention while faking. I then placed them back in my pocket. No one touched them besides myself.

"Do you think Geller ever bends keys psychically?" my friend asked.

I had to admit that I thought Geller did have some metal-bending ability. My mind raced over the Cox experiment in particular. So I again took out my keys, placed them on the table before us, and started to "stroke" one of them a la Geller. I was trying to demonstrate how he will often stroke a key while it is on a flat surface and make it curl up. I had stroked the key about three times or so when, all of a sudden, *both of us saw that the key was bent upward about 8 degrees.* I was amazed. The key, which unlocks a UCLA lab room, is extremely thick and I cannot bend it normally even using both hands. Now the key was not only bent up by several degrees, but was even slightly twisted to one side. It is my feeling that the key bend was PK-mediated.

I cannot ascertain when the key actually bent. I use my keys constantly during the day and certainly would have noticed this markedly deformed key before lunch. While I did not actually see it bend, *it did continue to bend slightly after we first noticed the deformity.* It seems likely that the key first bent while it was in my pocket between the two times I took my key ring out of my pocket.

I think it is indeed significant that the key apparently bent: (1) the day after I finished the final draft of my chapter on Geller and Geller effects; (2) during a conversation on the evidence for paranormal key bending; and (3) during a time when I had a suspicion that such a PK effect might occur.

This case, like so many others, represents another instance of PK metal bending indirectly related to Uri Geller. However, at least it is one case for which I can vouch personally!

8

Group PK

IN THE SUMMER of 1972 several members of the Toronto Society for Psychical Research embarked on a rather unusual experiment. They decided to see if they could conjure up a ghost! The upshot of their experiment was fascinating. The Toronto group discovered that, by hard and long practice, they could project a collective PK force even though none of them, individually, seemed endowed with any psychic ability. But this is getting ahead of our story, so let's go back and see just what factors led up to these novel explorations.

If you saw a ghost, how would you react? Would it appear real to you? Or perhaps misty and unreal? Would you realize that it was a hallucination? Or what? These were some of the questions that members of the society were interested in discussing. (The Toronto Society, like so many others in this country and Canada, is basically an amateur and privately run organization which offers open membership to the general public.) The Canadian group certainly took up a formidable challenge when they decided to tackle the subject of ghosts. Phantoms are perhaps the most enigmatic form of psychic phenomena. For instance, they seem to be illusions, yet real physical objects at the same time. A phantom may appear to one person, but will remain invisible to everybody else in the same room. Or it may be seen collectively by four or five people in a room, while remaining invisible to others. An apparition may appear lifelike, clothed and holding a walking stick or cane, or it may appear vapory and opaque. Phantoms are insubstantial enough to walk through walls, yet they sometimes pick up and move physical objects. The world of apparitions is a world of vast contradictions.

These were the puzzles which members of the Toronto Society tried to untangle as they met week after week to discuss ghosts and kindred phenomena. Finally they realized that in order to study ghosts they first had to find one. Needless to say, this was no easy matter! So ultimately they decided to try to conjure one up themselves. Now, you might ask, just how did they go about doing this?

By sitting week after week, meditating together, concentrating together, and forming a mutual emotional bond, the group hoped that they could produce a collective "thought form"—a ghost manufactured by the living, as it were. The leader of the project was Iris Owen, the wife of the well-known English-Canadian parapsychologist, A. R. G. Owen. The rest of the group consisted of other Toronto residents whose professions ranged from accounting to engineering. None of the group laid claim to any special psychic abilities. In order to make sure that the "ghost" they conjured up really was a projection from their own minds, they decided to create a wholly fictitious character whom they named "Philip." They would try to materialize Philip by invoking his name, and would consider him responsible for any psychic manifestations which might occur during their meetings.

In order to help themselves psychologically associate with the Philip personality, one member of the group wrote out a fictional biography for him. According to this story, he was an aristocratic Catholic nobleman who lived in seventeenth-century England, and frustrated by his beautiful but frigid wife, Dorothea, had taken a mistress named Margo. Eventually Dorothea discovered her husband's affair, denounced Margo as a witch and husband stealer, and had her burned at the stake. Philip, who had not defended Margo at her trial because of his dangerous political position, threw himself from the castle battlements in remorse soon afterward. One of the group members even drew a sketch of Philip as he was supposed to have appeared in life.

The group meditated together week after week. They studied Philip's life and loves, identified with him, and attempted to make him come to life in their minds. The procedures they used for the experiments were simple. They would sit around in a circle and mentally conjure Philip forth in the hope that eventually some sort of apparitional form would materialize in the circle. Often they would discuss Philip and his life among themselves, filling out and elaborating on the original story. In reminiscences about these sessions four years later, Mrs. Owen admitted that, "Not only had Philip himself become more 'real' to them, but . . . the story had become so familiar to them that the group members were beginning to find it more difficult to believe that Philip had never existed."

Eventually these meditation sessions began to pay off. Sometimes one or two members would feel some sort of intangible presence in the séance room or would receive a vivid mental picture of Philip. But, needless to say, no apparition ever actually materialized.

After months of sittings, the group decided to change strategy. Since the meditation practices hadn't worked too well, they thought that perhaps a different way of going about the experiments might fare better. By this time, Mrs. Owen had chanced upon some research reports written by a British investigator, K. J. Batcheldor, who had succeeded in witnessing strong PK effects. He achieved these results by seating a group of people around a table, having them place their hands on it, and having them joke and laugh until the table started to move under their fingers. He discovered that the table would eventually move, jostle about, emit raps, and even levitate. Of course, Batcheldor had discovered nothing new. "Table tilting" has been a parlor-room game since Victorian times. The Spiritualists of that era claimed that if a group of people sat around a table, placed their hands on it lightly, and addressed questions to it, eventually the table would rock and knock out answers. The table might raise a leg when a certain letter of the alphabet was called, for instance. Of course, during table-tilting sessions, the table usually only moves for the same reason a Ouija board indicator will slide across the board when hands are placed upon it. In both cases, the movements are produced by the sitters themselves who are actually pushing the table or board unconsciously. Sometimes table-tilting phenomena will present a greater mystery. Some practitioners have been able to make the table bounce about violently, rear up, and even levitate. But, unconscious pushing cannot account for a table rising in the air!

By following these old Spiritualist procedures, Batcheldor has been able to witness several levitations in full light while working with a group in England. Now, this group had no specific medium. Instead it seemed that the entire group was projecting a collective PK force which was, in turn, producing the manifestations, and Batcheldor believes that any group of congenial people is capable of generating this type of PK action.

After reading Batcheldor's reports, Mrs. Owen immediately realized that these table-sitting procedures would be a natural technique for the Philip circle to adopt. So the Toronto group changed battle plans. They followed Batcheldor's suggestions and sat around a table and made quite a social occasion of the experiments. Gone was the gloom and austerity that had typified their meditation sessions. However, even though the group was aware of Batcheldor's findings, they still expected Philip to materialize visually. The group's PK had different notions. As Mrs. Owen records in her book, *Conjuring Up Philip:*

> One evening, during the third or fourth new session, the group felt a vibrating within the table top, somewhat like a knock or rap. It is correct to say "felt" rather than "heard," because the group was making a degree of noise at the moment so that the unexpected action within the table took them completely by surprise. They were not expecting anything of that nature, so nobody could say for sure whether they *heard* the vibration as a noise, although everybody *felt* the vibration.

This was only the beginning. More and more knockings resounded from the table as the sittings progressed, and finally it began to slide under their fingers.

"I wonder if by chance Philip is doing this?" queried one of the sitters.

A rap resounded from the tabletop as though answering her.

The group became tremendously excited by this new development and by adopting a code—one rap for yes, two for no—they were soon communicating with an intelligence who claimed to be causing the table motions and raps. Of course, this personality claimed to be none other than their imaginary seventeenth-century nobleman.

As the group evolved psychically, they learned more and more about Philip and this strange new PK force they were liberating. Often the raps would freely answer questions asked by the sitters.

However, Philip would only answer in accordance with the basic story which the group had manufactured. If he were asked a question about his life upon which the group had never figured out an answer, the table would only emit annoying sawing noises. Raps would also greet people entering the room, and as the Toronto group continued sitting, the table motions also became more spectacular. It would sway to and fro, raise up on one leg, bounce about and so forth. The sittings would often become extremely animated. The table would move, rear about, and then raps would answer question after question put to it by the group. Sometimes these "conversations" would become rather lively as Philip began developing a distinct personality. If the group asked Philip about his life and loves, he might answer in any number of ways. The table would rap "no" loudly if a question were asked which Philip felt too private. On the other hand, forceful, enthusiastic raps would issue from the table when he was asked about his love for Margo. These raps, which sounded like loud wooden thuds, would come directly from the tabletop.

These developments highlighted the first phase of Philip's evolution. So before going on any further, let's critically examine the experiments up to this point and see what we can make of them.

When analyzing the Philip work, the first question we have to contend with is an obvious one. Can fraud account for the phenomena the Toronto group experienced? The answer to the question has to be affirmative. While I am not making any sort of specific accusation to this effect, neither do the early records of the Philip circle impress me as offering very good evidence for PK. (Later I will argue in favor of the genuineness of the Philip circle, but for now let me play the skeptic's role.)

First of all, let's take a look at the table movements the circle achieved. I find it is almost impossible to rule out subconscious or conscious pushing as an explanation for them. Michael Faraday, the famous British scientist, had to contend with this problem when he investigated table tilting in Victorian times. As a control he placed a rotating board on rollers on top of a table that some Spiritualists were using for table tilting. If the sitters tried to push the table in any way, the rollers would move this board about while the table remained unaffected. And this is exactly what happened when the table-tilting sessions began! This proved to Faraday that the sitters were pushing the table themselves, although they didn't realize it.

This same possibility applies to the Toronto group. Remember, it consisted of eight members. If any one of them started pushing the table, undoubtedly the others would follow suit automatically and unconsciously. I've seen this happen many times during my own investigations. In fact, you can prove this principle to yourself by trying a little experiment. Seat yourself and a group of people around a table and request everyone to place his hands on it. After a while, deliberately give the table little shoves. You will find the group will very often become excited by the vibrations and will inadvertently help them along. After a short while the table will rear up, move about, and proceed to engage in all sorts of motions. Yet, all these displays are caused by your own surreptitious pushings which the group is now unconsciously aiding and abetting. I am sure that just about everyone has, at one time or another, played with a Ouija board. If you have, then you know how hard it is to resist pushing the indicator even if you are consciously trying to keep your hand steady. Well . . . just think what happens when eight or ten people sit around a flimsy table and place their hands on it.

Mrs. Owen is apparently very aware of this problem and tries to counter it when she argues in *Conjuring Up Philip* that, "a strict watch was kept on the sitters to make sure that there was neither involuntary rapping or obvious pushing when the table was in motion." But how could such a watch be kept when everyone was busy working with the table? In order to control against fraud better, the Toronto group placed paper doilies on the table and under their hands during the Philip sittings. The table still shifted about, completely unaffected by the safeguard. But does this prove the genuineness of the table movements? Hardly. Paper doilies will not impede pushing. There is practically nothing you can put on a table which will prevent it 100 percent effectively. The only thing I know of that does work is liquid facial cleanser. Spread evenly over the tabletop, the liquid will keep the sitters from gaining any traction on it. Unfortunately, no tests using this substance were attempted by the Philip circle.

Although I have never had the opportunity to visit the Toronto group, I have seen a commercial film of one of their sessions and I am afraid that the film will be live ammunition for the skeptics.

Basically, it presents part of a table-turning session, while another segment shows the group receiving allegedly paranormal raps. Frankly, the film is so bad that it's almost embarrassing. The table movements are in no way very exciting. It jiggles, moves about, rears up off two legs, and carries out other maneuvers. In fact I can produce these movements myself with ease, though the documentary speaking for the group claims that some of the table movements depicted in the film cannot be imitated fraudulently. It certainly is apparent that the Philip circle are novices at table-tilting. A colleague and I went over the film a number of times and at several points saw indications that one or two group members could have been pushing the table.

Here I am only being critical in order to emphasize a point. The table motions filmed by the Philip group during the early phases of their development do not, in themselves, stand up as very good evidence for PK.

The raps, though, are harder to explain away. Unfortunately, it is almost impossible to prove whether the raps are paranormally produced or not, since they can be faked dozens of different ways. A short book could be written just on how to fake raps, so obviously I can't detail them all here. Even Hereward Carrington, who was one of the most experienced investigators of psychical research ever produced, admitted in his *The Physical Phenomena of Spiritualism* that ". . . Raps in the *home* of the professional medium can, in fact, be obtained in so many different ways that they are of no evidential value whatsoever." Mechanisms can even be fraudulently sealed inside tables which are absolutely undetectable unless the table is broken apart.

All of these considerations bore significantly on my own initial reaction to the Philip experiments. I found them tantalizing, but hardly very convincing. As the Philip experiments proceeded, though, the PK became more complex, and gradually the sitters encountered types of PK effects which are extremely difficult to explain away. For one thing, Philip eventually became endowed with ESP ability, or so it seems. (Since ESP and PK often work hand in hand, this should not strike the reader as odd.) One evening when Dr. A. R. G. Owen was visiting the circle and Philip was eagerly rapping out replies to his questions, Owen began challenging the entity with historical queries. In answer to one question Philip claimed that he had known Queen Elizabeth, yet moments later he denied having known Prince Rupert. This response puzzled Owen who believed that Rupert was the queen's brother-in-law. Nevertheless, Philip kept denying that he had known the prince even after Owen pointed out the apparent absurdity of the response. To resolve the matter once and for all, Owen hurriedly consulted an encyclopedia and discovered that he was indeed mistaken. So, Philip's answer had not only been correct, but historically consistent as well. Mrs. Owen believes that the sitters unconsciously knew that Owen was wrong. But, on the other hand, I think ESP is a distinct possibility for several reasons.

The intelligence behind paranormal raps seems able to use ESP when necessary. Another bit of evidence along these same lines was gained by Sir William Barrett, a founder of the SPR, while he was investigating a poltergeist which was haunting a little farmhouse in England. This geist delighted in knocking on the walls and ceiling of the house, much to the annoyance of the farmer and his family. Barrett, intrigued by the knockings, challenged the poltergeist to tell him how many fingers he had outstretched while his hand was hidden in his pocket. The raps answered correctly several times in a row.

Eventually Philip was able to produce raps on the walls of the séance room as well as on the table at the request of the sitters. On at least one occasion he was able to cause lights in the séance room to flicker, and spontaneous PK began breaking out in the homes of the individual group members. Even the table movements became more interesting. As Mrs. Owen recalls:

> During the January 1974 sessions there were again different movements of the table. On at least two occasions, *one* leg only was raised from the floor, causing some distortion of the table top, as the other three legs were still firmly on the ground. On each of these occasions much force was needed to push the table top down and the raised leg back into place. It felt as if the table was resisting the persons pushing down, and on one of these occasions four people were needed to push the leg down again. Once, when the table had flipped over, as described earlier, the group sat down with their hands on the exposed underside of the table and carried on a conversation with Philip. The raps became audible from the top side, which was lying flush with the carpet.
>
> During this session an experiment was made with the candies which Philip was supposed to like. Usually candies were placed

around the table for each member of the group, always with one set aside for Philip. Someone jokingly made a move to take "Philip's" candy, telling him to hang on to it. The table was at that moment tipped at an angle of 45 degrees, and the candy stayed on the table. Two or three different types of candy were tried, and care was taken to see that they were not sticky. All of them stayed put. Subsequently the table was tipped manually, and the same candies placed on the table. They slid off almost as soon as the table was tipped, and much before the 45-degree angle achieved by Philip in action.

I consider these phenomena very evidential. Very similar effects were noted by investigators who conducted séances with D. D. Home and others back in the nineteenth century. They, too, noted how the séance table would prop up on two legs and remain rigid, resisting any attempt by the sitters to push it back down to the floor. Tables would swing about during Home's séances, yet objects placed on top would remain stationary as though glued tightly in place. Needless to say, sham cannot easily account for these types of phenomena. On two occasions, the Philip group has even momentarily levitated the table completely.

I do not believe that the Philip circle is aware how closely the phenomena they are encountering match descriptions of table-turning phenomena recorded by the early Spiritualists over one hundred years ago. To me, these patterns make the Philip accounts more evidential.

The experiment is still continuing. Certainly the Toronto group has proved the efficacy of Spiritualist table-turning procedures, and only time will tell how much further their PK will develop. But there is a more important issue at stake, and one which I have raised several times in the course of this book. Just what is the Philip work telling us about PK?

Probably the most novel discovery by the Philip circle is that they can produce results by conjuring forth a totally imaginary communicator. These findings stand in striking contrast to the Victorians who, imbued by Spiritualist teachings and practices, usually thought that table tilting placed them in contact with discarnate intelligences. The Philip circle has also dramatically demonstrated that a group of nonpsychic people can develop formidable PK powers. (Or, as Iris Owen has termed this phenomenon, "PK by committee.") As I mentioned earlier, the Philip group found that none of their members seemed particularly endowed with PK. Nor did the absence of any sitter have an effect on Philip's ability to manifest. In fact, he can manifest even if only a few members of the group meet together.

But who is Philip? This is a question which I find extremely thought-provoking. Merely saying that he is a joint product of the sitters' minds tells us very little. How is the PK carried out? What personality traits has Philip developed? It is difficult to read accounts of the sessions without coming to realize that this imaginary ghost exerts a very real presence during the séances. He has his own likes and dislikes, yet he is downright amiable. But how can a group of eight people create a living presence week after week?

One possible solution to this puzzle was offered by Dr. Joseph Maxwell at the turn of the century. Although Maxwell formulated his theories from what he had observed while investigating several European home circles, his views are equally applicable to the Toronto group. He suggested that during a séance all of the sitters' minds link into a mutual psychic bond. Now each of us has a PK potential within our minds and bodies, but we normally have little access to this reservoir of power. However, during a séance a group mind is formed and this entity not only has access to our PK, but can manipulate it as well. This collective mind takes on the specific function of directing the PK and a medium present may serve more as the processor of the psychic force than the chief contributor. (This specific idea is only suggested by Maxwell, and is more my own.) This collective mind, argued Maxwell, takes on a "personification" molded by the thoughts and biases of the sitters, and will claim to be almost anything. As he points out in his 1905 book, *Metapsychical Phenomena,* if the group believes in spirits, the entity will claim to be a discarnate, and so on. Decades before the Philip experiments got under way Maxwell suggested that a group could conjure forth a purely fictitious being, and sometimes the intelligence will even claim to issue directly from the sitters:

> I have noticed that the role played by the personalification varies with the composition of the circle. It will always be a spirit of a dead or living person with spiritualists. But the roles are more varied if the circle be composed of people who are not spiritualists; it then sometimes happens that the communications claim to emanate from the sitters themselves. I am inclined to believe this is the real origin of the communications, and that a sort of collective consciousness is

formed... This forms part of an—as yet—undeciphered chapter on the psychology of crowds...

The findings of the Philip group are also consistent with a theory I have formulated and which I have already suggested to account for some poltergeist cases. This "personalifacation" of "group mind" may eventually take on an independent life of its own and may break away, wholly or partly, from its symbiotic dependence on the mind or minds which gave it birth. As I read Mrs. Owens' book, several questions kept coming to mind which I still have not been able to resolve. Is Philip only a name which the group uses to designate its collective PK? Or is Philip really a self-consistent, independent agency which they have unleashed into the world? Who directs the PK, the sitters or the Philip personality itself? And, of course, how much control does the circle have over this entity?

I am a little surprised that it only took the group a few table sessions before they started hearing raps, since many other groups report that they have had to wait months for anything to happen. However, we should remember that the Philip group had previously meditated together before they initiated the table sittings. No doubt these weeks acted as a gestation period for the PK, a period of time during which the group members psychologically prepared themselves for the emergency of the psychic force.

The Philip experiments, I hope, will reawaken parapsychology to the fact that there exists a proven methodology for developing PK. Ever since the Duke days, parapsychologists have thought that you had to throw dice in order to study or even achieve PK. We now know that this belief is false. But today, many parapsychologists are still playing host to an equally false premise: that to observe PK, you must first discover a gifted subject. The Philip work certainly proves that a group of people, none of whom are psychic, can develop startling PK abilities among themselves. This fact was perfectly well known a hundred years ago to the Spiritualists. Science can be arrogant. It often forgets the lessons it has learned during previous eras, and parapsychology is no exception.

Table titling can tell us quite a bit about the PK process as well as about the psychological dynamics which may help us to unfold and develop this elusive psychic ability. So I think it is worthwhile to take a somewhat detailed look at the history of table turning and see what the psychical investigators of previous generations learned about this interesting form of PK . . . discoveries which have nearly been forgotten by today's generation of laboratory-bound parapsychologists.

The art of table tilting dates back to the third century A.D. We know that the early Christians criticized their pagan contemporaries for prophesying by the use of tables, and European Jews practiced table turning during the seventeenth century. According to one contemporary source, the Jews would sit around a table singing psalms until it would "spring up even when laden with many hundredweight." However, table tilting first caught on in the United States during the Spiritualist epidemic of the 1850s when it became a fashionable parlor-room game. For a nice social evening, one or two families would sit around a table and table-turn all evening. The practice was as popular in the 1850s as Ouija boards are today. The groups would usually try to communicate with the intelligence behind the dancing table by asking simple questions. The alphabet was repeated and a table leg would lift up at the appropriate letter. By using this method, sentences would be laboriously spelled out. Less enterprising groups worked out simple codes. Usually one tilt stood for "yes," two for "no," and so on.

Even in these early years of the table-turning rage, many experimenters witnessed some rather bizarre and undoubtedly PK-mediated manifestations. Sometimes the table would move even when no one was touching it, and there were accounts of levitations galore. Often the tables would float in the air and could not be pulled down or, odder still, would become glued to the floor and could not be lifted by the sitters at all no matter how hard they tried to pry them loose.

One of the first scientists who studied table turning in any depth was Dr. Robert Hare, a chemistry professor emeritus from the University of Pennsylvania. In order to test the genuineness of table-tilting movements he mounted a plate on top of the table, and between the plate and the tabletop were placed several little balls which acted as rollers. If the subjects or medium shoved the table manually, the plate would roll on the balls while the table itself would remain stationary. Hare found that some of his subjects could move the table even when his foolproof guard covered its top, and it seemed clear to the chemist that somehow PK can be transferred to inanimate objects through physical touch.

Table turning quickly spread to England and continental Europe and by 1853 had become all the rage, especially in France and Germany. Although investigators in England discovered that sometimes the table could answer mentally asked questions, table tilting was dealt a severe blow when Faraday proved that unconscious muscular action could account for most of the phenomena. Nonetheless, other investigators were not so easily convinced that table tilting was purely hokum. For example, Sir William Barrett investigated a table-tilting case in 1876 which he felt could not be explained any way normally.

Barrett at first thought that the family's daughter was the principal cause of the PK but soon found that the table movements could occur even in her absence. As his report reads:

> ... One day, in broad daylight, her parents and I were sitting at the big mahogany table in the dining-room. Twelve persons could easily have been seated at it. Our hands were on the table, well in sight, when suddenly three feet of the table were lifted sufficiently high for me to pass mine under the castors. Anyone who tried to do it with all his force would find that even by grasping the table, which none of us did, it could not be accomplished without much difficulty, even by a clever and vigorous man.
>
> On another occasion we heard raps after we had withdrawn our hands and had moved away from the table. While the hands and feet of all were perfectly visible, *and nobody touched the table,* it started moving sideways unequally. It was a heavy four-legged table about four feet square. [Apparently a different table.—S.R.] At my request the two feet nearest to me rose up, then the other two, eight or 10 inches above the ground, and the table remained there for several seconds, while nobody touched it. I moved back my chair and it advanced toward me (nobody touching it) and finally got right in front of my chair, so that I could not leave it. When it was under my nose it rose up several times, and I could convince myself by touch and sight that it did not rest on the ground, and that no human being could be directing its movements.

The most detailed, systematic, and eye-opening studies of paranormal table turning were not carried out in England, but in Switzerland. Oddly enough, few contemporary students of psychical research seem at all familiar with the epoch-making research on table turning carried out in the 1850s by two Swiss investigators, Count Agénor de Gasparin and Professor Marc Thury. Both of these researchers spent months experimenting with table turning and both apparently witnessed some phenomenal PK. Yet, interestingly enough, de Gasparin and Thury came to very different conclusions about the nature of table turning and PK on the basis of their independent studies. It is a pity that their work is not better known among parapsychologists today, and I can but briefly summarize it here.

De Gasparin carried out his investigations between September and December of 1853 during the heyday of the table-turning craze in Europe. Only a year later he published detailed records of his experiments in a massive book entitled *Des Tables tournantes du surnaturel en general, et des Ésprits*. From these records one can see that de Gasparin's work was conducted under strict control.

De Gasparin experimented in full light with a thirty-two-inch-diameter oak table which rested on a three-footed column. The table-turning team consisted of between ten to twelve people. Instead of placing their hands on the table uncontrolled, de Gasparin made his sitters place their hands palms down with fingers outstretched. The thumb and little finger on each hand had to touch its neighbor's on either side, and the sitters had to maintain that position throughout the session. De Gasparin hoped that this procedure would help control conscious or unconscious pushing. Nonetheless, the team found that they could usually get the table moving after only about five minutes.

Even at the onset of his experiments, de Gasparin realized that the PK force which manipulated the table was extremely powerful. During one of their first sittings, a 190-pound man even sat on the table, yet it completely levitated from the floor, shoving him off in the process. The Swiss investigator also noted that the group members were unusually exhausted after a particularly active session. As he spent more and more time studying what factors helped or hindered the table turning, de Gasparin gradually became one of the first psychical investigators to appreciate the role that the individual psychology of the sitter plays in the production of PK.

"When a person is in a state of nervous tension, he or she becomes positively unfit to act upon the table," wrote de Gasparin. "It must be handled cheerfully, lightly, deftly, with confidence and authority, but without passion."

Notice how similar this prescribed setting is to the one the Toronto group employed. They, too, were not able to generate PK until they began experimenting in a lighthearted, sociable setting. De Gasparin also discovered that certain individuals completely inhibited table movements. The Swiss scholar also isolated a great many factors about the PK process. For instance, he observed that the table motions seemed sympathetically linked to the physical movements of the sitters. As he recorded:

> Seeing that everything was going according to our wish, and having decided to try the impossible, we next undertake an experiment which marks our entrance into a wholly new phase of the study and places our former experimental demonstration under the guarantee of a positive irrefutable demonstration. We are going to leave probability behind and dwell with evidence. We are going to make the table move *without touching it.*
>
> At the moment when the table was whirling with a powerful and irresistible rotation, at a given signal we all lifted our fingers, and continuing to form the chain at a height of say an eighth or a quarter of an inch above the table, we continued our circular movement. *To our great surprise the table did the same;* it made in this way three or four turns! We could scarcely believe our good fortune; the by-standers (witnesses) could not keep from clapping their hands . . .

De Gasparin went on to say that twice the table momentarily stopped swirling. On both of these occasions, he observed, the sitters had raised their hands a little too high above the table. The table resumed its revolutions when they lowered them. As he proceeded with these experiments, de Gasparin and his friends were able to produce several levitations, yet neither thermometers or compasses held near the table registered any peculiar readings.

However de Gasparin was more than merely interested in just witnessing PK table movements; he also wanted to discover the basic nature of the PK force itself and explore the nature of the intelligence that guided it. Like so many psychic investigators of the mid-nineteenth century, de Gasparin believed that the body houses a "psychic fluid" that could be exteriorized from the body. During table turning, asked de Gasparin, does the fluid reside within the sitters or does it saturate the table? He decided that this puzzle could be resolved by using two tables during a single session, and he had the opportunity to try out this experiment only a month or so later. The critical experiment was held in November 1853. That evening the group witnessed several levitations, but afterward the table became even more agitated and thumped about so much that its central column split in two. Undaunted, the group immediately placed their hands over *another* table which de Gasparin had brought along. It, too, began dancing about under their fingers. This incident proved to de Gasparin that the group was not manipulating some sort of psychic fluid which had specifically imbued the séance table. Instead, he argued, it indicated that the group was projecting the psychic fluid directly from their bodies and could make it act on any object they chose.

Discoveries such as these led de Gasparin to reject the popular notion of his day that table turning was caused by discarnate intelligences. Instead, he believed that the PK was produced solely by the sitters, and could be triggered by an act of will.

Professor Marc Thury published his researches into table turning in 1855 as a volume entitled, *Les Tables tournantes considerée au point de vue de la question de physique generale qui s'y rattache*. As might be guessed from its title, Thury's monograph was a critical examination of de Gasparin's experiments, highlighted by observations and evaluations drawn from his own personal experiences. Thury was a professor of natural history and astronomy in Geneva, so his primary interest was in discovering the physical principles underlying table turning.

Thury was certainly aware that de Gasparin had achieved full levitations of the table. However, most of de Gasparin's theories were based on table motions which were recorded when the group had their hands on the table. Thury correctly argued that these observations might be invalid. If the sitters were, in fact, pushing the table, as might well have happened, de Gasparin's observations would really not be telling us anything about genuine PK. So Thury suggested a new procedure for table turning and decided to initiate his own experiments. The first thing he did was to monitor a table mechanically in order to make sure that no one was pushing it, yet, despite his controls, he witnessed the same type of motions that de Gasparin had written up in his book. Convinced now of the genuineness of table turning, he embarked on a detailed study of the nature of the "psychic force."

Group PK 183

Just as de Gasparin came to believe, Thury also suspected that the table-turning force emanated from the sitters and was manipulated by their will. However, he also realized that the PK force might manifest spontaneously and did not necessarily have to be consciously conjured up by the group. Because of this discovery, he rejected his colleague's notion that PK could only be projected by a *conscious* act of will. Thury's views were based, in part, on studies he made with a family in Geneva who were accomplished table tilters. At first they achieved only rather conventional table swayings and rotations but, as Thury reports in his book, they were in for a surprise when one of their group lost conscious control of the PK:

> A week had scarcely rolled by, . . . when a child of the family, he who had formerly succeeded best in the table experiments, became the actor, or the instrument, in strange phenomena. The boy was receiving a piano-lesson, when a low noise sounded in the instrument, and it was shaken and displaced in such a way that pupil and teacher closed it in haste and left the room. On the next day, M. N. who had been informed of what had happened, was present at the lesson, given at the same time,—namely, when the dusk was coming on. At the end of five or ten minutes he heard a noise in the piano difficult to define, but which was certainly the kind of sound one would expect a musical instrument to produce. There was something about it musical and metallic. Soon after, the two front legs of the piano (which weighed over six hundred and sixty pounds) were lifted up a little from the floor. M. N. went to one end of the instrument and tried to lift it. At one time it had its ordinary weight which was more than the strength of M. N. could manage; at another, it seemed as if it had no longer any weight at all, and opposed not the least resistance to his efforts. Since the interior noises were becoming more and more violent, the lesson was brought to a close, for fear the instrument might suffer some damage. The lesson was changed to the morning and given in another room situated on the ground floor. The same phenomena took place, and the piano, which was lighter than the one up-stairs, was lifted up much more; that is to say, to a height of several inches. M. N. and a young man nineteen years old tried leaning with all their might on the corners of the piano, which were rising. Then one of two things happened: either their resistance was in vain, and the piano continued to rise, or else the music-stool on which the child sat moved rapidly back as if pushed or jerked.

As Thury noted humorously, "I do not think that anyone will

be tempted to attribute to the direct muscular effort of a child eleven years old the lifting up a weight of 440 pounds."

So long before psychic research became a psychological science, Thury had already discovered that PK was basically an unconsciously directed force. Basing his views on his Geneva investigations, the Swiss professor argued that the unconscious mind also had a will and can use it to direct and manipulate PK even without the aid or even knowledge of the conscious mind. In fact, he argued, at the psychic level there is really no difference at all between "unconscious desires" and conscious will.

Having unraveled the psychological nature of PK, Thury next attempted to explore the physical nature of the force. By studying de Gasparin's records and his own experiments, he extracted eleven principles about the nature of PK:

(1) It is a fluid produced from the brain and nervous system. (2) This fluid, which normally resides in the body, can be projected away from it over a considerable distance. (3) The force is controlled by the will. (4) It acts upon inert matter but is repelled by certain substances such as glass. (5) It usually produces a lifting motion when it acts on matter, but (6) it can also act to repel or attract objects. (7) By manipulating the internal structure of an object, the fluid can cause it to emit raps or other noises. (8) The force can be best excited into action by a group of people holding hands. (9) The force can be transferred from one person to another through physical contact. (10) We do not know the range of the fluid's possible movements, but (11) the force is probably the same as a nervous fluid residing in the body.

Many of Thury's ideas may seem naive to us when we evaluate them in the light of modern PK research. Nonetheless, he did hold several views about PK which I find thought-provoking even today. Are raps produced when PK alters the internal structure of wood or other material? Does PK work within the body to regulate the cells and nerves? The questions Thury raised in 1855 are virtually the same ones that parapsychologists are still asking today.

Thury and de Gasparin also had differing opinions about the intelligence which lay behind table turning. De Gasparin firmly believed that the group alone controls the PK. Thury was less sure. If this "fluid" could function outside the body, he thought, then it was theoretically possible that discarnate intelligences might also be able to manipulate it as well. In this respect, Thury's views are almost identical to those adopted by Hereward Carrington to account for Eusapia Palladino's phenomena.

Despite the pioneering work of de Gasparin and Thury, the actual source of group-generated PK is still rather a mystery. Does the group, as a whole, really generate a collective force? Or does only one member of the group become the generator of the PK? The issue could be argued either way. Take the Philip group, for example. They found that the PK was not inhibited by the absence of any particular member. So in this case we know that no one individual was responsible for the PK. However, we cannot be so sure in other instances. De Gasparin's or Thury's groups might have contained one or more members who were particularly gifted with PK. This certainly seems to have been the case with the Geneva family Thury studied. Obviously the boy, around whom ths pianos would rap and jump, was also the source of the table-turning force. Rarely have table-tilting or other PK groups deliberately and systematically excluded each of their members in turn to see if any specific absence would affect the PK. So, in these cases, one is left wondering how much PK was produced by the group and how much was contributed by a particular member.

In some groups, however, it does become perfectly obvious that one member is the principal source of the PK. Oddly enough, sometimes this focus person will not be able to produce the PK unless the group is in attendance. In other words, this person can only perform in a group setting and seems to draw and manipulate the force from the other members rather than serving as the source of the PK himself.

The most extensive investigations into this type of home circle were carried out between 1914 and 1920 by Dr. W. J. Crawford, who was a lecturer in mechanical engineering at Queen's College, Belfast, Ireland, where he had the good fortune to work with the Goligher family who had been practicing group table levitation sessions for some time. Mr. Goligher's eighteen-year-old daughter, Kathleen, was the primary source of the PK, but all the family members were instrumental in producing it as well.

The Golighers were a typical turn-of-the-century, working-class, Spiritualist family. Mr. Goligher ran the group and the sitters included his four daughters, a son, and a son-in-law. They would sit around a table in dim light, and sing and play music until the table began to move, levitate, make sawing sounds, or emit raps. Of course, the Golighers felt that the table movements were caused by discarnates and they communicated with these intelligences through raps similar to the way in which the Toronto group talks with Philip.

Crawford realized quite early in his investigations that young Kathleen was the focal point of the group's PK. For example, during the séance her weight increased proportionately every time the table levitated. (He made these measurements by placing Kathleen and her chair on a scale during the sittings.) Crawford was able to make this measurement time and time again. However, Kathleen's increase in weight did not exactly match the weight of the table. For one set of experiments, Crawford used several tables weighing successively 10 lb. 2 oz., 6 lb. 4 oz., 6 lb. 0 oz., and 2 lb. 12 oz. The medium's weight increased as each of these tables were levitated by 10 lb. 2 oz., 5 lb. 14 oz., 5 lb. 10 oz., and 2 lb. 14 oz. As you can see, one or two ounces would be added or lost from the total weight during the levitations. There also seemed to be a psychic bond between the medium's body and the levitated object. The floating table fell if Crawford passed his hand between it and the medium. However, he could explore the same area with a glass rod without disrupting the levitation.

After witnessing and monitoring several of these levitations, Crawford developed a theory that PK acts like a cantilever. When PK is projected and levitates an object, it first travels as a beam to the floor beneath the object, anchors itself, and then projects upward, raising the object along with it. Crawford felt this theory could explain many aspects of the Goligher phenomena. For instance, objects placed on top of the levitated table did not increase the medium's total weight. Somehow this added weight was being absorbed. A man could even sit on the table without causing it to descend. Once again, it looked to Crawford as though the table was braced by a force leading to the floor. Yet, on other occasions, the PK did not seem to anchor itself to the ground, but instead Crawford thought that it projected from Kathleen's body, proceeded directly under the table, and then lifted it up. When this occurred, the medium's body would fall forward from her chair if heavy weights were placed on the levitating table.

Crawford also believed that these PK levers could account for raps, thereby rejecting Thury's belief that PK manipulates the internal structure of an object in order to produce paranormal sounds. Crawford argued that the PK cantilever can consolidate and become hard. If it wants to create a rap, it then strikes any surface at hand. (Whenever a rap occurred in the Goligher circle, Crawford noted that Kathleen's body would jerk or contort momentarily.) These malleable cantilevers could carry out any physical action of which the human hand is capable. It could grasp, shove, hold, and pull as well as levitate objects. As Crawford wrote in his book, *The Reality of Psychic Phenomena:*

> The table, once levitated, strongly objects to being pushed to the floor, and few persons can push it there, no matter how they try. Then after a struggle with the levitating force the table again becomes tranquil on the floor and the visitor is invited to sit on it. But he does not sit long. In a moment or two it gently rises on two legs and slides him off. Finally it escorts him outside the circle, the "escorting" consisting of forcible ejectment by an overwhelming pressure against his body.

Notice how Crawford, the Toronto circle, as well as others, have all encountered this same phenomenon. If the table levitates or raises on two legs, it may be impossible for the sitters to press it back down. Practically all experienced table turners have encountered this phenomenon. It looks as though a field is being generated under the table which, once formed and stabilized, cannot be countermanded by physical pressure. My colleague, Raymond Bayless, was once table turning with a friend of his when he encountered a similar effect. The table had tilted up on two legs and he had to press with considerable force to make it return to the ground. As he described the experience to me, it felt as if he were fighting against a force pushing in the opposite direction. On other occasions the table would glide back to the ground as though floating through gelatin.

The Golighers' PK also had one other trick up its sleeve. It could secure the table to the ground so steadfastly that even three men working together could not pull it up or budge it.

Kathleen Goligher's body was drastically affected by the PK. She usually lost considerable weight during the course of the séance, sometimes as much as fifty pounds! But, most of this weight would be returned to her body by the end of the session, although she usually lost several ounces nonetheless. Crawford also made one curious observation about Kathleen Goligher's PK which I have never seen noted with any other medium. If she touched any levitating object it would immediately fall to the ground. It could be that by touching a PK-affected object, the contact acted like a conduit and the PK force immediately reentered Kathleen's organism.

Although the Golighers sat as a family team, it certainly looks as if the PK was produced solely by Kathleen. So why has this work been included here under the heading of group PK? The answer is simple. As I indicated earlier, Crawford eventually learned that somehow *all* the sitters, including himself, contributed to the PK process. After it became clear to him that Kathleen lost weight after a séance, he decided to check all of the sitters' weights before and after the experiment. Time after time he found that everyone in attendance during the séance lost a bit of weight, usually from two to six ounces. This indicated to him that during the table-levitation sessions either everyone was contributing a small amount of substance or energy to the PK, or that Kathleen was somehow drawing power from the group. No one seemed immune. So, even though Kathleen Goligher was the group's principal medium, some sort of collective action was also responsible for the PK. In order to prove that this loss-of-weight phenomenon had no normal explanation, Crawford weighed a group of people seated at a table for a card game. Their weights were the same before and after the session.

The history of the Goligher circle becomes somewhat controversial after 1920. Crawford had a nervous breakdown that year and committed suicide soon afterward. The Society for Psychical Research, encouraged by Crawford's report, decided to take up the investigations and sent another experimenter, Fournier d'Albe, to investigate the circle and make an independent report on it. D'Albe had a largely negative reaction to his meetings with the Golighers, and was constantly annoyed by their singing hymns during the séances. (D'Albe should have expected this since the Golighers were Spiritualists and the séances were religious observances to them.) In his report to the SPR, d'Albe argued that the singing was merely a maneuver by the Golighers to cover up noise they made while they faked the levitations. However, he did admit witnessing some genuine PK, and never saw any real evidence of fraud. Even the SPR officials—who had no great belief in physical phenomena—realized that the report was ridiculous and refused to publish it. D'Albe subsequently wrote a book on the Goligher work which incorporated his SPR report.

Before his death, Crawford had been able to photograph the PK levers in operation. These photographs were included in his last book, *The Psychic Structures at the Goligher Circle*. The rods look like they were constructed of flimsy material and then tied to the table. Frankly, they look phony as can be. Yet, another investigator, F. McC. Stevenson, replicated Crawford's experiments and independently photographed these same odd formations. These photographs represent another mystery about the Goligher circle . . . and one which will probably never be resolved either.

The Golighers produced PK in a totally different setting than the ones contrived by de Gasparin and the Toronto group. The Philip circle sits around a table laughing, joking, and keeping their minds free and open. De Gasparin even went so far as to admit that his group's table motions would cease if he concentrated too hard or intently on them. Both these groups operated in full light. The Golighers, on the other hand, approached the table sittings more reverently. As Spiritualists, they believed that their séances were sacred communions and they engaged in them with religious respect and solemnity. Unlike some table circles, they sat in only dim light, yet they observed no less remarkable results than what the Philip or de Gasparin groups attained. So, it is obvious that there is more than one way to produce group PK. The Philip experiments are certainly not, by any means, the last word on the subject.

Table turning is not a thing of the past. One contemporary parapsychologist who has had considerable experience with home circle PK is Dr. José Feola, whose unpublished work and experiences constitute an absorbing chapter in the history of group-PK research.

Dr. Feola is an eminently qualified scientist and parapsychologist. Born and raised in Argentina, he was educated at the University of La Plata. The physical sciences were his first love, so he enrolled at the University of Rochester (New York) and took his master's degree in radiobiology. In 1974 he earned his Ph.D. in environmental health from the University of Minnesota in Minneapolis, where he also taught. He now works in the Department of Radiation Medicine at the University of Kentucky in Louisville.

As a parapsychologist, Dr. Feola has worked at the Institute for Parapsychology in Durham.

Feola's interest in PK started when he was a young man in Argentina. Having read accounts about D. D. Home, Rudi Schneider, and other great mediums, Feola and a friend of his, Octavio, decided to see if they could develop similar powers. So starting in August 1951 Feola and his friend began table-tilting sessions.

"Our basic reasoning went like this," Feola wrote to me; "if psychokinesis is, in the final instance, mediated by human beings; then *every* human being should be able to develop this ability, or whatever it is. We will start with a group of people, and meeting every week, and trying different techniques, we will achieve, sooner or later, some results."

Feola soon came to realize, though, that developing PK just wasn't that easy. "We realized this," Feola added, ". . . after several months of weekly meetings, with only a few doubtful noises here and there which we could not explain."

The group consisted of Feola, his wife Olga, and Octavio; two other friends and a neighbor joined them later. Most of the group members were students at the University of La Plata. They followed rather conventional Spiritualist practices and sat around a thirty-five-inch square table which weighed about twenty-five pounds. They placed their hands on top of the table, played classical music, burned incense, and would address the table verbally now and then. "Is anyone here?" or, "Can you move the table?" were commonly asked incentives to prompt the PK into performing.

The first seven months of testing yielded nothing but blank sessions. To be sure, the table did emit some odd creaks, and once Feola's neighbor, Fernando, thought something had brushed up against his leg. But this hardly satisfied the group's great expectations. Finally Feola, in near desperation, consulted with two other friends, Alfred and William, who were running a successful home circle of their own in La Plata. The two men joined with Feola and two members of his group to see if they could help get the PK under way.

A special table sitting was arranged for this session, and Feola procured a larger and heavier table. Alfred, William, Feola, and his wife met with Octavio and table-turned at his house. They hoped that the presence of Alfred and William would be enough to get the table moving. It worked! After only a few moments, Feola and the other sitters could feel the table vibrating under their hands. Feola eagerly addressed some questions to the table, hoping that it would rap out answers by tilting one of its legs as the alphabet was called. Nothing happened though.

At this time, the group decided to rest for a while before continuing with the session. Perhaps this would allow the PK to gather strength. After two similar breaks during the session, the table finally began rapping out messages to the group. An intelligence manifested who claimed to be related to the Feolas, but its communications were interrupted by an unexpected development. The table suddenly started to reel about and bounce violently. A new intelligence now took over the table and communicated an ominous message. "Idiots! Stop! There is danger," it rapped. Then almost immediately afterward:

> . . . the table went fully in the air, with tremendous ease, and floated around, menacingly. I passed my hands and feet underneath, since, as you might have imagined, at this moment we were all standing and following the swings of the table levitating around.
>
> Of course there were no strings or gadgets of any sort; besides we could see table and friends clearly. At one point, I grabbed the table in the air, and tried to bring it down, but I could not change its course even by a hundredth of an inch.
>
> After about 30 seconds of the table flying around, it came down again, and started to knock on the floor with great strength. So we stopped, in fear that the owners of the house might call the police after such a lot of strange noises and knocks had been produced.

What are we to make of this dramatic turn of events? Was this a group PK effect? Or were either Alfred or William mediumistic? The latter explanation certainly seems to fit the facts better. Feola's group had achieved little during the past several months, but things sure got jumping as soon as Alfred and William joined them. Yet, on the other hand, Alfred and William were themselves part of another home circle which was apparently producing startling PK. Did they "carry over" some of that group's PK to Feola's? Or did they merely help generate a force already inherent in the Feola group which had been slowly developing during a lengthy gestation period? These are all possibilities which must, unfortunately, remain completely unresolved.

What about the strange message the table spelled out? Was there really any danger? It could be that the message was a reflection from Feola's or one of his comrade's unconscious thoughts. As I have suggested earlier, we not only resist the notion of PK consciously but unconsciously as well. Even if we readily admit that PK exists, we might still harbor subconscious resistance to the idea. This all commonly leads to what I call the "denial syndrome." I've been affected by this syndrome myself several times. I will witness a dramatic instance of PK, yet a few days later, after the initial excitement has worn off, I find myself rationalizing the experience away. "Did I really see what I thought I saw?" I will keep asking myself. Conviction often turns to doubt when the denial syndrome works its spell. This syndrome is nothing more than a conscious expression of our deep-rooted, unconscious resistance to believing in PK. Feola, Olga, and Octavio all probably had a great deal of subconscious opposition toward accepting PK, even if they consciously believed it existed. Feola and his group first witnessed strong PK manifestations when Alfred and William first levitated the table. It was an awe-inspiring moment. But, it also must have been a tremendous mental shock to them, and subconsciously they might have wanted to resist experiencing phenomena which they were not ready to handle psychologically. The only "danger" was to their psyches. Subconsciously Feola and his friends wanted the table movements to stop, and their unexpressed thoughts were reflected by the PK and the table's message.

A week after this tremendous success, Feola, Olga, and Octavio once again sat with all the members of their own group. They were very excited by what they had witnessed the week before and enthusiastically reported to the circle what had happened.

Eagerly, they all returned to the table. But it stubbornly refused to move even after two more months of experimenting. It wouldn't even emit a rap or squeak. Finally, after even more weeks of failure, Feola asked Alfred and William to join together with his entire group. The two men agreed, and a table session was scheduled. This added presence had an immediate effect on the table. It began to move, spell out messages, and bounce up and down. No levitations took place, but the group was at least confident that they were on the road to success. Their optimistic change of heart paid off. Two weeks later Feola and the circle, sitting without the presence of Alfred or William, succeeded in completely levitating the table. The group had suddenly graduated from failure to triumph.

There are three possible reasons why the Feola group succeeded so dramatically only two weeks after Alfred and William had attended one of their sittings. First, Feola's group may finally have been ready to begin producing PK after a year's development period. If this were the case, Alfred's and William's attendance at the key séance was purely coincidental. Secondly, the two visitors may have acted as catalysts or carriers of the PK, and their presence therefore acted beneficially on the power Feola's group was accumulating. There is also a third theory which can account for the circle's sudden development. It seems plausible that Feola's group was failing because some of the members harbored unconscious resistance to PK. After all, most of them had not had any real personal experience with the phenomenon. Alfred and William were probably mediumistic to some degree, and, during their participation in the Feola sittings, generated enough PK to move the table. This could have had a beneficial psychological effect on the group. Now, finally having experienced genuine PK, the circle could overcome the mental resistance which was blocking their development. In other words, the group was now psychologically prepared to unleash their own PK. And unleash it they did. A table levitation is nothing to sneer at!

After achieving their first table levitation, the circle's range of PK increased steadily. Raps and telekinesis developed, and a number of eminent scientists began to journey to La Plata to see the psychic wonders for themselves. On one occasion, Dr. Orlando Canavesio, a well-known Argentinian scientist, visited Feola's group to test the PK personally. For one key session, only Feola, Fernando, and Dr. Canavesio were present. According to what Feola wrote to me, here's what happened:

> He made Fernando sit at a corner of the room while he and I sat at the other end of the room. The table . . . was placed in between Fernando and Canavesio and myself, at a distance of about seven feet from anyone present. Under these conditions, the table literally jumped all the way towards Canavesio and me, and would have hit us had we not extended our arms and—fortunately—stopped it before collision. Fernando had been sitting without moving a muscle all the time.

On another occasion the table was placed outside the circle entirely. It proceeded to bounce by itself across the room and entered into the circle beneath their raised hands!

Feola carried out a rather exciting experiment when the curator of the La Plata Museum of Natural History visited the group. He asked the table, or the intelligence behind its movements, if it would levitate and stay suspended for as long as possible. The table rapped affirmatively, and, as Feola reported to me:

> Then, after a few seconds, this incredible levitation took place: the table rose slowly to about three feet from the floor. I was holding Fernando's left hand and the curator's right hand while Fernando's right hand was holding the curator's left hand. When the table levitated, we stood up; the table was following our hands at about a foot below. We could see everything quite clearly. As our hands went up, the table went up. The movement of the table was one like floating, slowly swinging to the right and to the left, and going upwards. All the time, I was counting slowly. As I had counted to 120, the table started to come down; then one of the legs stopped on top of a chair—as if it wanted to show us the exact height—finally descending to the floor. It must have been in the air more than two minutes.

Feola's circle didn't break up until 1956. So the physicist was able to make detailed observations on the PK for four years. Feola personally believes that Fernando was the key to the circle's success. One incident he witnessed, which transpired after a successful session was over, especially confirmed this in his mind. He and another sitter were arguing about the PK.

"No, José, you're wrong," the sitter declared.

"Yes, I am right, yes, yes," asserted Feola with equal conviction.

All during this friendly debate, Fernando sat passively on the sidelines. He obviously didn't want to take sides. But as the argument proceeded, the table, which was still resting in the middle of the room, suddenly jumped up and down of its own accord. It kept rapping out double bangs, the circle's code for "no." Feola believes that the table was being unconsciously manipulated by Fernando who secretly agreed with the sitter. However, it seems just as likely to me that any of those present could have caused the table to jump

The records of Dr. Feola's home circle teach us many lessons about PK. In this brief discussion I have emphasized the psychological dynamics behind the group's development and phenomena. This issue is crucial to parapsychology. But there is another point of question which is certainly equally as important. Why is it that groups can develop really sensational PK while most individuals cannot?

K. J. Batcheldor, the British investigator who has studied table-levitation phenomena and who has specifically studied the psychological dynamics behind group PK, has isolated several factors which he believes might explain why a group can produce PK more readily than an individual. First of all, Batcheldor argues that a group setting overcomes what he calls "ownership inhibition." We tend to resist believing that our own thoughts and will can have a real effect on our environment. This belief is against common sense, for one thing. Second, it is psychologically threatening for us to believe that our thoughts—especially our not-so-nice ones—can actually influence the world in which we live. The result of this psychological set is ownership inhibition. Few of us like to admit that we can indeed produce PK and will have to take responsibility for anything it carries out . . . good or bad. So we constantly shirk the responsibility by claiming that spirits or demons are the real culprits when PK occurs. However, this inhibition is somewhat overcome in a group situation. The individual can cast off responsibility for the PK onto the entire group. He doesn't have to feel personally accountable. Ownership inhibition also explains why table-tilting communications usually purport to be from spirits or other independent agencies. If the PK is directed by an independent intelligence, the group can argue, how can they be held responsible for what the PK might do? So you see, ownership inhibition also works at a group level as well. But it is not nearly as defeating a mechanism as it is for the individual.

There is another psychological factor which comes into play during group PK practices which I feel Batcheldor fails to appreciate. As Maxwell and others have argued, group-PK effects are often directed by a collective mind created by the sitters. By joining forces, several people may actually form some sort of semiautonomous will or mind which directs the PK. Now this "entity" is not "owned" by or dependent upon any single group member. It is, on the contrary, semi-independent of all of them. A PK group, therefore, can overcome ownership inhibition because the PK is really being architectured by an ego-alien personality.

Despite these psychological considerations, there are probably *paranormal* reasons why groups are better able to develop PK than individuals are. There are two psychic factors which I believe come into play here. First, while an individual may not have any appreciable PK himself, a group of people working together might be able to build up a formidable collective PK force as each person contributes his share of psychic force to the group's total PK output. In fact, we might *expect* a group of people to produce stronger PK than a randomly selected individual could.

Now let's turn to a second factor which I think contributes to the success of group-PK techniques.

Let us suppose that a group is sitting together and producing PK regularly. What process does the PK go through in order to manifest? Does it collect in some physical location in space? Or does it work through the organism of one or more persons in the group? Crawford proved through his weighing tests with the Golighers that, although Kathleen was the focus of their circle, all the participants contributed some of the energy. It could be that PK works best when a group of people are present who can contribute the PK while another person (or persons) is on hand who is able to process and manipulate it. It might be considerably harder for one single individual to contribute, generate, and channel PK all by himself. In a group setting, a division of these factors may take place. Some people will contribute the PK while others will take over the function of processing and directing it. These may not be set roles either. In some groups an interchange of functions might occur among the sitters from sitting to sitting. However, I do not believe this happens very often. A group may actually act like a PK machine, with each individual functioning as a different part of the motor. Thus the group would be able to function easier and more efficiently than any one individual taking on all these operations at once. Remember what Uri Geller said about his own PK? "Always it happened in class," he said. "Then I knew that things had to happen when people were around, because I'm using their energy." A few famous mediums of the past admitted that they couldn't produce *any* PK unless a group of sitters were present. Art von Szalay, a psychic whose talents I have studied over several years, has often told me that he works best when certain people are present. He believes these individuals act as "batteries" for his PK. As far back as de Gasparin's day, researchers investigating table turning realized that some people totally impede the PK. If they were present at a session, absolutely nothing would happen. Could it be that people like this somehow psychically disrupt the PK processing of a group?

Group-PK phenomena just may be the most important aspect of psychic phenomena we can explore. All through the history of parapsychology, investigators have attempted to locate and test gifted subjects . . . subjects who could levitate tables with a raise of their hand or move objects with the twinkling of an eye. But is this really necessary? It may not be. Table-turning practices and home circles are obvious ways of developing PK manifestations without the need for a gifted medium. In fact, a group may be able to produce PK more consistently than a psychic can. If so, a home-circle group might provide a perfect laboratory for the parapsychologist. José Feola's group contained no great mediums. Nor does the Philip circle. Yet, these circles produced PK every bit as sensational as Rudi Schneider or Stella C. exhibited. So maybe we don't have to wait for another D. D. Home to come along before we can explore the mystery of PK. We merely have to develop it in ourselves.

9

PK and Healing

SCIENTIFIC RESEARCH in this country is guided by our pragmatic needs. We tend to disdain the search for knowledge unless this knowledge has some practical application for improving our lives or advancing our technology. In our practical world, we tend to see purely pedagogical knowledge as useless or as some sort of intellectual game. The A-bomb was not developed as a by-product of our search to understand the atom. It was developed purposely to end the Second World War. The eminent British psychologist, Dr. John Beloff, has even suggested that any search for information and knowledge which does not have a practical application is "alien" to the "American ideal"!

What applications does PK have? Ever since the birth of psychical research, investigators have been asking this question. If PK exists, can it be put to any practical use? Can it serve a function in our lives? I am afraid, though, that no one has ever offered any workable ideas on how PK energy could be fruitfully used. However, many researchers have long suspected that PK might contribute to the healing process.

Psychic healing can be defined as a PK effect on organic tissue or matter which aids in its recovery from illness or biological damage. If PK can move an object or upset a quantum process, it might be able to rearrange cells and tissues or speed up the body's own regenerative abilities.

We do know, at least, that PK can exert a considerable effect on living or organic matter. A few simple experiments have neatly proved this aspect of PK. In 1953, Nigel Richmond carried out a PK-on-biological-systems experiment in England. He placed a drop of pond water under a microscope and then watched the paramecia, which live in the water, dart about. Richmond divided the water drop into four segments and then began "willing" the paramecia to travel into certain of the quadrants. Of course, he randomly selected the target quarter for each trial. Each attempt lasted fifteen seconds, during which time Richmond would pick out a paramecium which was temporarily immobile and would then will it to move in the direction of his choice. The British investigator made 1495 trials and was remarkably successful. By his will, Richmond had influenced the biological behavior of a single-celled animal.

An even more provocative biologically oriented test was conducted in France by Jean Barry, M.D., who carried out his experiment in collaboration with the staff of the Institute of Agronomy, Bordeaux, in 1968. His test, though, was designed along quite different lines from Richmond's. Instead of working with animal life, Barry focused his attention on fungus cultures. Petri dishes containing the cultures were prepared the day before the experiment and placed in an incubator where the cultures could thrive. The next day, each subject was given ten dishes. The subjects would concentrate on five of them for about fifteen minutes, during which time they tried to impede the growth of the cultures. The other dishes were left as controls. Eleven subjects participated in the study and a total of thirty-nine trials were made. By measuring and comparing the growth of the target and control cultures, Barry discovered that, by and large, his subjects had successfully inhibited the growth of the fungus populations they had concentrated upon. In short, Barry had demonstrated an incipient form of psychic healing.

There is, however, a vast difference between PK's ability to influence paramecia and fungus cultures and its ability to grow new bone or fight off an advancing cancer. Can PK be used to heal, regulate tissue, and alter the very structure of a biological system? This is the issue we have to confront next.

If anything, healing research is one of the trickiest areas in the field of parapsychology. Take the Lourdes healing for example. Some reported recoveries are nothing short of miraculous. But are they due to PK? Or to some mysterious biological or biochemical healing force generated by the human organism? Or to spontaneous remission? If either of the latter two possibilites do occur, we would not be talking about PK at all as it is normally defined in parapsychology. We usually think of PK as a "force" emanating from one person and influencing another individual or, more often, an object. Whether or not PK can be used by a person internally on his own body is another question entirely. While it is true that D. D. Home and Eusapia Palladino apparently could use PK to levitate their own bodies, how can we possibly monitor PK if and when it works purely within the body? In this case, are we entitled to talk of "PK" at all? The miracles at Lourdes do not generally offer us irrefutable evidence for a PK-mediated healing effect, to my mind. Paranormal healing, yes. But PK-mediated healing? The Lourdes cures could be due, instead, to some mysterious X factor which guides regeneration in the body. This force might hypothetically be related to PK, but not be one and the same with it.

Nonetheless, some of the Lourdes cures seem to be "paranormal healings" since our medical technology cannot account for them. And every so often a Lourdes cure comes to our attention which does seem to have entailed some sort of psychic process at work.

Probably the most phenomenal healing ever recorded at Lourdes is the case of Pierre de Rudder, a Belgian man whose left leg had been broken when he fell from a tree. A compound fracture resulted which later became infected, but he refused to allow the amputation of the leg. Although the poor man could hardly move about because of the injury, he made a pilgrimage to Lourdes in 1875. Before this journey was undertaken a surgeon, Dr. Affenaer, had removed a piece of fragmented bone that had lodged within the break in the leg. After its removal, there was a one-inch separation between the two parts of the leg bone which caused de Rudder intolerable pain. Doctors believed that amputation was the only answer. One doctor, Dr. Van Hoestenberghe, examined the patient in 1875 and reported,

> Rudder had an open wound at the top of the leg. In this wound one could see the two bones separated by a distance of three centimeters. There was no sign of healing. Pierre was in great pain and suffered this since eight years before. The lower part of the leg could be moved in all directions. The heel could be lifted in such a way as to

fold the leg in the middle. It could be twisted, with the heel in front and the toes in back, all these movements being only restrained by the soft tissues.

This opening in the leg was continually examined up until a week before de Rudder's journey to Lourdes.

Upon arriving at the shrine, de Rudder was in as bad a state as ever. The jostling about had irritated his leg no end, and it didn't help much when other pilgrims kept bumping into him as he sat before the grotto. Finally he prayed and, in a state of near ecstasy, walked up to the statue of the Virgin which adorns the Lourdes facilities. Because of the break in his leg, this act would have been physically impossible for him to maneuver normally. At that moment, he realized that he had been healed. His family was amazed, and Drs. Affenaer and Van Hoestenberghe were dumbfounded. It was medically impossible for the leg to heal, yet here it was, sound as could be.

Pierre de Rudder died in 1898, and the next year Van Hoestenberghe was granted permission to exhume the body in order to examine the healed leg. The doctor amputated both legs and photographs of them are still available. They very clearly show that the bones of the left leg are deformed but have been fused over by a new piece of healthy bone that has somehow grown and connected the two severed ones.

I am especially impressed by the de Rudder case for three reasons. First of all, the healing was of an incurable organic condition. Second, some sort of psychic process must have played a part in the cure. After all, spontaneous remission cannot account for the instantaneous growth of new bone. Third, the healing which was so fortunately bestowed on Pierre de Rudder revealed a willful and intelligent process at work. Whatever force molded or created the new bone knew exactly what it had to do biologically to repair the leg. Note how similar this process is to how PK often operates. It, too, has the ability to carry out not only physical acts but intelligent ones as well.

Despite the de Rudder case, though, only a few healings at Lourdes—or anywhere else for that matter—appear to be PK-mediated or even paranormal at all. One of the most scathing, though thorough, reports on Lourdes was made by Dr. D. J. West, a British psychiatrist, in 1957. In order to judge independently how well-authenicated the Lourdes miracles really were, he chose eleven healings which the Lourdes Medical Bureau had certified as miraculous. In all cases he discovered that the medical records for these patients were too insufficiently detailed for him to make a proper outside evaluation. In some cases the original diagnoses were questionable. In other instances follow-up investigations on the lasting effects of the cures were too superficial to mean anything. Some patients were healed of illnesses for which spontaneous remissions are fairly frequent. Since none of the eleven cases met his criteria for evidence, West felt justified in rejecting all of them as untrustworthy accounts.

According to West, the case of Rose Martin typifies the sloppy documentation on which most of the Lourdes miracles rest. In November 1945, Mme. Martin noticed an alarming loss of blood through her vagina, and a subsequent examination revealed a cancer in the cervix. The uterus was removed. Four days later a strangulating abdominal hernia formed when the abdominal wall broke open. A further operation was necessary and duly performed.

Six months later, Mme. Martin again fell ill and complained of rectal pains and constipation. She was confined to bed for the next several months and her condition gradually worsened. The pain was so intense that she went into convulsions, and she needed morphine injections to control the agony. Finally she was taken to Lourdes in June 1947. At this stage of her illness, Mme. Martin was wasted away and she was emitting fetid vaginal discharges.

The patient was immersed in the Lourdes pool three times and gradually appeared to be recovering. Her bowels returned to normal and the vaginal discharges stopped. Even the rectal swelling disappeared. In March 1948 an X ray was taken which indicated that her rectum was completely back to normal. It apparently was a spectacular recovery and the Lourdes Medical Bureau declared it a miraculous cure of an abdominal cancer.

However, Dr. West is less sure about Mme. Martin's purported miracle cure than the Lourdes Medical Bureau appears to be. He points out in his book, *Eleven Lourdes Miracles,* that Mme. Martin's doctors never really confirmed that her cancer had really returned. They merely assumed it on the basis of her complaints. No subsequent biopsy was made on her rectal tissue, and West feels that her symptoms were probably due to postoperative infections which cleared up of their own accord. There is even some evidence that her symptoms were to some degree psychosomatic. One doctor at Lourdes began giving the woman harmless camphor injections instead of morphine to help control the pain. The placebo worked just as well as the drug.

The Rose Martin case is only one of the eleven cases which West examined in depth. His conclusions about Lourdes are almost entirely negative:

"The rarity of the cures, and the incompleteness of the medical information on most of the cases put forward as miraculous, makes any kind of appraisal exceedingly difficult," West writes. "As far as it goes, and taking the dossiers at their face value, the evidence for anything 'miraculous' in the popular sense of the expression is extremely meagre."

I should add that I cannot support Dr. West's conclusions wholeheartedly since he rather snow-jobs many of the cases he is writing about and examining, and often makes unwarranted suppositions about certain medical aspects of the cures. However, his research exemplifies the difficulties confronting any scientist who hopes to document irrefutable proof of paranormal healing.

Despite his negative investigation of Lourdes, West does believe that some people have had recoveries at the grotto, but does not feel that these are in any way miraculous. As a psychiatrist, he argues that the recoveries might be telling us something very interesting about the regenerative powers of the mind and body.

Lourdes is, of course, not the only place where people have received—or thought they have received—paranormal healings. Many people claim that they have been miraculously cured by the ministrations of faith healers. Psychics, psychic healers, spirit healers, faith healers, shamans, and Christian Science practitioners all claim the ability to help individuals recover from disease through some spiritual power or ideal. Fact or superstition?

Unfortunately, few of these practitioners seem able to prove their claims when examined scientifically. For example, Dr. Louis Rose, a British doctor, investigated the healing abilities of the late Harry Edwards. (Edwards was one of England's most famous psychic healers.) Rose's study focused on ninety-five patients treated and allegedly helped or cured by Edwards. He could not procure any medical data for fifty-eight of the patients. As for the other thirty-seven . . . well, these cases presented quite an eye-opener. In twenty-two cases, the claims of the patient were totally different from what their medical records indicated; three patients improved but relapsed; in four cases there was no organic change in the patients' conditions; in another four cases the patients improved but were undergoing conventional medical treatment at the same time they were treated by Edwards; and one other patient continued to deteriorate. Only three patients were left whose improvement might have been due to Edwards's healing abilities. I am afraid this isn't a very good record for a psychic healer.

Even in those rare instances where people do improve after psychic-healing treatments, we still cannot be sure that the results are due to the healer's "psychic" abilities. We still have to ask ourselves an important question: Did the psychics actually use PK to induce healing, or did the sessions really benefit the patient by putting him in a more optimistic frame of mind wherein he stopped interfering with the body's own ability to combat illness? If the second possibility is the case, once again we would not be talking about a genuine PK effect at all.

Western medicine has long known that our state of mind can drastically affect our body and its ability to function. Duodenal ulcers, for example, are formed when acids, which normally activate when food is digested, act upon the tissues beneath the lining of the duodenum. The activation of these acids is, in turn, affected by tension and anxiety. So an ulcer, which is certainly a very physical problem, can be aggravated no end by purely psychological stress. Recovery from illness is complicated by several similar factors. Our very state of mind can cause all sorts of malignant physiological responses in our bodies which can impede it from recuperating from or warding off illness. So the purely psychological benefits a session with a healer might have for a patient could cause certain beneficial physiological effects within his body. Let's take a look at a hypothetical duodenal ulcer victim. He goes to a psychic healer, receives a "healing," and finds that his ulcer is gradually getting better. Now, it is possible that the healer used PK to "treat" the patients. But it is more likely that the patient's belief in the healer caused him to stop worrying so much about the ulcer. His mental relief acted biochemically on his body which stopped producing the acids which were irritating his condition.

Many people do not realize how sensitive to psychological factors a great many diseases really are. Take cancer, for one.

Cancer is probably the most dreaded disease of our times, even though most cancers are treatable and orthodox medicine is able to cure a great number of cases. Yet, cancer is extremely sensitive to our psychological ups and downs. Our minds may even play an instrumental role in the initiation and development of a cancer. Just take a look at the following studies:

> As far back as the 1930s, French cancer specialists realized that cancer might be activated by emotional traumas.
>
> In the 1950s, psychologist Bruno Klopfer found that cancer developed more rapidly in patients who were struggling with psychological conflicts.
>
> The noted American psychologist and cancer researcher, Dr. Lawrence LeShan, discovered that the widowed and divorced had a greater propensity for developing cancer than had the married or single. These findings indicated to LeShan that people who have suffered a deep psychological loss are more likely to develop cancer.
>
> In a further study, LeShan and Dr. R. E. Worthington discovered that 62 percent of their patients had developed cancer shortly after they had undergone the trauma of losing a spouse or other emotionally significant relation.
>
> David Kissen, a leading lung cancer expert, discovered that most of his cancer patients had "poor outlets for emotional discharge," which were playing an important role in their illnesses.

There are many more studies which have shown similar results, but these five reports will adequately make the point that cancer is somehow linked to psychological trauma. So, we might ask, can psychological therapy processes help eliminate cancer? Some promising leads have already been made by Dr. Carl Simonton, while working at the Travis Air Force Base hospital.

Simonton's cancer treatment may seen deceptively simple. He instructs his patients to meditate, to focus attention on the cancer while willing it to dissolve, to visualize it dissolving, and trains his subjects in relaxation and imagery exercises. Simonton has found that a vast majority of patients who cooperate in the exercises improve. Some recoveries are nothing less than dramatic. Uncooperative patients don't seem to benefit from the procedure at all. So, it does look as though meditation and relaxation somehow help the body resist cancer. Sometimes, Simonton has discovered, patients have been able to reduce the size of their own cancerous tumors up to 50 percent after only a week's meditation.

Now, what does any of this have to do with PK? Well, to begin with, it proves that healing is a complicated psychological as well as biological process which even medical authorities do not fully understand. This naturally bears on the problem we have when trying to isolate a PK factor in any single case of "psychic" healing. It is now clear to us that a great many factors and variables—biological, physiological, psychophysiological, and psychological—come into play during the process of healing. In fact, so many variables complicate biological healing that it is nearly impossible to isolate what role PK plays, if any at all, in cases of spontaneous or abnormal healing. Simonton's patients might be using some sort of PK on themselves, but it would be impossible to prove it. And since this *is* impossible to prove, we really have little scientific right even to suggest it.

The work of Dr. Simonton also bears significantly on the results claimed by such miracle workers as Kathryn Kuhlman, Harry Edwards, and others. It is impossible to prove that they used any nonphysical force to help their patients recover. It could always be argued that they merely helped these people achieve a frame of mind which helped their bodies heal more efficiently. Certainly, the self-healing results of Dr. Simonton's patients are every bit as staggering as those claimed by psychic and faith healers.

To my mind, there is only one way that a healer can be scientifically tested to see if PK plays any role in his results. The patient must be treated without his even knowing it. This is not too much to expect since many healers claim the ability to heal over great distances. The phenomenon of "absent healing" is part and parcel of Spiritualist and Christian lore alike. If through absent healing a patient miraculously recovers, then some sort of action-at-a-distance has obviously come into play. And that, naturally, indicates a psychic process at work.

No one has yet tried the rather simple experiment I have in mind. One would need a healer, a doctor, an experimenter, and a group of patients all suffering from the same disease in the same stage of development. One patient would be chosen by the experimenter as the subject and would be given several absent healing treatments. The others would serve as controls. None of the subjects would know which one of them was chosen. This would be kept a secret between the experimenter and the healer. Even the doctor would remain blind. His role would be to judge which patients seem to be recovering most rapidly after a month's time. At this time he would rank the patients in order of improvement. (Of course, all the patients must be given exactly the same medical treatment during the time of the experiment.) If the target subject rates first or second on the doctor's ranking, then we can accept that the healer's action-at-a-distance *may have* helped him. However, the experiment would have to be run several times and always with the same results before we would be entitled to believe that some sort of PK healing has taken place. Since PK can work over distance, this test is an obvious one for some parapsychologist to carry out.

One experiment run along vaguely similar lines has been conducted by Joyce Goodrich, as part of her doctoral work at the Union Graduate School in Ohio. (Like many innovative schools, UGS does not have national accreditation and its Ph.D. program does not entail the same type of course work or examinations most universities require.) Miss Goodrich set up several teams consisting of a healer and one patient. Over the next several weeks, the healers tried to "merge" or "heal" their patients even though they were usually miles away from them. The patients kept diaries in which they recorded their experiences while they were separated from the healers. They registered their thoughts about the experiment and especially noted times when they felt that their healers were trying to contact them. Blind judges read over the diaries and designated the times when *they* felt the healers were actively trying to make contact with their patients. The results of the experiment were statistically significant.

Miss Goodrich's experiment was clever, but I am afraid that it will not serve as very good evidence for healing PK. Her test does not prove distant healing, since the results could have been due to ESP just as easily. Next experiment please!

I do, however, like the general design of the Goodrich experiment. At least the experiment was carried out in such a way as to demonstrate that some sort of psychic interaction between healer and subject was taking place. These types of tests are sorely needed in parapsychology, but only a few have been carried out so far.

Probably the best controlled, systematic, and original research into the phenomenon of healing was carried out in the 1960s by Dr. Bernard Grad. Dr. Grad has long been an associate professor in the psychiatry department of McGill University in Montreal and is an expert on experimental morphology. During his early career, he spent considerable time working with Dr. Wilhelm Reich, a rather unconventional psychiatrist who was trying to prove the existence of a life-force he called "orgone." Reich believed that orgone was a force which permeated both man and the universe and which was vital to his survival. Although Grad is hardly an out-and-out disciple of Reich's, his interest in psychic healing was sparked by the possibilities suggested by Reich's work. Most of Grad's work has been designed to explore the gifts of a single subject, Oskar Estebany, a retired Hungarian military officer who claims that he can heal by using the ancient art of the laying on of hands.

For one test, Grad asked Estebany to try his art on mice which had been fed an iodine-deficient diet. This deficiency causes goiters, and all the mice used in the study had developed them. The rodents were divided into three groups: an experimental group on which Estebany would work, and two control groups. In order to treat the goiter-afflicted mice, Estebany merely held the cages in which they were deposited (eight to ten animals per cage) but was never allowed to gentle the animals directly. Five 15-minute periods per week were scheduled. After twenty days of this procedure, one of Grad's lab workers, who seemed to have the same power as Estebany, continued the treatment for another twenty days. One of the control groups was left completely alone, while the other mice were administered heat treatments. All in all, seventy mice were used in the experiment.

The overall results of the experiment were consistent with Estebany's claims. The goiters on the target mice increased in size less quickly than those afflicting the control mice.

In order to replicate the experiment, Grad used another thirty-seven mice. However, Estebany did not even hold the target cages in this test. Instead, he held wads of paper and wool which were then deposited in the target cages. Untreated cuttings were placed in the cages housing the control mice. Once again, the goiters on the target mice increased in size more slowly than those afflicting the controls.

For his next test, Grad decided to determine the effects of psychic healing on wounds. Estebany was the only subject for the experiment and his task was to "heal" mice which had been surgically wounded. This all may sound much more gruesome than it really was. The "wounds" were made merely by removing patches of skin from the animals. Pieces of transparent plastic were placed over the wounds and the boundaries traced with a grease pencil. Estebany held the cages of several target mice, while the other animals served as the controls. The mice treated by Estebany healed quicker than the controls.

In order to replicate his findings, Grad utilized three hundred additional mice which he also divided into three groups. One set was treated by Estebany, one by selected, skeptical medical students, and one was left completely untreated. The cages were, in turn, placed in paper bags. Half of the time the bags were open and the "healers" placed their hands inside them and over the cages. On the other trials, the bags were held—cage and all—by the healers. The results of this test were similar to those of the earlier one. The mice treated by Estebany healed faster than the control mice, while the mice treated by the skeptical students healed more *slowly* than the controls. (This finding, though, only held true for the "open bag" series. The "closed bag" series yielded no significant effects, probably because the condition agitated the animals. They might have warded off any incoming PK influence through their heightened vigilance.)

It certainly looks as if, in this experiment, the skeptical students actually impeded the healing process by PK. That is, they used PK to inhibit the healing influences.

For his next large-scale project, Grad decided to focus attention on plants instead of animals. Barley seeds were chosen as the target material. They were planted in a series of plots which were then watered with a 1 percent sodium chloride solution to inhibit their growth. After several days of treatment, tap water was substituted. However, early in the experiment some of the beakers holding the saline solution were psychically treated by Estebany. (He merely held and concentrated on them.) Sure enough, plots watered with the treated solution gave a richer yield of plants than did those fed with the straight solutions. In subsequent tests, Grad found that the treated water helped plants grow taller.

These plant tests with Estebany actually served as pilot experiments for an even more enterprising experiment. For his final tour de force, the same experimental design was used, but now three very different subjects were drafted. One was the same lab worker who had shown promising healing powers during the original mice experiments; the other two participants were mental patients. One of the mental patients was a depressive neurotic, while the other suffered from psychotic depression. Grad believed that healing might be affected by mood, and expected the depressives to inhibit plant growth.

Each of the subjects held bottles containing the saline solution for thirty minutes. Sets of seeds were watered respectively with these solutions. The results were pretty much as Grad expected. The seeds treated with the water held by the lab assistant grew the most successfully. The seeds assigned to the psychotic grew the worst of the lot and considerably below the growth rate of control plants which had been watered with untreated solution. However, the neurotic depressive's plants grew a bit better than the controls, and this result baffled Grad until he realized that the woman's mood had been radically altered by the experiment. The patient's mood and demeanor improved after she first learned about the nature of the test, and she cheered up and was almost excited about it. Could it be, Grad thought, that this enthusiasm caused the patient to exert a beneficial PK effect on the solution she was holding?

Dr. Grad, though, does not speak in terms of PK or "psychic forces" when discussing his work. Drawing on his association with Wilhelm Reich, he is more prone to believe that paranormal healing is the product of some life force . . . a force which, I am sorry to say, Grad has never defined very well. Speaking at a public symposium sponsored by the American Society for Psychical Research and held on May 18, 1974, Grad urged science to consider once again existence of a universal life-force. He reminded his audience that such a concept had been propounded by such innovators as Mesmer, Hans Driesch, and Wilhelm Reich. He warned:

> Obviously, the question as to whether or not a life force exists can only be solved by further experimentation. Unfortunately this is easier said than done, for persons with a materialistic-mechanistic viewpoint find the idea of a life force unacceptable a priori and this creates difficulties for research even at the present time of greater

freedom. Mechanists, along with some vitalists, have repeatedly claimed that it is not possible to conduct experiments testing the existence of a life force. Reich and others have shown that this is not so . . .

Grad believes that his experiments do offer experimental evidence which supports the basic correctness of Mesmer's and Reich's theories. As he stated in his concluding remarks at the ASPR symposium:

> In our experiments with the laying on of hands, the simplest explanation would seem to be that there is in fact a life force emanating from the hands of people, probably more in some than in others . . . It would seem that if there is such energy, it is somehow very intimately associated with momoeostatic mechanisms; that is, it tends to operate so as to maintain the organism at its optimal level . . .

My own reactions to Dr. Grad's remarks are varied. On one hand, it would seem that he is postulating something akin to, but not quite the same as, PK. PK is usually thought of as a mental or biological force, not as an all-pervading cosmic energy existing in the universe. We usually think of it as a force unique to living organisms. I am therefore always uneasy when people start talking about life-forces, cosmic energies, and the like. These terms tell us very little and, as Grad realizes, it is often difficult to prove experimentally the existence of such forces. However, remember too that *psychokinesis* is merely a word, not an explanation. I would say that Grad's test demonstrated PK for one simple reason. I define PK as an interaction between man and a material object not mediated by physical contact or by any known energy. Now this definition does not in any way limit or define the nature of PK. It could be cosmic, biological, or anything else. We should also keep in mind that what we call "PK" may encompass many different types of interactions. Perhaps some PK-mediated effects are produced by a purely mental force ignited by the will; other forms of interaction might be caused by some sort of superbiological force such as "bioplasma"; and at other times, perhaps the activity of some sort of cosmic force comes into play. I'm only suggesting these as possibilities. But it seems to me rather arrogant and premature to assume automatically that all PK effects are due to the same process at work. There may be numerous types of ultraphysical forces which we control or have access to. If you study parapsychology long enough, you will realize that possibilities far outnumber hard facts.

Although Dr. Grad's work certainly demonstrates some sort of psychic healing effect, his research tells us rather little about the nature of the process. A more process-oriented research project into the realms of healing was the brainchild of Sister Justa Smith, of Rosary Hill College, Buffalo, New York. A biochemist by training, Sister Justa was exploring the nature of the enzyme trypsin when her attention was diverted into research on paranormal healing. She discovered that trypsin, which is produced by the pancreas in order to assist digestion, is damaged when given untraviolet radiation treament, but increases its activity rate when subjected to a magnetic field. It struck Sister Justa that psychic healing might be initiated when a healer somehow speeds up enzyme activity in the patient's body. Such an acceleration would help the body recover from organic damage.

Sister Justa soon procured the services of Oskar Estebany in order to test her theory. Four trypsin solutions were used. Estebany treated one similar to the way he had dealt with Grad's solutions. He merely held the flask containing the enzymes for a period of seventy-five minutes. A control bottle was given no treatment at all, while the other two bottles were treated by a magnetic field and with ultraviolet radiation respectively. After analyzing her results, Sister Justa discovered that the activity rate of the enzymes focused on by the healer matched the heightened activity rate of those treated with the magnetic field. Estebany also treated the enzymes damaged by the ultraviolet radiation, and their activity increased almost to a normal level. However he was not able to repeat his success when the experiment was replicated.

Another experiment designed by Sister Justa offers us even more tantalizing data about PK-induced healing. Nicotinamide-adenine dinucleotide (NAD) was used instead of trypsin for this test. NAD acts to remove hydrogen from carbohydrates. The rate of this reaction is carefully regulated in the body, but the process takes place quickly in a pure controlled solution. Sister Justa found that when her healers concentrated on the NAD, they retarded its reaction rate in this controlled solution. In other words, the healing force affected the NAD in such a way as to impede its reaction rate back to the level used most effectively within the organism.

This experiment exemplifies PK's vast complexities. As I said earlier, PK is different from any other known energy in one striking way. Physical energies can produce physical effects, but they cannot carry out intelligent or cognitive ones. Even though Justa Smith's healers had little knowledge about NAD's function in the body, *the PK process discovered its nature and probable use in the body before influencing it in the best interests of the organism.* So, either the healers used ESP unconsciously to gain this information, or the PK force itself is endowed with some sort of cognitive ability. One is reminded of the pioneering biologist, Hans Driesch, and his concept of the "entelechy," a term which he used to designate some semi-intelligent force in the body comparable to the soul which directs man's biological development. Of course, today, we know that man's development is governed by certain laws of genetics which were unknown in Driesch's day. But is Justa Smith's experiment offering us some experimental evidence for some force in the body akin to Driesch's entelechy? This is a provocative possibility, and a few biologically minded parapsychologists are beginning to wonder if some sort of intelligent psychic force might be a factor in guiding physical evolution.

We do know that PK and ESP work hand in hand, but we don't know if the subject first employs ESP and then projects PK when necessary, or whether the PK force itself is endowed with cognitive ability. If PK is some sort of life-force, it might well have a primitive form of intelligence or instinct. But then, too, we may be making a mistake in drawing any dichotomy whatsoever between ESP and PK. They might both be products of the same force which take on different attributes depending on the task at hand. One PK experimenter I know designed a test which could be converted from a PK task to a precognition (ESP) task without the subject knowing it. The subjects, especially one participant, scored well no matter which condition was used.

Graham and Anita Watkins, two former research associates at the Durham-based Institute for Parapsychology, have also explored the healing effects of PK. Mice were used as the principal targets. For their main study, pairs of the little rodents were first anesthetized and then placed side by side on a platform. The subjects were asked to focus their attention on the pair assigned to them and use PK to awaken one of them sooner than the other. For each series of trials several different pairs of mice were used one after another. Either the right-hand or left-hand mouse was randomly chosen as the target for the entire session of several attempts. (The Watkinses had found that their subjects could not achieve any results if they alternated their PK between the two sides of the platform in the course of the trials.) All in all, the Watkinses found that a few subjects, notably those who had been successful on more conventional PK tests, could successfully use their psychic abilities to help the target mice overcome the effects of the anesthesia. They also made two other discoveries. First, the PK seemed to be spatially located. As just mentioned, the PK could only affect one side of the platform at a time during an experiment just as though the PK effect were accumulating there and helping the mice. Second, the PK also lingered on in the experimental area. If pairs of mice were placed on the platform after the experiment was over, the mice left immobile on the target side would still awaken sooner than the control mice. This linger effect lasted for about thirty minutes. After that, the mice roused equally as often between the two sides.

Parapsychologists have designed other healing experiments which have offered a host of different findings. Healers seem able to affect hemoglobin counts in the blood, and there is some tentative evidence that they can even rebond water molecules. But, despite these interesting leads, I don't think that parapsychologists are ready to formulate a general theory which can account for how paranormal healing takes place. There does seem to be two general ways that PK can help the body heal, though. Either PK acts on the organism in such a way as to speed up its normal regenerative abilities, or the PK directly interacts with the organism and remolds organic tissue and restructures it until a healing is imminent.

I think there is good evidence for both these types of healing. Take Grad's experiments, for instance. The mice wounds treated by Estebany did not miraculously close up by themselves. They merely followed an apparently normal biological course of healing, but did so abnormally fast. Similarly, Sister Justa Smith's experiments demonstrate that PK can interact with organic matter on a biochemical level and influence the organism to function more expediently in its own best interest. However, there are some extraordinary cases of paranormal healing which indicate that some paranormal force can bypass the body's normal biological functions altogether. The PK might then work a more direct and spectacular effect directly on the body. No matter how much regenerative power the body houses, how can it generate new bone almost instantaneously, as apparently happened to de Rudder? On an even more speculative level, we might even suggest that the body is really a manifestation of some ultraphysical blueprint. (This would be similar to the Soviet concept of a bioplasmic body.) PK might act directly on this blueprint and, by modifying it, exert an empathic healing effect of the physical body itself. This theory is intriguing, but would be impossible to prove or even test experimentally.

PK can take numerous forms and can draw upon a variety of mechanisms. It might just as well draw upon different processes, depending on the specific task it is confronting. So, while we do know that PK can be used to heal, we don't know the hows, whys, or wherefores. But then . . . that seems to be an old refrain in parapsychology, doesn't it?

10

The Range of PK

PSYCHOKINESIS might just be the most versatile and powerful force in nature. Its range seems limitless. Just look at the effects it can produce. It can influnece the fall of rolling dice and levitate tables. It can interfere with the decay rate of a piece of radioactive material and, apparently, decompose physical matter and then reassemble it. It can heal biological tissue yet cause burns on the skin as well. It can start fires, but grant immunity from the flames at the same time. It can knock on wood or tear it apart. It can bend metal or cause rocks to fall from the sky. It can work invisibly or appear as a mist. It can function like a lever or take on the properties of a field. It can manifest as an energy yet appear as a biological plasma. I know of no other force in nature which has so many faces, guises, or manifestations. In the universe the only comparable phenomenon with this versatility is man's own imagination. Perhaps this is the reason we think of PK as a mental force. It seems guided by our thoughts and even unverbalized desires. PK might be capable of carrying out any task we want or think it can perform. It might not necessarily be only the physical force of our will, but the physical manifestation of our very imagination as well.

I doubt whether any parapsychologist would say that we know the entire range of PK. Even in the limited confines of the laboratory, experimenters have watched it affect a wide variety of substances, including wooden dice, fungus cultures, animal tissue, metal balls, plastic discs, drops of water, and so on. I doubt that there is anything which PK can't affect. It is highly likely that it can influence any level of matter, from large objects to subatomic processes. There is, for example, some evidence that PK can even offset the action of subatomic particles, the very fabric of the universe.

The first controlled experiments on micro-PK, as I call this range of phenomena, were carried out in the early 1960s. John Beloff, a psychologist at the University of Edinburgh, was the primary experimenter. In one of his tests a spinthariscope was used. This device contains radioactive source material. As particles decay and shoot off from the material, a count can be made of them as they strike a phosphorescent screen. For another experiment, he used a conventional Geiger counter. In both tests subjects tried to increase the rate of particles registering on the devices. Such an increase would indicate that they were speeding up the decay rate of the radioactive material by PK. None of the subjects, unfortunately, were able to succeed at the task.

On the other hand, research conducted in France during the 1960s fared better. Two researchers, Remy Chauvin and Jean-Pierre Genthon, used a Geiger counter to register subatomic emissions from a piece of uranium nitrate. Since a Geiger counter records radiation striking it by producing blips on its counter, each subject's task was to increase the number of these blips by concentrating on the uranium. If he could do so during a specified period of time designated by the experimenters, it would indicate that his mind was interacting with the uranium and speeding up its decay rate. Right after this task, the subject was asked to slow down the decay rate of the uranium nitrate, thus producing fewer blips on the counter. Seven subjects were used for the test, all children between the ages of eight and seventeen. Two of them were eminently successful at the test.

Revealing a more powerful force at work, PK can also make moving objects fall in certain willed positions. This finding, of course, prompted the famous Duke University dice-throwing project which followed on the heels of the ESP tests. The Duke PK project came about after a young gambler visited Rhine and claimed that he could "will" dice to fall on certain faces. So Rhine, always the keen experimentalist, rounded up some dice and, huddled together in a corner of the psychologist's laboratory, the two were soon rolling them. We don't know the exact results of this rather informal experiment, but we do know that Rhine was apparently impressed enough to begin active PK experimentation. Soon everyone at Duke got hooked on the dice-rolling craze. Cups were used to throw them, a rectangular rotating cage was invented to flip the dice from one end to the other, dice were thrown down baffled boards, and so on. Several lengthy studies were made on the PK effect solely on dice rolling.

These tests didn't really reveal much about PK or the PK subject until Betty Humphrey, a bright young helper at the Duke University Parapsychology Laboratory working at the direction of J. B. Rhine, made a significant discovery when she started examining all the results. All of the dice-rolling data were recorded on score sheets which were divided into several columns. Each column was divided into twenty-four segments, one each for each die (or dice) throw for a series of twenty-four trials. There might be, say, ten columns per sheet, which constituted the results for one entire experiment. Miss Humphrey found that by dividing the score sheet into four equal quarters and comparing the scores, the first quarter of the experiment yielded significantly more successful dice rollings than the last quarter. For example, if a subject were rolling dice for 3s, he might have ten successes in the first quarter, eight in the second, three in the third, and none in the fourth. Intrigued by her discovery, Miss Humphrey began reevaluating the results of several more PK tests and found that the same pattern was present there as well. The decline or quarter distribution (QD) effect had been occurring right under the Duke workers' noses, but only now had it been discovered.

Rhine had found this same pattern in his ESP tests. Subjects invariably did better at the beginning of the ESP experiment than at any other time during the session.

The next step in the Duke PK research was the development of "placement PK" tests. These experiments do not test whether PK can make dice land on a certain face, but rather test to see if the force can influence them to land in certain areas on a platform as they fall.

The first systematic examination of placement PK was made by W. E. Cox, a research associate at the Institute for Parapsychology in Durham. He has been one of parapsychology's most inventive "gadgeteers," and has a passion as well as a penchant for inventing PK-testing devices. His office sometimes looks more like a patent museum than a lab room, and he is always eager to share his little inventions with anyone who visits the institute.

One of Cox's first PK tests used a typewriter case placed upside down. A checker-board was drawn on the bottom and each square was numbered successively from 1 to 6 until each of them was numbered. Cox then threw twenty-four dice into the case while his subjects willed them to land on designated faces which matched the numbers on the squares. In other words, if the subject threw for 3s, he tried to make more than an average number of dice land on squares also numbered 3. Cox's subjects were able to succeed at the task.

For another experiment, Cox invented a three-tiered platform. Dice were placed on a chute leading to the top tier. When pushed off, they would bounce through the chute to the first tier, then fall down a corrugated runway to a second tier, and then fall onto the bottom platform. This platform was also checkerboarded into several squares, each marked either A or B. So, of course, the subject tried to make those dice which made it through the tiers to the bottom land on either the A or B squares more often than chance could account for. (The same number of dice should fall, on the average, on both sets of squares.) Of course, several of the dice would be trapped on the upper tiers.

Cox had a specific theory in mind when he designed this test. He believed that if several dice are thrown at the same time, only *some* would be significantly influenced by PK. But what about the other dice? These cubes might be negatively affected by the force (PK-missing). If that happened a cancellation effect would result. The scores of the positive PK-influenced dice would be offset by those of the PK-missing dice and the overall result would not be significant. For example, say you were throwing two dice on a checkerboard for those squares marked A. One die is positively PK-influenced and always lands on the A squares. But your other die always PK-misses over to the B squares. This is certainly significant when the results of each die is considered alone. But if the results of the experiment are pooled, the results from both dice will cancel each other out and will only show, numerically, a chance result.

Cox theorized that, by using a tiered platform, any negatively influenced dice would be trapped on the upper levels, and only positive influenced dice would make it to the bottom. These dice would have the highest likelihood of responding to the PK command. All in all, Cox released some twenty-four thousand dice, twenty-four at a time. Subjects did seem able to make them land in the designated squares on the platform more often than chance could account for. However, whether or not the results really confirmed Cox's theory is a moot point.

Cox's ingenuity is almost as versatile as PK itself. Inspired by his earlier successes he quickly ran back to his drawing board and soon came up with an even more original PK testing device. This contraption also tested for tiny PK influences on moving systems. The target was a spray of water. Cox used an ordinary bathroom spray which shot the water through a grid. The slits of the grid were, in turn, connected to two glass tubes. Ordinarily the tubes would fill at the same rate when the water was turned on and sprayed through the grid, but Cox wanted to see if PK could make one tube fill quicker than the other. If one tube did fill quicker, this would indicate that PK was deflecting water droplets into the tube of the subject's choice. As Cox predicted, his subjects were able to deflect the water drops into the target tube about 53½ percent of the time instead of 50 percent of the time. Over so many trials, this result is astronomically above chance expectation.

Working independently in Sweden, Haakon Forwald was also actively investigating placement PK during the 1950s. Forwald, like his American colleague, is quite an inventor, and has over five hundred patents to his name throughout the world. His attention turned to PK after he and some friends started table turning. He found the table motions so extraordinary that he contacted J. B. Rhine at Duke University, who convinced the Swedish inventor to focus his attention on the possibilities of placement-PK work. Since then Forwald has published a consistent stream of research reports on several different aspects of PK.

In his first test, Forwald used a platform which led to a tabletop via a runway. A series of dice were placed at the top of the platform and would, when pushed, fall down the runway, bounce about, and land on the table surface. The table was divided down the center, and Forwald tried to make the dice fall more often on the right (A) or left (B) side alternately. He discovered that he could do this successfully. In a replication of his test, he used dice of different weights by fashioning them from wood, paper, steel, aluminum, and so forth. The composition of the dice didn't seem to affect his PK performance, but he did discover an odd quirk about his newfound force. He was successful if he threw the dice willing them first to land on the A side of the table and then, for the next trial, on the B side. But he couldn't get any results if he first threw for the B side and *then* for the A side. Although Forwald thought this effect was due to his own psychological preference for the AB sequence, I am less sure. As he began his test, could his PK have actually become locked into place? If so, his will might not have been strong enough to reverse the PK's action when he changed the target sequence.

For a third test, Forwald also used cubes composed of different material. For each throw he used six dice, a set of three each made from different materials. As he threw the dice he willed his PK to affect only one set of them. For instance, if he used wood and steel cubes, he might will only the wooden ones to deflect to the target side of the table. Forwald was just as successful at this test as he had been on his previous ones. The engineer also once again verified that PK was not inhibited by the composition of the dice. You might expect that paper cubes would be easier to deflect than steel ones. But this principle, to which a physical force would adhere, didn't seem to burden Forwald's PK. His power worked equally as well on both materials.

After carrying out several more successful tests, Haakon Forwald traveled to Duke University in 1957 in order to replicate his work in the presence of independent witnesses. While at first he didn't seem able to perform well in his new surroundings, his PK eventually made a dramatic recovery and he ultimately succeeded in replicating his earlier success while being stringently controlled.

A very different approach to the study of micro-PK has been made by Raymond Bayless. Back in the 1950s Bayless theorized that some PK effects, notably raps, might often manifest below our sensory threshold. Although these effects might not be gross enough for us to see or hear, they might be strong enough to register on sensitive recording equipment. Bayless formulated this theory after working with Attila von Szalay, a psychic living in Los Angeles. While tape-recording conversations or leaving the tape running while he sat quietly with von Szalay, he discovered that extra voices were often found on the tapes when they were replayed. These voices were sometimes quite loud, commented directly on the conversation, or would even answer direct questions. On rarer occasions the voices would become audible to the naked ear. These findings indicated that some sort of PK activity was affecting the tapes or the microphone. Bayless came to believe that the von Szalay voices were physical voices that were acoustically produced almost imperceptibly in front of the microphone, and were not some sort of PK effect directed onto the tapes themselves. It was during these experiments that Bayless suggested that raps and other psychically produced sounds might also occur on a microlevel.

Bayless wasn't able to obtain evidence supporting his theory until 1975 when he discovered a young man named Wesley Frank, who could produce low-intensity raps while sitting at a table. Although the raps could only be heard audibly on rare occasions, they could be easily recorded on a sensitive cassette recorder. Bayless carried out a complete set of tests with Mr. Frank which he reported in the June 1976 issue of *New Horizons*, the official journal of both the New Horizons Research Foundation and the Toronto Society for Psychical Research.

In his report, Bayless chronicles several experiments with Frank in which raps were recorded. Usually he and Frank sat at a small table with a microphone between them. They sat in full light. (A Sony Panasonic RQ-2365 recorder was used.) Sometimes human voices were also recorded. However, the raps were Bayless's main focus of attention. Literally hundreds of them were recorded, from tiny pops to loud drummings. Based on his early work with Frank, Bayless came to several conclusions about the phenomenon: (1) The sounds made by the raps do not always match the materials on which they are produced. For instance, if the recorder is placed on wood the raps might sound metallic and vice versa. (2) The intensity of the raps may range considerably from clicks to poundings. (3) The raps can manifest randomly or can produce intelligent patterns and rhythms: (4) On rare occasions the raps will become audible to the ear. (5) Paranormal voices are sometimes recorded along with the raps. (6) If Mr. Frank leaves, the raps will cease. (7) Mr. Frank can increase the intensity of the raps by verbally coaxing them on.

After completing his work with Wesley Frank, Bayless discovered that he too could produce these raps, and he has continued on with his research, using himself as subject. As in his previous work, Bayless's raps are usually not audible to the ear but will be readily picked up on tape. (Bayless, however, has been able to produce tiny, clicklike raps which are clearly distinguishable to the human ear.) The raps that he has recorded sound like sudden pops or wooden knocks. As he continued on with his research, a new sound began appearing on the tapes. These sonications sound like sawing noises, as though something is rubbing the table. This phenomenon has now become Bayless's new focus of attention. If you recall, both the Philip circle and the Golighers reported that their séance table would produce sawing noises. So Bayless's new discovery does adhere to a pattern.

Influenced by Crawford's work with the Goligher circle, Bayless also believes that these tape-recorded raps and other noises are produced when some physical force, which emanates from the body, strikes or rubs against the table. He is now exploring ways to test this theory experimentally.

At about the same time Bayless was examining the phenomenon of low-intensity acoustical raps, another parapsychologist made a similar discovery. At the 1975 convention of the Parapsychological Association held on the campus of the University of California at Santa Barbara, Dr. J. Gaither Pratt and Dr. John Palmer reported on a poltergeist case they had investigated in the Midwest. Paranormal rappings were one of the poltergeist's key manifestations and Pratt tried to record them. He was in for quite a surprise when he replayed his tape. He found that extra raps, which he had not heard audibly, had been recorded clearly.

As well as affecting tapes and microphones, PK can also play havoc with photographic plates and film. Black and white photographic plates are covered by silver halide particles. Their chemical properties are altered when light reaches them and they turn either dark or light, thus creating images. Color film works along similar, but much more complex, lines. In order for someone to print a mental image onto a photographic plate, all he would have to do is use his PK to affect these particles. In chapter 4 I pointed out that Nina Kulagina has been known to "fog" film placed over target objects during her PK demonstrations. This would indicate that her PK interacted with the film, partially exposing it, while carrying out other tasks such as moving objects telekinetically. All through the history of psychical research there have been psychics who claim that they can willfully exert a PK influence on film.

"Psychic photography," as the phenomenon is called, is a fascinating study in its own right.

One of the most carefully controlled explorations into the realm of psychic photography was made by Hereward Carrington. The subject for his research was a young mechanic named Joseph Ruk, whom Carrington discovered in New York sometime during the 1940s. Ruk claimed that, by his will, he could impress streaks, foggings, and images onto photographic plates and Carrington was quick to put him to the test. According to his own claim, Ruk had discovered his psychic gift after becoming a Rosicrucian. Intense concentration was a practice he had been taught by the order, and it was while perfecting these exercises that he decided to see if he could affect photographic film. He was joined by a group of enthusiastic coexperimenters and together the group had produced odd light streams and other peculiar markings on film. However, at the time when he first met Carrington, he had not practiced psychic photography for many years.

Since Ruk felt that he could work better with photographic plates than film, Carrington first used twelve standard Eastman 4 x 5, No. 50 plates which he acquired from a commerical supply house in New York. An official of the firm numbered the plates, wrapped each in opaque black paper, sealed the paper with adhesive tape, and then numbered the packages on the outside. After all these controls had been prepared, the plates were tied together, placed in a box, and sent to Carrington. Carrington also allowed his coexperimenters to bring their own plates for use during the tests. These impromptu trials would offset any criticism that Ruk and the photographic supply house were in collusion. Ruk, of course, was not allowed to touch the plates at any time unless specifically requested to do so by Carrington. Sometimes the plates, still sealed in their paper wrappers, were tied to Ruk's head, but more often they were dangled eighteen inches or so in front of him. Pairs of plates were used at one time for some of the trials. Before being developed, the wrappings around the plates were examined once again by Carrington and by the supply house official who had prepared them.

Carrington discovered that Ruk was not exaggerating when he claimed that he could imprint shafts of light or other odd streaking effects onto photographic plates. But that wasn't all he could do. On rare occasions he could imprint the plates with outlines of objects chosen by the experimenters. Although Carrington reported few of these striking successes and never mentioned much about them in his published report, he showed some of these treasured plates to friends and colleagues toward the end of his life. One of these unpublished photographs shows a perfect imprint of a key.

In order to test the parameters of Ruk's abilities, Carrington carried out several experiments in which he shielded the plates from his subject by placing metal, plastic, cork, or other substances over them. Only glass disturbed the psychic's ability to expose the plates. Also, Carrington noted, Ruk's PK most often affected a specific corner of the plates instead of streaking the entire surface at random. In a further series of tests, Carrington placed two plates side and side and asked Ruk to affect only one of them. Ruk could selectively guide his PK to the correct target and never accidentally exposed or streaked the control plate.

Of course, Ruk's ability is not unique. Back in the 1910s, Professor T. Fukurai of the University of Tokyo experimented with several amateur psychics who could imprint Japanese characters, faces, and images of buildings directly onto photographic plates. Fukurai even discovered that some of his subjects could imprint figures on one specific plate placed within a stack of controls. Resistance to the notion of PK was so strong in Japan that, when he published his work, a scandal resulted that almost ruined his academic career.

The subject of "thoughtography," as the phenomenon became known, had a resurgence in the 1960s when Dr. Jule Eisenbud, a Denver-based psychoanalyst, began working with a Chicago bellhop named Ted Serios, who could impress psychic pictures onto Polaroid Land Camera self-processing film. Serios merely stared into the camera lens, sometimes through a black paper cylinder he called the "gismo," and snapped the shutter when he felt he had projected an image onto the film. Although critics suggested that Serios had a lens in the gismo, some of Eisenbud's experiments precluded fraud altogether.

For one test in 1965, Serios was asked to try his hand at a combined ESP-PK thoughtography experiment. Target subjects were written down on slips of paper, but kept from Serios's view or knowledge. He was then asked to imprint one of the hidden target subjects onto the Polaroid film. One slip turned out to have "staggerwing airplane" written on it. Serios produced a spidery-looking image which at first didn't seem to be an airplane. However, Serios and Eisenbud found photographs of some staggerwing planes in a book, *The American Heritage History of Flight*, two years later, and Serios's psychic snapshot matched part of the photographs. Sometime after the Eisenbud tests, Serios lost his abilities but now seems to be regaining them.

Dr. Eisenbud was able to study another case of thoughtography in 1968. This fascinating case first came to the psychoanalyst's attention when a young man, Richard Veilleux, wrote to him from Maine, claiming that his entire family were psychic photographers. The power, he explained, seemed to ebb and flow. Sometimes his family would go through a dry spell, while at other times they could produce a multitude of psychic photographs almost at will. The family consisted of his wife and himself, his brother Fred and his wife, and his parents. Apparently Fred and Richard were the main psychic photographers, but the whole family could produce them as well. The Veilleuxs, who are Spiritualistically inclined, first began practicing psychic photography after they received Ouija-board communications urging them to try. The family doesn't engage in any occult rituals, though, when they take their pictures. They merely point the camera at a wall, object, or family member, snap the shutter, and wait to see what comes out. Eisenbud soon realized that psychic photography was only one of the Veilleuxs' phenomena. They had also formed a home circle and were achieving some encouraging minor PK results.

Eisenbud journeyed to Waterville, Maine, in September 1968 to meet with the Veilleuxs personally. For their first demonstration the family took the researcher to a local cemetery, which had been the scene of some of their best results, and started working the Ouija board. Communications from an entity named William D. Gittings was the first order of the day. Gittings claimed that he had hung himself when only thirteen years old and had been buried in the cemetery. The communicator assured the Veilleuxs that he would help them procure a psychic photograph if they would take a snapshot of his tombstone. Eisenbud and the Veilleuxs had no difficulty finding a grave marked with a stone bearing Gittings' name. Eisenbud loaded up a 100 Polaroid camera he had brought along, and Fred, pointing it at the grave, started snapping pictures. The fifth photograph was oddly bleached and had a barlike mottling along its left border. The next shot was perfectly normal, and Eisenbud was duly impressed. However, most of the Veilleuxs' most surprising results have not been procured under test conditions. Nevertheless, some of their results are very provocative. As Eisenbud writes in the November 1975 issue of *Fate* magazine:

> That fall, November 1968, I received a phone call from William Cook, then with North American Rockwell in California and in charge of photogrammetry for the upcoming Apollo VIII moon shot, asking if I could induce Ted Serios to try something on the moon before Apollo got there. Since Ted for all intents and purposes was on the dark side of the moon at the time I put the matter to the Veilleux. Richard, whom I phoned, was anything but hopeful as target shots were not in the family repertoire. A couple of days later, however, I received in the mail from him three prints which looked like different blowups of one scene although each was taken separately. As fast as I could I had these attested to, copied, and shot out to Cook, to make sure they got to a review board before Apollo's pictures started coming in.
>
> Whether they are anything like the photos beamed back by Apollo VIII or resemble any other moon shot apparently will remain one of NASA's most closely guarded secrets. But Cook who says he got them shown around at NASA assured me that at least they were not copies from some book or magazine, as they showed the stereoscopic effects to be expected from a "live" scene.
>
> The Veilleux claimed Fred simply went outside his house on an overcast night and pointed the camera at the sky. No terrain in Maine, even along the shoreline, could provide a picture of this sort.

Although the Veilleuxs usually work alone and unobserved, some of their pictures are evidential in spite of the loose conditions under which they were taken. For example, the family produced a "rock painting" type of image on a snapshot taken on July 23, 1968. The Veilleuxs could not identify what the images represented at the time. To them, the picture was just another oddball psychic result which they filed away with their hundreds of other photographs. However, it did match pictures of Australian cave paintings which were eventually reproduced in Erich von Daniken's *Gods from Outer Space*. Yet this book was first published over a year *after* the Veilleuxs' photograph had been taken. After a painstaking inquiry, Eisenbud discovered that the original pictures, from which von Daniken's reproductions were probably taken, were in a Munich museum. It is very doubtful that the Veilleuxs were aware of the Munich museum's holdings. The psychic photograph most likely "precognized" the widely publicized von Daniken book. But there is another psychic twist to this unusual story as well. The Veilleux picture was taken on the very day that Eisenbud was having difficulties with the publishers of his book on Ted Serios and psychic photography who were also the eventual publishers of the Daniken book. This entire sequence of events appears to me more than coincidental. It looks more like the result of a grand network of psychic interactions among Eisenbud, the publishers, and the Veilleuxs.

The Veilleuxs visited Eisenbud in Denver in July 1969. It was during this trip that the psychoanalyst made another weird discovery: many of the pictures and faces produced by the family, although unrecognized by them, matched photographs printed in a rare book, *The Album of Gunfighters*, which they discovered in the Western History Department of the Denver Public Library. However, the Veilleux photographs were not exact copies or replicas. Many details were either changed or distorted in the psychic photos.

Eisenbud also took the Veilleuxs to an office at the University of Colorado Medical Center. The staff member who formerly occupied the office had died a few days before, and Eisenbud hoped that the room might act as a trigger for the Veilleuxs' thoughtographic ability. The family was able to photograph a white cloudy formation in the office, but little more. But, as Eisenbud hints, these odd clouding effects ". . . could be embryonic versions of what might have become full representations of a face or figure."

In conclusion, the Veilleux photographs are not as evidential as the Ruk or Serios productions. Most of their best results are made when they are working uncontrolled and the family has not been able to perform well when visited by investigators. The fact that so many of their snapshots seem copied or linked to existing photographs is a bit suspicious as well. But, what are we to make of cases such as the von Daniken photograph, psychically produced a year before his book ever appeared? And on the same day that Eisenbud was arguing with the book's eventual publisher over his own book on psychic photography?

The Range of PK

If PK can alter the chemical properties of photographic film, it might also be able to manipulate other sorts of image-producing devices as well. If so, PK can explain an even more unusual phenomenon . . . a phenomenon few parapsychologists are even aware of.

Over the last few years, a few startled people have been shocked to find odd images somehow burned onto their TV screens! Vincent Gaddis, a well-known writer on Fortean and psychic topics, has collected at least two well-documented cases of this odd phenomenon which he reported in the May 1975 issue of *Probe* magazine.

The first case was originally reported from South Carolina. There, in the little town of Geoffrey, a poltergeist plagued a family a few years ago. For several days the family could only look on helplessly as glass objects in the house shattered before their eyes. At the height of the poltergeistery an apparitional figure was seen imprinted on their television screen. It lasted for several days before fading out.

An even more astounding case was reported by the Travis family of Blue Point, New York. Their three children were up early one morning to watch TV when they reported to their mother that a face was imprinted on the screen, obscuring the program being broadcast. Mrs. Travis didn't know exactly what to make of this rather odd story. But, as she approached the set she stopped dead in her tracks. . . . There, indeed, was a human face apparently "burned" into the screen. The regularly scheduled program could be seen behind the figure on the screen as well. The female face, silhouetted in profile, was superimposed right over the regular telecast. The face remained even after the set was turned off.

News of the Travis's haunted TV set spread quickly over Blue Point, and soon TV repairmen, technicians, newsmen, and photographers were invading the home to see the face for themselves. The onlookers recognized the phantom face as that of singer Francey Lane, whom the family had watched on a program the day before. The picture finally faded away after remaining on the screen for fifty-one hours, during which time it was photographed several times.

There are other reports on record of similar TV high jinx, but I think these two examples are fairly typical of the phenomenon. In some cases people report that the phantoms appearing on their sets resemble deceased friends and relatives. In every case, though, the pictures appear like photographic images. They don't move, alter position, or anything else. They seem riveted into position as though impressed directly on the screen and usually fade away after a few hours or days.

I don't think that parapsychologists can afford to laugh off these cases. Nor do I feel that these incidents are as totally inexplicable as the newspapers and psychic press try to make them sound. During the Travis investigations, TV experts argued that the image was probably produced when freak explosions of electrons, which occur during television broadcasts, literally burned into the phosphorescent coating over the picture tube. In other words, they believed that the image was an anomalous, but normal, physical oddity. However, this explanation cannot account for all cases of TV ghosts, nor even why it was only a day after Francey Lane's TV appearance that her picture showed up on the screen. It seems logical to assume that PK can manipulate the coating on TV tubes. The evidence we have for the existence of psychic photography certainly points in that direction. Perhaps on rare occasions TV tubes can be used instead of photographic plates to record images projected from our minds. I don't think this is an outlandish possibility at all.

As you can see, PK can probably affect any and all objects in the known universe. I don't know anything that is exempt.

Even plants are not immune to our PK powers. Dr. Grad's experiments tend to prove that PK can accelerate or inhibit plant growth. So, we might ask, to what extent can PK accelerate plant growth? The answer to this puzzle has not been discovered in the laboratory. But there are a few spontaneous examples of PK on plant growth or development which indicate that PK can exert an almost unbelievable force on them. One such report comes from Mrs. Amarya Fodor, the wife of the famous psychoanalyst and psychic investigator, Nandor Fodor.

Fodor died on May 17, 1964. Mrs. Fodor's apartment was plagued by telekinetic displays shortly after his death, and she naturally thought that these phenomena were signs from her dead husband. It is just as likely, though, that Mrs. Fodor was producing the PK herself. It was during this outbreak that her terrace flowers became the focal point of some rather bizarre phenomena. As Mrs. Fodor explains:

> On our terrace there are flowers. The climbing roses usually last four days, then lose their petals and new buds form. But (after my husband's death) the roses, about 150 of them, bloomed at once and lasted for several weeks.
> For that period of time no rose dropped a petal. Then one day they all withered together. I cut them off and as I did so I asked for just one rose. I got it one week later—just one rose, which also lasted several weeks.

A similar case has been reported by the noted novelist, Taylor Caldwell, whose husband, Marcus Reback, died in April 1970. Writing in the October 1972 issue of the *Ladies' Home Journal*, Miss Caldwell claimed that a shrub of resurrection lilies, which had not bloomed for twenty-one years, suddenly blossomed forth radiantly the day of her husband's funeral. There seemed to be a deeply personal meaning to the blooming. Before his death, Reback had joked about the shrub. "You can't prove the resurrection by these lilies!" he quipped. Indeed, someone was using PK that day to prove the resurrection!

In both of these cases, it is likely that the distressed widows used their own PK to cause the abnormal blooming of the plants. When someone is sick, we send him or her flowers. They are a symbol of consolation. Could Mrs. Fodor and Miss Caldwell have used PK to give themselves the consolation they needed so badly?

Since PK can accelerate plant growth, I see no reason why it cannot also cause abnormal blooming or flower preservation. There is even some experimental data which indicate that PK can offset the decay of dead tissue or can preserve living matter longer than normal. These studies might help us understand why Mrs. Fodor's flowers survived so long. This research is not very well known and was chiefly the work of two Bordeaux physicians, Dr. L. Clarac and Dr. B. Llaguet, who published their findings in 1912. The two scientists worked with a single unnamed subject they called Mme. X. in their report. Like many pioneering psychical investigators, these two physicians did not talk in terms of a psychic force but, like Grad, more in terms of a mysterious "human fluid" or "life-force" housed in the body. Mme. X. was a

Bordeaux housewife who discovered her ability when she noticed that plants and little animals that died in her house did not decompose. In order to test her abilities experimentally, Clarac and Llaguet invited Mme. X. to their laboratory where she could be carefully observed. Her hands were first checked for chemicals and then various materials were placed in front of her on a table. Mme. X. would either place her hands directly on them for about twenty minutes or, less often, over or away from them. Then the materials were locked away and carefully guarded and watched by the experimenters.

Using this procedure, Mme. X. was able to preserve permanently the color of plucked snapdragons. Control flowers, untouched by the subject, desiccated rapidly. Wine treated by Mme. X. was not acidified after eleven days, while untreated wine acidified in seventy-two hours. Dead oysters were mummified and did not putrefy at all. Other oysters, already in the process of decay, were given to Mme. X., who was able to stop the decay process. Dead fish held by the subject did not decompose even after several months. Mme. X. could even liquify coagulated blood!

It is hoped modern experimenters will take a cue from the work of Drs. Clarac and Llaguet. It wouldn't be hard to demonstrate experimentally whether or not a psychic can preserve a flower or prevent it from desiccating for an abnormally long period of time. All one need do is have the subject concentrate on one flower, and then compare its rate of decomposition to untreated control flowers. (Remember, though, that all the flowers must be taken from the same plant. Furthermore, they must be flowers which blossomed on the same day.) Some pilot research along these lines has been carried out at the UCLA Neuropsychiatric Institute with promising results. Researchers at the institute have found a few subjects who can delay or accelerate the decomposition rate of a leaf or flower. However, this research is still unpublished.

Mme. X.'s "life-force," which caused such odd biological results, is probably the same force which Bernard Grad monitored during his tests with Estebany. No normal force can account for these mummifications and preservations. Instead, I believe that Mme. X. could use her PK to alter the biological composition of organic matter or permanently restructure it. Preserving the color or texture of dead tissue may not be as unusual a phenomenon as you might think. After all, there are quite normal ways of processing certain types of tissue in order to preserve it. Amateur insect collectors, for example, will tell you that dragonflies, once killed and mounted, will lose their color and their abdomens will shrivel and dry up. In order to offset the process which occurs in a matter of hours, collectors take the insects right after they have been killed, place them in an oven, and heat them at a high temperature. After several minutes of heat treatment, their color and form will be perfectly and infinitely preserved. They will not fade or shrivel. Freezing is another normal method of preserving tissue. PK may be able to produce the same biochemical effect as heating or freezing in order to preserve organic material.

This chapter has surveyed a considerable array of PK effects: from placement tests to subatomic PK; from tape-recorded raps to psychic photography; from PK on plant growth to PK-induced mummification. The inclusion of this wide range of phenomena has not been by accident or happen-chance. I have included them to illustrate the incredible versatility of PK. In one respect, PK actually seems to be some sort of "life-force." It often reveals a type of adaptability which only a living creature possesses. It adapts to its surroundings, alters its behavior at will, and reacts differently to each task it confronts. Of course, you could say, aren't *we* the ones who direct the PK? Isn't it a force coming from our minds and bodies? Yes, this is true. But remember, PK can carry out acts which show knowledge most of us do not possess. How many of us know what biochemical changes affect living tissue after death? Or what processes lie behind the decay of a radioactive element? The PK force apparently does, and can offset or accelerate these processes. PK may be like a genie in a magic lamp. It carries out the desires and wishes we are too limited or ignorant to execute ourselves. PK is not merely an energy, it is something infinitely more complex.

I began this chapter by posing a question: What is the range of PK? I am afraid that this question will have to remain unanswered. So far we have found no parameters or substances which can consistently inhibit its power. Nor have we found any object too small or too large to withstand its influence. But as we study this sometimes elusive and invisible force, a few things do become clear. PK is not some sort of power which manifests merely according to our will and motivation. It is probably affecting our whole world every minute of every day—manipulating it, interfering with it, possibly even helping it along. Likewise, we probably use PK to affect each other in our daily lifes although we are unaware of it. This is one of PK's most remarkable attributes. It is such a horrendous force in the world, yet we conveniently have been able to overlook its power for hundreds of years.

11

PK Theories: Mind Energy? Physical Energy? Or Cosmic Energy?

BECAUSE OF ITS almost unbelievable complexity, I don't think anyone working in parapsychology today could possibly offer a comprehensive theory that could explain how PK operates. Such a theory would have to account for all its different manifestations as well as explain the mechanics it uses to carry them out. PK is too big a mystery to be explained by any neat, trim, and facile theory. When and if we do fully understand PK, it will probably take hundreds of pages just to outline the physics behind its operation. Nonetheless, we are beginning to understand at least a few things about the nature of PK. These facts will, in turn, help guide us as we speculate a bit about its function in the world.

The first question we have to ask about PK is a crucial one. Is it really an energy or force at all? There are two ways of looking at this issue. Either PK uses or *is* some sort of material energy or biological force generated by the organism which mediates between mind and matter, or PK manifestations are the product of a *direct* interaction between mind and matter. If the latter turns out to be the case, we can dump such concepts as bioplasma, psychic fluids, psi energy, and the like. These concepts would have about as much use to us as the theory of an all-pervading physical ether had for the physicists of yesteryear. However, it seems unlikely to me that our minds can directly interact with matter without having to rely on some mediary force. The research of such investigators as Crawford, Watkins, Roll, and others indicates that PK is a measurable force, albeit one which adheres to laws distressingly different from any which govern physical forces and energies. When Kulagina moves an object across a table, I don't believe that her mind is directly interacting with the object on some nonphysical psychic level. She is probably ejecting some physical force from her mind and body which is moving it. This model would certainly fit in more neatly with the ontology which guides Western science and thinking.

However, a few contemporary parapsychologists are beginning to wonder if there really is such a thing as a "psychic energy" at all. They argue that PK can be explained more easily if we accept the idea that the mind can directly affect matter. We wouldn't have to worry, for instance, why PK doesn't conform to the laws of physics since it really isn't a force at all. Dr. John Beloff believes that this might be the most fruitful approach to the study of PK. In his 1975 presidential address to the Society for Psychical Research, Dr. Beloff pointed out that physical science is guided by certain assumptions, principal among these being that the world and all that transpires in it must be explainable by "impersonal forces." But, as he also points out, PK may represent a complicating factor, namely that

> ... under certain conditions, still to be established, an idea or intention in the mind can automatically constrain a physical system to act in such a way as to express the idea of intention. That this is, in the last resort, an ultimate fact about the world; there is no further 'bridging mechanism' to be invoked to make this fact intelligible.

As for the concept of a psychic energy? Beloff has a rather disdainful attitude about its existence. As he suggests,

> ... some theories like to explain psychic healing as due to a flow of "psychic energy" from the healer to the patient, a view, incidentally, that is encouraged by many healers themselves. Yet, unless there were independent evidence for the existence of such a psychic energy—and, despite the efforts of those calling themselves psychoenergeticists, no such evidence exists—such an assumption strikes me as grossly unparsimonious.

Actually, Dr. Beloff is not saying anything truly novel. In fact, his views accord fairly well with the world view outlined in Mahayana Buddhist thought. Buddhist thought underwent a considerable schism in India when the philosopher Nagarjuna began advancing his *Madhyamika* doctrine ("the doctrine of the middle way") around the second century A.D. Nagarjuna was reacting against the prevalent *Abhidharma* thought which taught that the objective world, its constituents, and the individual should be regarded as real entities for the sake of expediency (that is, investigating the world and its realities) even though they have no underlying substance. Nagarjuna taught that man's basic error is seeing or positing the existence of an objective world as *apart* from his own subjective world. In other words, all physical phenomena and attributes of our world are only aspects of our own minds. There is nothing "other than self," and our belief in the existence of an outside world is merely an error of categorization which we have fallen into.

This concept, which Nagarjuna termed *prapanca* (false imagining) underlies man's whole misery. He cannot understand the world because he distinguishes between himself and the world in thought and language. This, in turn, leads to the basic tenet of Madhyamika thought, *Pratitya sumatpada*. This doctrine, grossly simplified, means that everything is interdependent and interrelated in the Universe. When we overcome our nasty habit of categorical reasoning, we reach nirvana, or liberation from worldly desires. This is the "Void" (*sunyata*) about which Buddhist philosophy speaks so often, but which is a doctrine very much misunderstood by many Western students. It does not mean "oblivion" and "nothingness" as is often suggested. It means the surrender of our individual views and discriminations.

Students of Western mysticism will immediately recognize the parallel between the concept of the Void and the mystical experience described in Christian thought. Catholic saints and other Christian aesthetics talk about entering into a nontemporal, blissful "oneness" with all things. They speak of merging with all nature and life during which the basic truth behind the universe is revealed to them. This experience is little different from the Buddhist concept of entering the Void.

Buddhist philosophy was revised further in the fourth or fifth centuries A.D. by Maitreya and Vasubandhu with their *Yogaçara* school of thought which argued that consciousness is the basis upon which the phenomenological world generates into existence. But, it also teaches, consciousness really does not exist. That is, it does not exist separate from the world . . . both came into being together.

I think that these concepts bear significantly on Dr. Beloff's theory about PK. If the mind (subject) and matter (object) are really one and the same, mind should be able to manipulate matter directly because they are dependent on one another. We usually do not exhibit PK because the very way we think about the world limits the mind's ability. The way we experience reality prohibits PK from occurring. But this is a mental censor, not a physical one. A person who could enter into a state of sunyata, who at that time becomes free from mind-matter discrimination, might easily be able to manipulate matter directly. His reasoning would no longer prohibit the possibility. *Other* people would see the results as an act of PK. Felicia Parise once told me something about her PK which is very consistent with Buddhist thought. She described to me how she "merged" with the objects she was moving and that all sensory awareness became distorted and numbed. Could this be a result of her entering a vastly altered reality-concept in which PK becomes possible to her?

Despite the fact that this Buddhistic theory may work philosophically, I don't think it works practically for several reasons. If Beloff's theory is correct, many facts about PK and PK subject would make no sense. Take Palladino, Nina Kulagina, and Felicia Parise as examples. They had to strain, stress, and force in order to ignite their PK into activity. Why? If PK is a result of a direct mind-matter interface, why did these psychics have to go through such a physiological ordeal to produce the PK? That is, unless they were liberating "something" from their bodies? Why does PK have physical properties such as a linger effect? Or measurable perimeters of influence such as Graham Watkins found while working with Miss Parise? Why do temperatures fluctuate when PK goes into operation? And why are only a few people gifted with PK? What makes their minds any different from yours or mine? How too could Beloff's views explain materialization phenomena? His views would be tantamount to a belief in the spontaneous generation of life, a theory few biologists would care to entertain. No, we are not dealing with a direct mind-matter interaction when we study PK. We are dealing with some sort of semiphysical force which can act on matter, interact with physical energies (such as electricity), and mold itself into different forms. Now, just what is the basic purpose this force serves in nature?

The theory that PK is a force which is usually used within the organism to help regulate it is one of the oldest ideas about its primal nature. This concept is still entertained today by many parapsychologists. For instance, Hereward Carrington believed that PK was a vital force whose main function was to regulate the internal functioning of the cells within the body. It was, as it were, the basic force of life.

J. B. Rhine holds a related view about PK. He maintains the philosophical position that man is comprised of a nonphysical mind which somehow controls a physical body. But how can it do this? Rhine suggests that PK might be the mediary by which mind, brain, and body cofunction. PK is the energy that converts thought into action.

A very similar theory about the nature of PK has been offered by J. C. Eccles in his book, *The Neurophysiological Basis of Mind*. Eccles, like many thinkers, is fascinated by the puzzle the mind-brain relationship poses for us. Are mental events real occurrences? he asks. To answer his own question, he goes as far as to argue that "mental events" could be as valid as physical events. Such acts as thinking or willing are mental events, but are physical events as well since they initiate neuronal activity in the brain. To explain this phenomena, Eccles argues that there must be some sort of direct interaction between a mental activity and brain activity. Drawing upon the evidence from laboratory PK tests which were then being reported from the Duke University Parapsychology Laboratory, he argued that PK was the elusive force which mediated between the mind and the brain, thus creating a two-way channel between them.

While all these ideas are clever, they don't really help us understand PK. Nor do I believe that they are fundamentally correct. If PK links mind and brain, what happens to the brain when PK is ejected from the body? We might expect considerable neurological disruption to occur. Could this be why there might be a link between poltergeist attacks and epilepsy? Roll's data might be used in support of the Rhine-Eccles theory, but subjects engaging in the usual run-of-the-mill laboratory PK experiments don't seem to exhibit any neurological dysfunction. I have yet to see any successful PK subject thrown into an aberrant brain state, such as suffering an epileptiform seizure or exhibiting the dissociation caused by an organic brain syndrome, while being tested. Maybe this might be too overt a response to expect. But, if PK works between the brain and the mind, we should expect to find some sort of aberrant brain activity in *any* subject producing a PK phenomenon. As of now, there is no evidence that this ever occurs.

On the other hand though, Rhine's and Eccles' views do make the idea of PK somewhat understandable. They answer one annoying question that has plagued parapsychologists for years: what does the PK force do when it is not operating in the physical world? Does it merely "sit around" like potential energy, waiting to be activated? Or what? Rhine and Eccles attribute a basic role in the life process to PK. They also explain why PK occurs rather rarely. (Of course, PK might be occurring all the time even though we don't realize it.) Since PK is a force used within the body, we wouldn't expect it to manifest into the external world very readily. Any such activity would be clearly abnormal both for PK and for us. This might explain why physical mediums were plagued by drastic physical repercussions while they worked their wonders. They were severely disrupting the body's basic neurological functionings. Unfortunately, most poltergeist phenomena mitigate against the Rhine-Eccles view. Poltergeist agents usually seem to be as physically normal as can be—even while rocks are tossing about, fires are starting, and tables are floating around!

Another line of evidence which might support the Rhine-Eccles concept comes to us from an-psi research (psi experiments that use animal subjects). If it can be shown that animals possess PK powers, this fact would indicate that PK is a force distributed throughout the entire animal kingdom. This, in turn, would indicate that PK is a force normal to animal life, that it is a force inherently linked to the life process, and that it has an important role in it. An-psi experiments are notoriously hard to evaluate, though. It is often hard to tell whether the animals used PK in a particular test or whether the experimenter used his own PK to influence the results to make his experiment a success.

Dr. Helmut Schmidt pioneered the development of PK tests which use animal subjects while he was working at the Institute for Parapsychology in Durham. He designed one test which tried to circumvent, to his mind at least, the experimenter's influence over the results of his own experiment. To begin with, Schmidt used a binary random number generator (RNG) which oscillates back and forth between two positions in a random sequence during any set period of time. These positions are marked as +1 or −1. (The machine bounces between the two positions but stops when it registers the arrival of a decaying particle from a piece of strontium 90. The PK task is to regulate the time of arrival of the electrons from the radioactive source to make the machine generate either more +1 or −1 positions than chance could account for.) Schmidt then hooked up the RNG to a 200-watt lamp. Every time the RNG stopped in the +1 position, the lamp would light up. When a −1 position was generated, the lamp would switch off. Schmidt placed the lamp in a cold shack where it served as the room's only source of heat. The RNG, which was connected to the lamp, was placed in a house some sixty feet away. At the same time, another light was placed outside the shack. Everytime the shack light lit up, this light went out and vice versa. Schmidt elected his one-year-old pet cat to be the PK agent for his experiment and placed it alone in the shack. He theorized that the cat, if it had PK ability, would use it to make the lamp inside the shack stay on more often than 50 percent of the time in order to stay warm. The cat could only do this by exerting a PK influence on the RNG. Each test lasted thirty minutes and several sessions were run on consecutive afternoons. Schmidt discovered that the lamp did stay on more than the expected 50 percent of the time for the first five sessions. After that, the lamp flickered on and off at a normal rate. Schmidt suggested that the cat stopped using PK after the first five sessions when it finally became annoyed at the flashing lamp. (He found that the cat gradually grew to dislike the lamp, while during the first tests it usually settled down next to it for warmth.)

It is impossible, though, to rule out the possibility that Schmidt was the real PK agent in this test. There is no reason why he could not have used his own PK to affect the generator. The decline in scoring may not have been due to his cat's eventual dislike for the lamp, but could have been due to his own PK which, keeping the QD in mind, would be expected to decline over a space of time. Later, Schmidt conducted animal experiments which were run automatically while he wasn't even in attendance to offset this possibility. But he based the design for this experiment on two faulty assumptions: (1) that PK cannot occur over distance and (2) that the experimenter cannot project a PK influence when he sets up his test, and which can manifest even after he has left. We know that PK can work over distance. This fact throws Schmidt's first assumption into question. The existence of a PK linger effect indicates that PK can occur even in the physical absence of the agent. This fact counters Schmidt's second premise.

Although there is no firm evidence that we use PK to regulate the body and mind-brain interaction, it is clear that PK does at least emanate from us. So the next question we have to ponder would be: What is the basic nature of this force? There are three ways to answer this question. PK could be (1) a mental or psychic energy, (2) a biological plasma, or (3) a mental agency which manipulates normal forces and energies in the world, redirects them, and makes them act in certain prescribed ways according to the will of the subject. What is even more complicating is that a good case could be made for all three of these theories.

There can be little doubt that PK does have many characteristics of an energy. It is usually invisible, causes overt effects on material objects, and so forth. In other words, it carries out work. W. G. Roll has also found evidence in some of his poltergeist cases that PK acts like an energy. In these cases, objects displaced by the poltergeist often moved in the same direction or followed similar trajectories, while objects closer to the agent moved more often than those which were farther away from him. This all indicates that poltergeistic PK is an energy directed out from the agent which takes on the properties of a field and whose power declines with distance. Roll and his associate, Dr. John Artley, discovered that the movements of poltergeist-affected objects seem to be guided by some form of exponential decay. (If an energy such as light travels through a medium such as water, it converts to heat in the process and gradually its strength is reduced until the force peters out. The calculation which predicts the rate of the process is called exponential decay.) Roll and Artley found that most objects moved by the poltergeist are rather close to the agent. In some cases the number of objects moved systematically decreased as their distances increased from him. This is just what would be expected from an exponential decay function. As Roll has stated:

> If we are dealing with an exponential decay function, then in one respect there would be method in the poltergeist madness. Poltergeist distrubances would then conform to an old and established rule: The principle of conservation of energy. It is easy to see why this is so. In poltergeist disturbances kinetic energy is produced. If the

energetic process is similar to known types, then the creation of kinetic energy should result from the expenditure of some other form of energy and the number of such energy conversions should lessen with increased distance from the source. In other words, we should expect our data to follow a curve such as the exponential decay function, rather than the inverse function which describes the dispersal of energy in empty space and not its conversion to some other form of energy.

So you see, PK might conform to a few basic laws which also govern known physical energies.

Felicia Parise's PK also seemed to be guided by some sort of energy field. Her PK could only affect a limited spatial area, and Graham Watkins could even mark off its boundaries by exploring the PK's sphere of influence with a compass. Linger effects also indicate some sort of energy at work. It looks as though PK dissipates gradually once its power source is cut off, just as any known energy would. So it does appear that on certain occasions PK can function like a physical field.

Not all parapsychologists, however, agree that linger effects are caused by an energy-dissipation process. Dr. Rex Stanford, a young researcher who until recently was an associate professor of psychology at St. John's University in Jamaica, New York, has argued that the linger effect is actually a psychological phenomenon. Stanford came to this conclusion when he discovered an odd aspect of PK that he calls the "release of effort" phenomenon, a principle he uncovered while testing to see if his subjects could use PK to offset a random number generator. To his surprise, he found that sometimes the generator departed from randomness more noticeably after the subject had stopped trying to influence it and thought that the test was over. This phenomenon indicated to Stanford that PK works better on an unconscious level. Willful motivation initiates the PK process, but the PK itself functions better once the subject's mind is taken off the experiment altogether. Linger effects would, according to this theory, be a "release of effort" phenomenon as well.

One can easily argue against Stanford's position though. He is really only offering us a chicken-egg paradox. Are linger effects really release of effort manifestations, or are release of effort manifestations really dissipation effects? There would seem to be no way of resolving this issue. However, Graham Watkins did make one discovery which throws crucial light on this puzzle. He found that the linger effect uncovered in his tests with anesthetized mice lasted about half an hour. In this experiment, several different subjects were used. He also found that Felicia Parise's linger effect also lasted for about thirty minutes. Stanford's theory simply cannot account for this consistency. How could it be that many different subjects all seem to show a specific thirty-minute release of effort phenomenon? We would expect to find that the duration of a release of effort manifestation would vary considerably from one subject to another. But this just isn't the case. Instead it looks as if the same physical process occurs no matter who is projecting the PK. This indicates that the thirty-minute residual PK activity is due to a function of the PK force itself, and is not psychologically mediated. And this indicates some sort of energy at play.

PK researchers have also amassed considerable evidence that PK is a biological force as well as an energy. It can interact with living matter and can appear as a mist, plasma, or as a mock tissuelike structure. Furthermore, PK seems linked more to the body of the agent than to his mind. The type of physiological ordeals many mediums went through speaks for itself. However, there is even stronger evidence that PK is some sort of biological plasma. Once again, though, we must look back into parapsychology's rich history for this evidence.

Franek Kluski, a Polish writer and poet, was born in 1877, but it wasn't until 1918 that he attended a séance conducted by the famous Polish medium, Jean Guzik, who was the talk of Europe. Guzik could produce mists, pillars of light, and materializations to order. Kluski witnessed all of these manifestations and, experimenting with some frineds after the séance was over, discovered that he could produce similar phenomena himself.

The best-controlled experiments ever run with Kluski were conducted by Gustave Geley, Count de Gramant, and Charles Richet in 1920 at the Paris-based Institute Metapsychique Internationale. Camille Flammarion, René Sudre, and other notable figures in French psychical research attended some of the sittings as well. Kluski's most impressive phenomena were the production of lights, the materialization of arms and other body parts, and the appearance of luminous forms in the séance room. Some of these phantom limbs took on the exact characteristics of living tissue.

Since the séances were held in darkness, the experimenters developed a foolproof way to test these phantom forms and hands. They brought a bowl of hot paraffin into the séance room and, once the sitting was in progress, asked the entities manifesting through Kluski to dip their materialized limbs into the paraffin and then into a bath of water to cool it. A paraffin glove would be produced which could be examined by the experimenters after the séance was over. A typical séance with Kluski was run something like this: The medium would sit in a chair and would be held by two experimenters. Bowls of paraffin and water would be placed at the opposite side of the room. The lights would be turned out and soon telekinesis would occur: lights would dart about the room, raps would resound, and so forth. Soon splashing water would be heard, and the séance would come to an end or be momentarily discontinued. The gloves would usually be found deposited in areas of the séance room beyond Kluski's reach. Obviously some physical structure resembling a hand had dipped into the paraffin to create the glove.

These gloves had several remarkable characteristics. First of all, their wrist openings were usually so small that no person could have humanly withdrawn a physical hand from them. Whatever created the gloves must have disintegrated within them. Second, the gloves were so thin that, to this day, no one has ever figured out a way to manufacture them fraudulently. Artificially created molds are much thicker than Kluski's were, and the wrist openings have to be large enough for the hand to be withdrawn. (A hand-shaped balloon can also be used. After the glove forms, the balloon can be removed by releasing its air. The wrist opening in this case would be very narrow. The result, though, is a distorted, almost laughable caricature of a hand. Kluski's molds were perfectly formed appendages.) Third, interlocking hands, childrens' hands, miniatures, and so on were also produced by Kluski. Often times Geley and his collaborators would even secretly place dye in the paraffin. Yet Kluski's hand molds were always the same color as the tinted paraffin, so we know that he was not smuggling prepared gloves into the séance room beforehand. Kluski could also produce molds of other body parts as well as hands. Feet and partial head molds were also part of his psychic repertoire.

As phenomenal as it may seem, even the lines of the skin could be seen on the molds. Whatever produced the gloves obviously took over the form and exact shape of living tissue before dissipating. Kluski could also materialize full-form animal-like and humanoid forms. Some of these phantoms were photographed and look oddly two-dimensional or manikin-like. Some of the animal forms were more animated.

There is little doubt that Kluski's PK was some sort of biological force or substance. If PK can take the form of a "bioplasma," then Kluski's phenomena become more intelligible to us. Let's say that the body possesses a bioplasma system, as some of our Soviet confreres believe, and that this system forms a duplicate body within the physical organism. (Now, of course, we are using the word "plasma" very loosely and in the biological sense, not in the sense it is used in physics.) This plasma might have the ability to leave the body and build into tissue-like structures, that is, arms, legs, forms, animal phantoms, and so forth. The plasma might be like clay, a substance that can be molded by the psychic's or experimenter's mind. It can leave the body, solidify, and then become tenuous before returning to the body. It might become more visible to the human eye when it does solidify, but might remain invisible when it vaporizes.

Dr. Jule Eisenbud is one of the few parapsychologists who has tried to figure out what materialization phenomena are telling us about PK. Dr. Eisenbud addressed himself to the problem of the "mind-matter interface" when he lectured before the Institute for Research on the Dissemination of Human Knowledge on October 10, 1973. In his address, he urged his audience to remember that materialization phenomena, despite how extraordinary they may seem, do apparently follow normal biological processes. He compared the development of a materialized form to the development of a fetus or cancer. Materialization phenomena, he argued, indicate that our psychic powers are an intergral part of biological life. Eisenbud has even suggested that aeons ago PK may have initiated the biological beginnings of life as we know it.

Of course, Dr. Eisenbud's ideas are only speculative in nature. But his suggestions might also be pointing out a fundamental truth. PK might be a force which is not only fundamental to life, but perhaps even necessary for it to continue.

Today, however, a few parapsychologists are developing a third explantory model to account for PK, and one which drastically differs from the way we have conceptualized it in the past.

Perhaps PK is not a force at all. Perhaps its job is not to expend large amounts of energy or manipulate matter directly. Perhaps PK manipulates and processes normal forms and sources of energy, reorders it, and then directs it to carry out our mental wishes. This idea may sound a bit confusing, but look back to Dr. Gertrude Schmeidler's experiments with Ingo Swann. Swann tried to use PK to make thermistors become hotter or cooler. Each time a specific thermistor changed temperature, outlying thermistors in the same general area altered temperature in the opposite direction. Did the PK directly affect the target thermistors, or did it actually redirect energy from the atmosphere which really carried out the task and which resulted in these sympathetic temperature changes?

Veteran physicist Dr. Joseph Rush has become a rather outspoken proponent for this theory, although he doesn't promote it dogmatically. He argues that PK is not a force complete in itself, but merely acts intelligently to reorder random but physical energy. Rush certainly should know what he is talking about. He has been an associate physicist at the Tennessee-based Clinton Laboratories, a professor of physics and astronomy at Denison University in Granville, Ohio, and has worked both at the High Altitude Observatory and at the National Center for Atmospheric Research in Boulder, Colorado. He has also had a longtime interest in parapsychology. Back in the 1940s he conducted a series of highly successful ESP experiments. He also witnessed some of Eisenbud's thoughtographic experiments with Ted Serios.

Dr. Rush thinks we might be making a mistake by conceptualizing PK as an energy system complete within itself. He outlined a very different conception for PK when he delivered an address, "Physical Aspects of Psi Phenomena," at an ASPR symposium on May 18, 1974:

> It seems that quantum theory cannot now account for psi effects. Yet certain peculiarities of PK suggest a tantalizingly close relation to the statistical processes that are the basis of quantum physics. PK influence has been observed in many kinds of situations. These indicate that, at least in experiments, it is easier to influence a situation that already involves random or near-random motion than a static arrangement. Successful experiments have used tumbling dice or unmarked cubes, random electrical impulses derived from

radioactive decay (Schmidt, 1969b), Puthoff and Targ's pendulum driven by random "noise" vibrations, and apparent changes of temperature in air in which molecules are in random motion (Schmeidler, 1973).

In each of these situations there is the suggestion that the PK perturbation is accomplished through an alteration of the probability describing the system rather than application or abstraction of energy directly. The effect suggests information more than energy. Clerk Maxwell fantasized a supernatural "demon" who could defeat the Second Law of Thermodynamics by operating a tiny door between two vessels of gas, admitting only fast molecules in one direction and only slow ones in the other. He would thus raise the temperature of the gas in the first vessel (full of more energetic molecules) at the expense of the second, which would become cooler.

We know now that Maxwell's demon is a fantasy: informing himself of the locations and velocities of the gas molecules would dissipate more energy than he could concentrate by this process. Yet the PK experiments mentioned above, as well as some others, inescapably suggest the intervention of a Maxwell demon that works. This observation is not intended to imply a breakdown of the Second Law of Thermodynamics; rather, it suggests that the PK practitioner may be able to intervene in somewhat the role of the demon, introducing information and order into the random situation, but at the expense of a compensating degradation of energy in his own system. In the case of Schmidt's random-number generator, the PK influence ostensibly interferes with the normally completely random process of radioactive decay that is described statistically by quantum theory. As Schmidt (1969a) remarks, "This [experiment] implies that quantum theory does not give, at least for systems that include human subjects, a complete description of nature".

The PK experiments with dice never have yielded extraordinarily high scores, in curious contrast to the comparable ESP card-guessing tests which sometimes have yielded scores of 100 per cent in a run. This observation suggests the possibility that PK is inherently a statistical phenomenon, whereas clairvoyance may be "all or nothing"; however, the observed difference may be an artifact of the experimental procedures. The concept of informed manipulation of energy already in the target situation finds some further support in Eisenbud's experiments (1967) with Serios' "thoughtography," in which the camera shutter was operated normally. Serios sometimes got abnormal exposures on film in an opaque package, but not pictures. The difference in performance could be psychologically motivated; but it suggests that manipulation of the light energy normally entering the camera is less difficult than directly influencing the film. Also, reports of paranormal voices on tape recordings usually indicate that the voices are barely distinguishable from the noise background—again suggesting, to the extent that such observations are valid, that the voices have been created by imposing some degree of order upon the random noise energy. The familiar reports of cool sensations during séance phenomena further support the impression of an intelligent ordering of randomly distributed energy.

Dr. Rush's views are certainly thought-provoking. But he does leave one crucial question unanswered. What is the force that the psychic uses to reorder normal energy? There must be some mediating link between the psychic's will and this energy-manipulating process. So we soon find ourselves back to Dr. Beloff's dilemma. Does mind interact directly with energy? Or does it use a mediating force to process it? I believe that to make Rush's theory intelligible we must still think in terms of some force which emanates from the psychic and which physically acts on normal energy sources. However, Dr. Rush's model is attractive because it explains the information aspect or cognizant ability of PK. However, how could even a colossal energy-reordering and information-processing system account for materialization phenomena? Could PK skim off and manipulate molecules from the medium's body, the sitters, and nearby objects and then reorder them into a new structure? Maybe parapsychologists will have to study Einstein's view that energy and mass are interchangeable. Perhaps a clue may lie there.

Another theory about PK which drastically differs from our normal conception is what I call the "cosmic PK theory." This theory states that PK is not a force peculiar to biological life at all. It is a cosmic energy which is sometimes *channeled through us*. We are not the source of the PK, we only use it. The force itself permeates all life and matter in the universe. This conceptual model for PK is the newest fad in some parapsychological circles.

This theory is not a new one. Progenitors can be traced all the way back to many ancient civilizations. The medieval and Reformation occult philosophers also developed concepts about cosmic forces and energies. Paracelsus (1493–1541) taught that there existed a substance he called "munia," a cosmic power permeating the universe which could control, which could heal, and which could be made to act on other people and over long distances.

The belief in an all-pervading universal fluid became popular in European thinking in the eighteenth century when Franz Anton Mesmer discovered "mesmerism," a psychophysiological state which today we would call hypnosis. Mesmer found that his subjects entered a trance when magnets were passed over their bodies. Instead of realizing that psychological suggestion caused the entrancement, Mesmer developed highly complex theories about a magic "fluid" which permeated the body as well as the universe. Magnets could act upon this fluid and man could project this fluid into other people and into inanimate objects as well.

During these early years, the most notable contribution to the study of this hypothetical cosmic energy was made by a German scientist, Karl von Reichenbach (1788–1869), who wrote several books on such topics as magnetism and electricity, and experimented with several psychics he had discovered. Reichenbach began his research by following up on Mesmer's discoveries. Ultimately the German scientist discovered that his subjects could distinguish between the taste of magnetized water and untreated water, and could see odd, flamelike emanations dancing about the poles of magnets. Based on these investigations, Reichenbach, like Mesmer, theorized the existence of an all-pervading cosmic substance he called *od* or *odyle*. He believed that this odic force has the following features: it is a universal force permeating all matter; it cannot be eliminated from anything; specific sources—such as electricity, friction, and so forth—can concentrate it; it possesses polarity; conducts through metals, glass, and fabric; it can radiate over distance; it can be transferred from one body to another; is sometimes luminous; and it is particularly stored by the human body. Since both Mesmer and Reichenbach witnessed psychic displays during their experiments, their theories were structured to help explain psi.

In our own times, Dr. Wilhelm Reich, an offbeat disciple of Sigmund Freud, developed similar concepts while working in Europe and later in the United States. Reich's work is important since he tried to discover physical evidence for the existence of the universal force. And this evidence bears significantly on our understanding of PK.

Dr. Reich began his controversial career as a psychoanalyst and as one of Freud's favorite disciples. While studying the mysteries of human sexuality, he posited the existence of a life-force he called orgone. Like Reichenbach before him, he came to believe that this life-force pervaded all space and could exert a physical effect on man, plants, and even on nonorganic structures. While working at the University of Oslo from 1934–1936, he studied microscopic life and learned that all life seemed to follow an "orgasmic response" of tension and release. For example, he believed that the contractual movements of the amoeba were one and the same to the human orgastic response. His belief in a "biological pulsation" which guided all life eventually led him to assert that orgone was the energy igniting this pulsation. Later while still working in Norway, Reich thought he had discovered the basic units of orgone energy, which he called bions. While studying various organic and nonorganic substances under a microscope, he began seeing vesticles forming around the material and immediately decided that these were the basic units of his life-energy. Eventually he claimed that he could see orgone everywhere—around his body, emanating from walls, from clothing, and so forth.

Reich's work became exceedingly controversial in the United States when he began developing apparatuses to harness orgone energy and built orgone accumulators which he asserted would help heal organic diseases. (The accumulators were merely boxes lined alternately with layers of organic and inorganic material.) By sitting in the accumulator or by placing a diseased limb into a smaller orgone box, claimed Reich, orgone would permeate the tissue and help it to heal.

Reich didn't stop there, though. He went on to develop orgone devices to control weather, and even got Albert Einstein at least superficially interested in his work. He founded a laboratory in Maine where for several years he and his followers carried out experiments on the healing properties of orgone, its physical effects on man and the world, its ability to change weather, and so forth. To Reich, orgone was a universal force which could be harnessed to help and benefit man.

Was Reich a genius or a madman? This is a hard question to answer. Reich began his career as a brilliant disciple of Freud, but was later expelled from the Vienna clique when he began promoting his radical views on sex, character, society, and other psychological issues. Above all else, Reich was an experimentalist. His writings consist of experiment after experiment into the properties of orgone, successes and failures alike. But he rarely followed up the leads offered from his own work. He rarely replicated his experiments, reported them sloppily, based his views on a few anomalous findings, and was often unsystematic in his work. Today it is clear that many oddities which Reich saw was evidence of orgone in his experiments were normal physical reactions. He also harbored weird beliefs about orgone for which he had no experimental evidence. His theories that static electricity and the aurora borealis are orgone manifestations are hard to take seriously.

Today, there is a growing movement to replicate Reich's experiments. This resurgence, though, has been a steady downhill battle. Government funding agencies throughout the world have been reticent about granting money to experimenters interested in exploring Reichian concepts. Dr. Bernard Grad has unsuccessfully tried for many years to find any agency willing to fund him to replicate Reich's work. However a few European scientists are beginning to carry on with Reich's work, and some psychiatrists in the United States still practice Reichian therapies which focus on liberating life-energies within the patient's body. Orgone accumulators are being used experimentally to treat organic diseases in Italy. So, whatever the truth or fiction about orgone, the case of Wilhelm Reich will long remain one of the most curious stories in the history of modern science.

Now, what has any of this to do with PK? Reich endowed his orgone energy with properties which seem identical to PK. Most students of orgonomy do not realize that Reich made several PK-like claims for orgone energy. In 1949 he published the first issue of the *Orgone Energy Bulletin* in which he asserted that orgone could become a motor force. He even invented an orgone motor, a strange device complete with a rotating armature. Ola Raknes, one of Reich's disciples, claims in his *Wilhelm Reich and Orgonomy* that he saw the motor in operation. Reich hooked it to an orgone accumulator, and the armature began rotating by itself! Reich also believed that atmospheric orgone could self-manipulate and organize into systems. The orgone, which normally has no mass, could then develop into a material substance. This concept could conceivably help explain materialization phenomena. Dr. Raknes also claims that he watched Reich change wind direction by projecting orgone into the air through one of his inventions. Other writers on Reich, such as Professor Edward Mann of York

University, Ontario, more than suggest that what we call PK is often really orgone manifestations. (See his book, *Orgone, Reich, and Eros.*)

But what about this motor that moved by itself? Was it a hoax? Did Reich learn how to harness his orgone energy? Or did Reich himself possess some PK ability?

It is hard to determine what role the experimenter plays in his own experiments. It is perfectly conceivable that Reich might have used PK to cause some of the odd results he witnessed during his experiments with orgone healing, with his motor, and could even explain some of the odd biological responses he observed under his microscope. This is the inevitable problem we face when trying to analyze any theories about the existence of cosmic energies. It is impossible to test these concepts experimentally. Any results could be due to the PK ability of the experimenters. Reich could have influenced the outcome of his tests just as easily as Cox or Dale could have contributed to the success of their dice-throwing experiments.

Nonetheless, there is a growing movement in some more radical parapsychological circles that not only believes in the existence of cosmic energies, but that we should start studying them full time as well.

Unfortunately, the evidence for the existence of some type of PK-mimicking cosmic energy is extremely weak. Take all the furor over "pyramid" power, for instance. Pyramid power is the most popular fad in the recent tide of pop occultism. Enthusiasts of pyramid power claim that pyramidal-shaped structures generate a mysterious energy which helps rejuvenate the body, wards off illness, stalls the decomposition of organic matter, and even sharpens razor blades.

According to Sheila Ostrander and Lynn Schroeder in their *Psychic Discoveries Behind the Iron Curtain,* Czech scientists have discovered that pyramid structures can sharpen razor blades, mummify living tissue, and act as a lens for nonphysical energy.

Now these are all very wondrous claims, but just where is the documental experimental evidence in support of them? Frankly, there isn't any. The Toronto Society for Psychical Research began studying pyramid power at the height of the craze. They found that pyramids had no effect on either razor blades or food preservation even when they followed the directions for using the pyramids set down by pyramid-power promoters. As Dr. A. R. G. Owen reports in his *Psychic Mysteries of the North:*

> In all tests the members of the research team, who performed their experiments independently in their various homes and offices while following the same agreed-upon procedures, were unable to discover any significant difference between material placed in a pyramid and material placed in control containers. If anything, they had only rediscovered the "Cookie Jar Principle", that is, any substance placed in a container which keeps out air currents does not spoil as quickly as in the open air.

As for sharpening razor blades, Dr. Owen has this to report:

> Dale Simmons tackled the problem of the alleged sharpening of used razor blades by a very direct method. With the aid of a metallurgical microscope with an attached Polaroid camera he photographed the edges of blunted razor blades before and after they had spent time in the model pyramids. The resulting photographs made it obvious that the effect of sitting under a pyramid for even as much as a week was negligible. If there was any rounding off of the jagged protuberance it was no more than that which occurred with a control blade sitting in the open. However, it should be stressed that it was very difficult to see any change in a blade whether it had rested inside or outside a pyramid. Simmons carried out all the instructions laid down by pyramid suppliers very precisely and to the letter. He oriented his pyramids to the magnetic north. He did not think it worth repeating the experiments with orientation to the true north because in the dehydration experiments this had given no results. We may note that in pyramid literature there seems to be some confusion between geographical and magnetic north; some say one and some say the other.

Alan Vaughan, articles editor for *Psychic* magazine, reported on the Toronto work in the February 1974 issue and was soon deluged by letters from pyramid-power exponents. They urged him to read the positive literature on the subject. As Vaughan reported in a subsequent issue of *Psychic,* he looked over the literature recommended by his correspondents but couldn't find any claims in the books which were backed up by experimental evidence.

Another experimenter who claims to have learned to control some form of cosmic energy is Robert Pavlita, a Czech inventor. He has made little metal devices which can theoretically monitor, harness, store, and project this force. These gadgets, which he calls psychotronic generators, look like little metal sculptures and vary in size and shape but are all small enough to be held in the hand. Several witnesses, including American parapsychologist Dr. Stanley Krippner, have visited Pavlita and report the same thing. They have seen him put the generators to his head to charge them and then move little objects about by pointing the generators at them! The well-known Czech parapsychologist, Dr. Zdenek Rejdak, is also a firm supporter of Pavlita's work. However the inventor's own claims are a little bizarre. He has assured his colleagues and news reporters that he learned how to construct his generators and harness psychotronic energy by studying old alchemistic and occult writings. What writings, you may ask? Dr. Rejdak, Pavlita's self-proclaimed confidant would only tell Ostrander and Schroeder, " . . . we can't tell you that." This is hardly a very encouraging attitude and a totally unscientific one to boot.

For a typical demonstration, Pavlita or his daughter will charge up a generator mentally and then point it at mobiles and other small metallic or nonmetallic objects. The mobiles will turn, the objects will slide by themselves, or the generator will act like a magnet or magnetize the object it is moving. However Pavlita always works completely uncontrolled, and has never submitted to one single scientifically supervised test. His demonstrations are little more than stage performances. His claims—such that his generators once partially paralyzed his daughther and that the secret of the generators can be found in esoteric occult writings which he refuses to produce or name—are suspicious to say the least. Furthermore, he always demonstrates phenomena which can easily be faked if only a magnet were secreted in his hand or in the generator. Pavlita's main tour de force is using a generator to move a small piece of wood across a table. But no one has ever had the initiative, or opportunity, to see whether or not a metal sliver had been imbedded in the wood. If there was, the wood could be made to move if a magnet were in Pavlita's hand or in the generator.

Has man's search for cosmic energy in the world about us borne any fruit? From the standpoint of evidence, the answer has to be no. On the other hand, though, there can be little doubt that our world houses energies and forces that we are simply unaware of. We don't know about them because we can't detect or monitor them. To believe that modern science has discovered *all* the forces of nature and that no other energies remain to be uncovered is ludicrously naive. However, I don't think that we are entitled to believe that such energies, if they exist, can account for all PK manifestations. There is simply no evidence to warrant this assumption. Psychotronic energy, orgone energy, pyramid power all *may* exist. But scientists of the future will have to devise much more rigorous experiments to prove it than have been carried out to date. Only time will tell.

What, then, do I think PK is? This is a difficult question to answer. It is much easier to ask questions in parapsychology than to answer any of them. One thing is clear to me though: PK can manifest itself in different ways in order to handle best each task it tries to perform. There might be little connection between the force employed to levitate a table and the energy released to Gellerize a key.

I doubt if PK is a uniform process at all. Please remember that PK is a term we use only to label and categorize a certain class of phenomena which are, as yet, inexplicable according to the known laws of science. That is all the term denotes. Different PK effects may not be due to the same force, so I don't think that there is any one explanation for PK. To the contrary, the evidence indicates that man controls a complicated *system* of hitherto unrecognized energies. I also think that man controls three basic types of PK. The first type might be some form of energy, let's call it psi energy as Rhine does, which is ignited by a conscious or unconscious act of will. This psi energy could take two guises. It may either generate power to achieve its end, or it may manipulate and redirect normal sources of energy. The second type of PK power we possess may be some sort of biological plasma which is capable of exteriorizing from the body. This force could be linked to psi energy. According to modern physics, mass and energy are interconvertible. So it is conceivable that somehow we can convert psi energy into mass. This process would probably occur within the body as the PK readies itself to project into the world. This mass might account for mists, materializations, and other rare séance room phenomena. Third, I can't dismiss the possibility that man might also have the ability to channel some sort of cosmic force or life-force as well.

PK Theories

This force might pervade the universe and, on certain occasions, we might act as batteries or generators for it. This theory must remain only a possibility, though.

I realize of course that this scheme is contrived. I don't mean it to be anything but that. By structuring this hierarchy of PK forces, I am trying to make the point that I think there are many kinds of PK forces, each of which draws upon different mechanics and each of which is governed by different principles.

Will we ever discover the true nature of PK? I don't think that anyone in the near future is going to pop up with an equation or formula which will—zap!—suddenly make PK understandable. It's not that I think PK is a totally incomprehensible group of phenomena. It's just that twentieth-century physics is obviously not advanced enough to account for PK. Parapsychologists who study PK will probably not be the ones who will ultimately discover the mechanics of PK. No doubt this understanding will come as physicists learn more about quantum processes, plasma physics, and as the discipline of theoretical physics develops. As these scientists learn more and more about the fabric of the universe, PK will gradually become more intelligible and explainable. When we truly understand the physical world, we will also understand PK. Eventually some breakthrough will come in our understanding the physical universe. This discovery may come suddenly or gradually. New physical principles which underlay our world will become clear to us and many of our most pressing questions about the universe will be answered. PK may become another "old problem" at that time as well.

As the study of physics evolves, the PK mystery will gradually be taken under its wing. We can see this happening today. Parapsychology, which in the 1930s became a psychological discipline, is now evolving away from psychology and is nurturing a tender romance with biology and physics. More and more parapsychological research is being carried out by physicists and I doubt if this trend will soon end.

But let's not get too wrapped up in the future. We still have many problems to confront as we travel that almost infinitely long road toward understanding psychic phenomena. For now we must still investigate PK every way we can: by throwing dice, investigating poltergeists, monitoring Gellerized metal, and by trying to use our minds to disrupt quantum processes. And we must do this without any preconceptions about where our findings will lead us.

I can't end this book without adding an ominous note, though. PK is certainly an awesome force. It can even interplay with the molecular structure of matter. And it is a force that is controlled by our sometimes primitive unconscious desires and will. When we finally understand PK, we will then be in a position to harness and willfully control it. I cannot help but wonder: Will man be mature and wise enough to control the force he will be unleashing? I pray that he will be.

References

References

1. FROM SKEPTICISM TO BELIEF

Bell, M. "Francis Bacon, Pioneer in Parapsychology." *International Journal of Parapsychology* 6 (1964):199-208.

Dale, Laura. "The Psychokinetic Effect: The First A.S.P.R. Experiment." *Journal of the American Society for Psychical Research* 40 (1946):123-51.

Eisenbud, Jule. "The Case of Florence Marryat." *Journal of the American Society for Psychical Research* 69 (1975):215-34.

Rhine, J. B. *The Reach of the Mind.* New York:William Sloane, 1974.

Schmeidler, Gertrude. "PK Effects Upon Continuously Recorded Temperatures." *Journal of the American Society for Psychical Research* 67 (1973):325-40.

Schmidt, Helmut. "Mental Influence on Random Events." *New Scientist*, June 24, 1971, pp. 757-58.

———. "A PK Test with Electronic Equipment." *Journal of Parapsychology* 34 (1970): 175-81.

2. PK IN EVERYDAY LIFE

Fisk, G. W., and Mitchell, A. M. J. "The Application of Differential Scoring to PK Tests." *Journal of the Society for Psychical Research* 37 (1953):45-60.

Flammarion, Camille. *Death and Its Mystery*, vol. 2: *At the Moment of Death.* New York: Century, 1922.

Jung, C. G. *Memories, Dreams, Reflections.* New York: Random House, 1961.

Laurent, Emile. "Remarks on Certain Common Telepathic Manifestations." *Annals of Psychical Science* 5 (1907):79-96.
McConnell, R. A. "Remote Night Tests for PK." *Journal of the American Society for Psychical Research* 49 (1955):99-108.
Nash, Carroll. "Position Effects in PK Tests with Twenty-four Dice." *Journal of Parapsychology* 10 (1946):51-57.
―――, and Richard, Alice. "Comparison of Two Distances in PK Tests." *Journal of Parapsychology* 11 (1947):269-82.
Rhine, Louisa. *ESP in Life and Lab.* New York: Macmillan, 1967.
―――. *Hidden Channels of the Mind.* New York: William Sloane, 1961.
Rogo, D. Scott. *The Poltergeist Experience.* New York: Penguin, in press.
Stanford, Rex, et al. "Psychokinesis as Psi-Mediated Instrumental Response." *Journal of the American Society for Psychical Research* 69 (1975):127-35.
Targ, R., and Puthoff, H. "A Perceptual Channel for Information Transfer Over Kilometer Distances: Historical Perspective and Recent Research." *Proceedings,* Institute of Electrical and Electronics Engineers 64 (1976):329-54.
Tietze, Thomas. "Ursa Major: An Impressionistic Appreciation of Walter Franklin Prince." *Journal of the American Society for Psychical Research* 70 (1976):1-34.
White, Sarah Parker. "Elwood Worcester and the Case for Survival." *Journal of the American Society for Psychical Research* 43 (1949):78-107.
Wilkins, Hubert, and Sherman, Harold. *Thought Through Space.* Hollywood, Calif.: House-Warven, 1951.

3. THE MYSTERY OF THE POLTERGEIST

Bayless, Raymond. *The Enigma of the Poltergeist.* West Nyack, N. Y.: Parker, 1967.
Bender, Hans. "Modern Poltergeist Research," in John Beloff, ed., *New Directions in Parapsychology.* London: Elek, 1974.
Fodor, Nandor. *On the Trail of the Poltergeist.* New York: Citadel, 1958.
Gaddis, Vincent. *Mysterious Fires and Lights.* Philadelphia: David McKay, 1967.
Palmer, John. "A Case of RSPK Involving a Ten-Year-Old Boy: The Powhatan Poltergeist." *Journal of the American Society for Psychical Research* 68 (1974):1-33.
Quinlin, James M., and May, Marsha. "Baffling Ghost Wrecks a Home." *National Enquirer,* January 14, 1975.
Rogo, D. Scott. *The Poltergeist Experience.* New York: Penguin, in press.
Roll, W. G. "Poltergeists," in Benjamin Wolman, ed., *Handbook of Parapsychology.* New York: Van Nostrand, 1977.

———. *The Poltergeist.* New York: New American Library, 1974.
Solfvin, G., and Roll, W. G. "A Case of RSPK with an Epileptic Agent," in J. D. Morris et al. (eds.), *Research in Parapsychology–1975.* Metuchen, N. J.: Scarecrow Press, 1976.
———. "The Smithfield Teleportations." *Theta,* Winter–Spring 1975.

4. SCIENTISTS, MEDIUMS, AND PK

Bottazzi, Philipe. "The Unexplored Region of Human Biology: Observations and Experiments with Eusapia Palladino." *Annals of Psychical Science* 6 (1907):149-56, 260-90, 377-425.
Carrington, Hereward. *The American Seances with Eusapia Palladino.* New York: Garrett Publications, 1954.
———. *Eusapia Palladino and Her Phenomena.* New York: B. W. Dodge, 1909.
———. *The Problems of Psychical Research.* London: Rider, 1914.
Crookes, William. *Researches into the Phenomena of Spiritualism.* London: James Burns, n.d.
Dunraven, Earl of (Lord Adare). *Experiences in Spiritualism with D. D. Home.* London: Society for Psychical Research, 1924 (reprint).
Flammarion, Camille. *Mysterious Psychic Forces.* Boston: Small, Maynard & Co., 1907.
Honorton, D., and Barksdale, W. "PK Performance with Waking Suggestions for Muscle Tension Versus Relaxation." *Journal of the American Society for Psychical Research* 66 (1972):208-14.
Osty, Eugene. *Les Pouvoirs inconnus de l'esprit sur la matrière.* Paris, 1932.
Price, Harry. "An Account of Some Further Experiments with Rudi Schneider." *Bulletin No. 4 of the National Laboratory of Psychical Research.* London, 1933.
———. *Rudi Schneider.* London: Methuen, 1930.
Rogo, D. Scott. "Eusapia Palladino and the Structure of Scientific Controversy." *Parapsychology Review* 6, no. 1 (1975):23-27.
Venzano, Joseph. "A Contribution to the Study of Materializations." *Annals of Psychical Science* 6 (1907):75-119.

5. NINA KULAGINA: THE SOVIET PK BREAKTHROUGH

Herbert Benson. "Kulagina Cine Film 'A.' " *Journal of Paraphysics* 3 (1969):89-95.
———. "Kulagina Cine Film 'B.' " *Journal of Paraphysics* 4 (1970):16-24.
———. "Notes on the Kulagina Films." *Journal of Paraphysics* 3 (1969):67-68.

262 *Minds and Motion*

———. "Report on Nina Kulagina." *Parapsychology Review* 3, no. 6 (1972):8-10.

———. "Spring in Leningrad: Kulagina Revisited." *Parapsychology Review* 4, no. 4 (1973):5-10.

Inyushin, V. "Bioplasma, the Fourth State of Matter, from the Point of View of Physics." Unpublished paper available in translation. See Edward Mann's *Orgone, Reich and Eros*, pp. 298-311, New York: Simon & Schuster, 1973.

Keil, J. H. J.; Herbert, B.; Ullman, M.; and Pratt, J. G. "Directly Observable Voluntary PK Effects." *Proceedings of the Society for Psychical Research* 56 (1976):197-235.

Kolodny, Leo. "When Apples Fall." Journal of Paraphysics 2 (1968):105-108.

Kulagin, Ing. V. V. "Nina S. Kulagina." *Journal of Paraphysics*, special issue: *Symposium on Psychokinesis* (1971):54-62.

Moss, Thelma. "Searching for Psi from Prague to Lower Siberia." *Psychic*, June 1971.

Ostrander, S., and Schroeder, L. *Psychic Discoveries Behind the Iron Curtain*. Englewood Cliffs, N. J.: Prentice-Hall, 1970.

Pratt, J. G. *ESP Research Today*. Metuchen, N. J.: Scarecrow Press, 1973.

Rejdak, Zdenek. "The Kulagina Cine Films." *Journal of Paraphysics* 3 (1969):64-66.

———. "Telekinesis or Fraud?" *Journal of Paraphysics* 2 (1968):68-70.

6. THE PK EPIDEMIC

Adamenko, Victor. "Controlled Movement of Objects in Bio-electrical Fields." *Journal of Paraphysics* 6 (1972):180, 225-26.

Herbert, Benson. "Alla Vinogradova: Demonstration in Moscow." *Journal of Paraphysics* 6 (1972):191-96.

———. "Cleio and Kulagina." *Parapsychology Review* 2, no. 5 (1971):20-23.

———. "Electrical PK." *Parapsychology Review* 3, no. 5 (1972):18-19.

———. "Psychokinesis in Bratislava." *Parapsychology Review* 3, no. 1 (1972):9-12.

Honorton, Charles. "Apparent Psychokinesis on Static Objects by a 'Gifted Subject,'" in J. Morris et al. (eds.), *Research in Parapsychology—1973*. Metuchen, N. J.: Scarecrow Press, 1974.

Maigret, Pamela de. "PK Training in Russia." *Fate*, May 1976.

Ochorowicz, Jules. "A New Mediumistic Phenomenon." *Annals of Psychical Science* 5 (1909):333-99.

Watkins, G., and Watkins, A. "Apparent Psychokinesis on Static Objects by a 'Gifted Subject': A Laboratory Demonstration," in J. Morris et al. (eds.), *Research in Parapsychology–1973*. Metuchen, N. J.: Scarecrow Press, 1974.

7. EXAMINING THE GELLER EFFECT

Byrd, Eldon. "Uri Geller's Influence on the Metal Alloy Nitinol," in C. Panati (ed.), *The Geller Papers*. Boston: Houghton Mifflin, 1976.

Christopher, Milbourne. *Mediums, Mystics and the Occult*. New York: Crowell, 1975.

Coohill, Thomas. "Filmed and Non-filmed Events: On Uri Geller's Visit to Western Kentucky University," in C. Panati (ed.), *The Geller Papers*. Boston: Houghton Mifflin, 1976.

Cox, E. W. "Notes on Some Experiments with Uri Geller." *Journal of Parapsychology* 28 (1974):408-11.

Leslie, Leo. *Uri Geller*, exerpted in C. Panati (ed.), *The Geller Papers*. Boston, Houghton Mifflin, 1976.

Moss, Thelma. "Uri's Magic," in C. Panati (ed.), *The Geller Papers*. Boston: Houghton Mifflin, 1976.

Panati, Charles (ed.), *The Geller Papers*. Boston: Houghton Mifflin, 1976.

Price, E. Alan. "The Uri Geller Effect," in C. Panati (ed.), *The Geller Papers*. Boston: Houghton Mifflin, 1976.

Randi, James. *The Magic of Uri Geller*. New York: Ballantine, 1975.

Rogo, D. Scott. "A Critical Examination of the 'Geller Effect.'" *Bioenergetic Systems*, special issue no. 3 (1977).

Targ, Russell, and Puthoff, H. "Information Transmission under Conditions of Sensory Shielding." *Nature*, October 18, 1974.

Taylor, John. "A Brief Report on a Visit by Uri Geller to King's College, London, June 20, 1974," in C. Panati (ed.), *The Geller Papers*. Boston: Houghton Mifflin, 1976.

———. *Superminds*. New York: Viking, 1975.

Wilhelm, John. *The Search for Superman*. New York: Pocket Books, 1976.

8. GROUP PK

Barrett, William. *On the Threshold of the Unseen*. London: Kegan Paul, 1917.

Batcheldor, K. J. "Report on a Case of Table Levitation and Associated Phenomena." *Journal of the Society for Psychical Research* 43 (1966).

Crawford, W. J. *Experiments in Psychical Science*. New York: Dutton, 1919.

———. *The Psychic Structures at the Goligher Circle*. New York: Dutton, 1921.

———. *The Reality of Psychic Phenomena*. New York: Dutton, 1918.
Feola, José. *PK: Mind over Matter*. Minneapolis: Dillon, 1975.
———. "Physical Phenomena in La Plata, Argentina." Unpublished manuscript sent to author.
Flammarion, Camille. *Mysterious Psychic Forces*. Boston: Small, Maynard & Co., 1907.
Maxwell, Joseph. *Metapsychical Phenomena*. New York: Macmillan, 1905.
Nisbet, Brian. "Table-Turning, a Brief Historical Note." *Journal of the Society for Psychical Research* 47 (1973):96-106.
Owen, Iris, with Sparrow, Margaret. *Conjuring Up Philip*. New York: Harper & Row, 1976.
Rogo, D. Scott. *In Search of the Unknown*. New York: Taplinger, 1976.

9. PK AND HEALING

Barry, Jean. "General and Comparative Study of the Psychokinetic Effect on a Fungus Culture." *Journal of Parapsychology* 32 (1968):237-43.
Carrel, Alexis. *The Voyage to Lourdes*. New York: Harper & Brothers, 1950.
Goodrich, Joyce. Doctoral dissertation (unpublished). Yellow Springs, Ohio Union Graduate School, 1975.
Grad, Bernard. "The Biological Effects of the 'Laying On of Hands' on Animals and Plants: Implications for Biology," in G. Schmeidler (ed.), *Parapsychology: Its Relation to Physics, Biology, Psychology and Psychiatry*. Metuchen, N. J.: Scarecrow Press, 1976.
Kuhlman, Kathryn. *I Believe in Miracles*. London: Lakeland, 1968.
Mann, W. Edward. *Orgone, Reich and Eros*. New York: Simon & Schuster, 1973.
Nolen, William. *Healing: A Doctor in Search of a Miracle*. New York: Random House, 1975.
Richmond, Nigel. "Two Series of PK Tests on Paramecia." *Journal of the Society for Psychical Research* 36 (1956):577-88.
Simonton, Carl. "The Role of the Mind in Cancer Therapy," in Stanley Dean (ed.), *Psychiatry and Mysticism*. Chicago: Nelson-Hall, 1975.
Smith, Justa. "Paranormal Effect of Enzyme Activity Through Laying-On-of-Hands." *Human Dimensions*, Summer 1972.
Vallee, Jacques. *The Invisible College*. New York: Dutton, 1975.
Watkins, G., and Watkins, A. "Possible PK Influences on the Resuscitation of Anesthetized Mice." *Journal of Parapsychology* 35 (1971):257-72.
West, D. J. *Eleven Lourdes Miracles*. New York: Garrett Publications, 1957.

10. THE RANGE OF PK

Bayless, Raymond. "Tape-Recording of Paranormally Generated Acoustical Raps." *New Horizons* 2 (1976):12-17.

Beloff, John, and Evans, L. "A Radioactivity Test of Psychokinesis." *Journal of the Society for Psychical Research* 41 (1961):41-46.

Carrington, Hereward. *The Story of Psychic Science.* London: Rider, n.d.

Chauvin, R., and Genthon, Jr. "Eine Untesuchung uber die Moglichkeit Psychokinetscher Experiemente mit Uranium and Geigergahler." *Zeitscchift fir Parapsyologie and Grenzgebeite de Psychologie* 8 (1965):140-47.

Cox, W. E. "The Effect of PK on the Placement of Falling Objects." *Journal of Parapsychology* 15 (1951):40-48.

———. "The Placement of Falling Water." *Journal of Parapsychology* 26 (1962):266.

Eisenbud, Jule. "The Marvelleux Veilleux: Their Psychic Photography." *Fate*, November-December 1975.

———. *The World of Ted Serios.* New York: Morrow, 1966.

Fodor, Amaya. "Does Dr. Fodor Communicate?" *Fate,* January 1965.

Forwald, H. "A Further Study of the PK Placement Effect." *Journal of Parapsychology* 16 (1952):59-67.

Fukurai, T. *Clairvoyance and Thoughtography.* London: Rider, 1931.

Gaddis, Vincent. "When TV Tunes to Another Dimension." *Probe*, May 1975.

McConnell, R. A. et al. "Wishing with Dice." *Journal of Experimental Psychology* 50 (1955):269-75.

Pratt, J. G., and Palmer, J. "An Investigation of an Unpublicized Family Poltergeist." Paper delivered to the 1975 Annual Convention of the Parapsychological Association.

Rhine, J. B. "The Forwald Experiments with Placement PK." *Journal of Parapsychology* 15 (1951):49-52.

Rhine, J. B., and Humphrey, B. M. "The PK Effect: Special Evidence from Hit Patterns. 1. Quarter Distribution of the Page." *Journal of Parapsychology* 8 (1944):18-60.

Rogo, D. Scott. "Paranormal Tape-Recorded Voices: A Paraphysical Breakthrough," in J. White and S. Krippner (eds.), *Future Science.* New York: Doubleday Anchor Books, 1977.

11. THEORIES ABOUT PK: MIND ENERGY? PHYSICAL ENERGY? OR COSMIC ENERGY?

Bayless, Raymond. *Experiences of a Psychical Researcher.* New Hyde Park, N. Y.: University Books, 1972.

Beloff, John. "On Trying to Make Sense of the Paranormal." *Proceedings of the Society for Psychical Research* 56 (1976):173-95.
Eccles, J. C. *The Neurophysiological Basis of Mind.* Oxford, N. Y.: Clarendon Press, 1953.
Eisenbud, Jule. "The Mind-Matter Interface." *Journal of the American Society for Psychical Research* 69 (1975):115-26.
Geley, Gustave. *Clairvoyance and Materialization.* New York: Doran Co., 1927.
Greenfield, Jerome. *Wilhelm Reich vs. the U.S.A.* New York: Norton, 1974.
Mann, W. Edward. *Orgone, Reich and Eros.* New York: Simon & Schuster, 1973.
Matsunaga, Alicia. *The Buddhist Philosophy of Assimilation.* Rutland, Vt.: Charles E. Tuttle Co., 1969.
Ostrander, S., and Schroeder, L. *Psychic Discoveries Behind the Iron Curtain.* Englewood Cliffs, N. J.: Prentice Hall, 1970.
Owen, A. R. G. *Psychic Mysteries of the North.* New York: Harper & Row, 1975.
Raknes, Ola. *Wilhelm Reich and Orgonomy.* Baltimore: Pelican Books, 1970.
Rhine, J. B. *The Reach of the Mind.* New York: William Sloan, 1947.
Rhine, Louisa. *Mind over Matter.* New York: Macmillan, 1970.
Roll, W. G. *The Poltergeist.* New York: New American Library, 1974.
Rush, Joseph. "Physical Aspects of Psi Phenomena," in G. Schmeidler (ed.), *Parapsychology: Its Relation to Physics, Biology, Psychology and Psychiatry.* Metuchen, N. J.: Scarecrow Press, 1976.
Schmidt, Helmut. "PK Experiments with Animals as Subjects." *Journal of Parapsychology* 34 (1970):255-61.
Tweedale, Charles. *News from the Next World.* London: Psychic Book Club, 1947 (2d ed.).

Index

accordion experiment, 72—73
Adamenko, Victor, 118—19, 136
Adare, Lord, 70—71
an-psi research, 240—41
Artley, John, 242

Baggally, W.W., 81
Barksdale, Warren, 97
Barrett, William, 174, 179
Barry, Jean, 199
Batcheldor, K.J., 169—70, 195
Bayless, Raymond, 27, 147, 149—50, 187, 221—23
Beloff, John, 62, 198, 217, 236, 238, 249
Bender, Hans, 48, 51—53, 59, 160
bioplasma, 86, 133—36, 211, 235, 242, 244, 246, 256
Blum, Gerald, 136
Blundon, J., 36
Bottazzi, Philippe, 80
Buddhist philosophy, 236—38
Byrd, Eldon, 155—57

Caldwell, Taylor, 231
Canavesio, Orlando, 193
cancer, 205—6
Carrington, Hereward, 81—85, 134, 173, 185, 224—25, 239

Cassirer, Manfred, 111—12, 115—16
Chauvin, Remy, 217
Chiaia, Ercole, 75—76
children: metal-bending, 159—62; and poltergeists, 47—49, 52—54, 57—63
Clarac, L., 231—32
Cleio, 122, 130—31, 137
clock stoppings, 32—36. *See also* death coincidences.
cockroach experiment, 39
compass experiments, 104—5, 115, 127—29 145—46
Coohill, Thomas P., 157—58
Cox, W.E., 154—55, 218—20, 253
Cranshaw, Stella, 86—91, 99
Crawford, W.J., 185—89, 235
Croiset, Gerard, 101
Crookes, William, 72—75

Dale, Laura, 23, 253
d'Albe, Fournier, 188
Damiani, M., 75, 99
de Gasparin, Agénor, 180—82, 184, 189
de Maigret, Pamela Painter, 119-20
de Rochas, Albert, 83, 131
de Rudder, Pierre, 200—1
death coincidences, 27—36, 97—100, 230—31

denial syndrome, 192
dice experiments, 21—24, 36, 217—21
Dingwall, Eric, 92
displacement, 110
Driesch, Hans, 211, 213
DT (down-through) test, 20

Eccles, J.C., 239—40
ectoplasm, 85
Edwards, Harry, 203—4, 206
Eisenbud, Jule, 19, 225—29, 246
electrostatic fields, 118—24
energy, and PK, 91, 135—36, 235—37, 242—43, 256—57
entelechy, 213
ESP, 30—31; and PK, 19—35, 39—40, 89, 101, 173—74, 213, 225—26
Estebany, Oskar, 208—12, 214, 232
experimenter PK, 37—39
exponential decay function, 242—43

Fahler, Jarl, 116
Faraday, Michael, 717, 179
Feilding, Everard, 81, 132
Feinberg, Gerald, 140
Feola, José, 189—95
fire immunity, 72
Fisk, G.W., 36
Flammarion, Camille, 26—28, 77—78, 244
fluidic double, 131—32
Fodor, Amarya, 230—31
Fodor, Nandor, 58, 230
Forwald, Haakon, 220—21
Fox sisters, 67—69
Frank, Wesley, 223
fraud, allegations of: and Geller, 144—54, 159; and mediums, 79, 86, 90, 93; and metal-bending children, 159—62; in Philip circle, 171—73; and poltergeists, 49, 52—53
Fukurai, T., 225

Gaddis, Vincent, 55, 229
Gardner, Martin, 157
Garrett, Eileen, 101
Geley, Gustave, 97, 244—45
Geller, Uri, 100, 139—66, 196
"Geller effect," 162—66
Genthon, Jean-Pierre, 217
ghosts. *See* phantoms
gloves, 244—46
Goligher, Kathleen, 100, 185—89
Goodwin family, 42—45
Goodrich, Joyce, 207
Grad, Bernard, 17, 208—11, 214, 230, 232, 252
Gregory, Anita, 96
Grottendieck, W.G., 50—51, 57
group PK, 84, 167—97; theories about, 181—85, 193, 195—97
Grunewald, Fritz, 93
Guzik, Jean, 244

Harary, Blue, 121
Hare, Robert, 178
Harper, Randall, 60
Harribance, Sean, 20
Herbert, Benson, 104, 111—17, 119, 124, 136—38
Hodgson, Richard 79
Home, Daniel Dunglas, 69—75, 97—98, 100—2, 175
Honorton, Charles, 38, 97, 126—28, 243—44
Humphrey, Betty, 218
hydrometer experiments, 113—15
Hyman, Ray, 145—46
Hyslop, James H., 33

infrared, and PK, 94—95
Inyushin, V., 133—36

Johnson, Alice, 79
Joseph of Cupertino, Saint, 17
Jung, C. G., 19, 40—41

Keil, Jürgen, 108—11, 117
Kirlian photography, 133—34
Kluski, Franek, 244—46
Kogelnik, Fritz, 99

Krall, Karl, 93
Krippner, Stanley, 255
Krmessky, Julius, 123—25
Kuhlman, Kathryn, 206
Kulagina, Nina, 102—17, 121—22, 129, 133, 223, 238; PK principles of, 107—8, 117

Laurent, Emile, 28—29
Lawrence, George, 145—46
Leonard, Gladys, 101
Leslie, Leo, 158
life force, 210—11, 232—33, 250—53, 256—57
linger effects, 71, 108, 111, 117, 128—29, 214, 242—43
Llaguet, B., 231—32
Lodge, Oliver, 78—79
Lombroso, Cesare, 76
Lourdes healings, 199—203

McConnell, R.A., 36
Martin, Rose, 202—3
materializations, 71, 77, 80—81, 84, 89, 94, 244—46
Maxwell, Joseph, 84, 176, 195
mediums, 66—101; decline of, 98—101, 137; effects of, 75; theories about, 82—86, 96—98
Mesmer, Franz Anton, 210, 250
metal-bending, 145—46, 148—50, 154—66
mice experiments, 208—9, 213—14
micro—PK, 217—34
Mikhailova, Nelya. See Kulagina, Nina
Mitchell, A.M.H., 36
Mitchell, Edgar, 140—42
Morselli, Enrico, 84, 100
Moss, Thelma, 103, 104, 153
mummification experiment, 231—32
Myers, F.W.H., 78—79

NAD experiment, 212—13
Nash, Carroll, 36
Nitinol wire tests, 156—57

Ochorowicz, Julien, 131—33
odic force, 250
organisms, PK effects on, 107, 111—13, 116, 198—99. See also psychic healing
orgone, 208, 252—53
oscillator experiments, 24
Ossowiecki, Stefan, 101
Ostrander, Sheila, 103, 104, 253, 255
Osty, Eugene, 94—95, 100
Owen, A.R.G., 168, 173—74, 254
Owen, Iris, 168—50, 172, 174
ownership inhibition, 195
ozone, and PK, 122

Palladino, Eusapia, 75—82, 90—91, 97—100, 102, 105, 107, 121, 131, 137, 238
Palmer, John, 60—61, 223
Paracelsus, 249
paranormal healings, 200—3. See also psychic healing
Parise, Felicia, 125—30, 238, 243—44
Pavlita, Robert, 254—55
phantoms, 167—77
"Philip", 168—77
picture-drawing tests, 143—44, 147—48, 150—52
PK, in animals, 240—41; as cantilever, 186—88; and death, 26—36; effects of, 216—17; and ESP, 19—35, 39—40, 89, 101, 173—74, 213, 225—26; fields of, 111, 129, 136, 243; historical aspects of, 16—17; mimicking aspects of, 122—23; physiological aspects of, 22—23, 105—7, 116, 117, 186—88, 244—47; principles of, 107—8, 184; psychological aspects of, 17—19, 58—64, 106—7, 110, 138, 164, 180—81, 195—97; range of, 216—34; spontaneous, 26—41; theories about, 82—86, 96—98, 133—38, 235—58; as unconscious process, 31—34, 37—39, 106, 110, 123,

138, 164, 183—84. *See also* group PK; micro-PK
PK mediums, 66—101
PK—missing, 219
placement PK experiments, 218—21
plant experiments, 209—10, 230—31
"poltergeist theft," 51
poltergeists, 42—65, 164—65, 242; description of, 46—47, 59—60; and electrical mimicking, 122—23; and epilepsy, 63—64, 239; fire, 47, 54—57, 61; object'throwing, 42—47, 49, 51—52; rapping, 47—49; stone-throwing, 47, 49—51; teleporting, 47, 50—53; as unconscious process, 58—64, 97—98; water, 47, 53—54, 61
Pratt, J.G., 46, 108—11, 117, 162, 223
Price, E. Alan, 162—64
Price, Harry, 58, 86—91, 92—96, 99
Prince, W. Franklin, 40
psychic fluid, 83—84, 181—82, 184—85, 235
psychic healing, 112, 113, 198—215; psychological aspects of, 204—5
psychic photography, 108—9, 113, 128—29, 133, 223—30
psychokinesis. *See* PK
psychotronic generators, 255
Puharich, Andrija, 139—40, 144
Puthoff, Harold, 31, 141—44
pyramid power, 253—54

quarter distribution (QD) effect, 218

Raknes, Ola, 252
Randi, Amazing, 146, 161
Ransom, Champe, 108—9
raps, 221—23. *See also* poltergeists, rapping; table-rapping
Reback, Marcus, 231
Reich, Wilhelm, 208, 250—53
Reichenbach, Karl von, 250
Rejdak, Zdenek, 104—7, 113, 255
release of effort phenomenon, 243
Rhine, J.B., 17, 21, 46, 134—35, 217, 220, 239—40

Rhine, Louisa, 29, 31
Richet, Charles, 76—78, 100, 244
Richmond, Nigel, 199
Riggs, Jon, 147—48
Rogo, D. Scott, and Geller, 147—53, 165—66
Roll, W.G., 46, 57, 59—63, 235, 239, 242—43
Rose, Louis, 203—4
Rosenheim poltergeist, 122—23
Ruk, Joseph, 224—25
Rush, Joseph, 247—49

Schmeidler, Gertrude, 25, 247
Schmidt, Helmut, 24, 240—42
Schneider, Rudi, 86, 91—99, 102
Schneider, Willi, 86, 91—92
Schrenck-Notzing, Albert von, 91—93, 99, 100, 132
Schroeder, Lynn, 103, 104, 253, 255
Sergeyev, Grenady, 107—8, 112—15, 135—36
Serios, Ted, 225
Sherman, Harold, 30—31
Sidgwick, Henry, 79
Simonton, Carl, 205—6
skin vision, 103
Smith, Justa, 212—13, 214
Society for Psychical Research (SPR), 69, 78—79, 81, 106, 188—89
Solfvin, Gerald, 63
Soviet Union, PK studies in, 102—23, 133
Spiritualism, 68—69, 98—99, 169, 175, 188—89, 207
Stanford, Rex, 39—40, 243—44
Stevenson, F. McC., 189
Stevenson, Ian, 162
Strang, Shipi, 144, 150
Sudre, René, 244
Surrency family, 165
Swann, Ingo, 91, 247
Szalay, A. von, 196—97, 221—22

table-rapping, 170—71, 173, 186—87
table-tilting and -turning, 169—73, 175, 177—97

Tanagras, A., 130
Targ, Russell, 31, 141—44
Taylor, John, 160—61
telekinesis, 17
telekinetoscope, 87—88, 90—91
telepathy, 30—31
temperature changes, 25, 87, 88, 247
Teresa of Avila, Saint, 17
thoughtography, 223—30
thunderstorms, and PK, 117, 121
Thury, Marc, 180, 182—85
Tietze, Thomas, 40
Tomczyk, Stanislawa, 122, 131—33, 137
Toronto Society for Psychical Research, 167—77, 189, 253—54
trances, 137—38
Travis family, 229—30
trypsin experiments, 212
TV, images on, 229—30

Ullman, Montague, 117

Van De Castle, Robert, 145—46
Vasiliev, L.L., 103—4
Vaughan, Alan, 254
Veilleux family, 226—29
Venzano, Joseph, 83, 97, 100
Vinogradova, Alla, 118—23
voices, 221—22

Watkins, Graham and Anita, 128—29, 213—14, 235, 238, 243
West, D.J., 201—3
Whitton, Joel, 61—62
Wilkins, Hubert, 30—31
Willey family, 55—56
Wimberley, Mary, 121
Worcester, Elwood, 33

X, Mme., 231—32

Zorka, Arthur, 157
Zugun, Eleanore, 58